D0910087

the BRANDEIS reader

The life and contributions of

MR. JUSTICE LOUIS D. BRANDEIS

[CENTENARY EDITION]

Edited with Commentary by

ERVIN H. POLLACK

Professor of Law,
The Ohio State University

DOCKET SERIES
Volume 7

Oceana Publications
New York City
1956

TO JAY AND JOAN

*and all other Jays and Joans
in the world who are too young
to understand fully the meaning
of democracy yet share in its
blessings.*

ACKNOWLEDGMENTS

The editor acknowledges with appreciation the permission granted by the following copyright holders, publishers and authors to reprint copyrighted material in this volume:

To Vanguard Press, Inc., for "The Menace of the Trusts" (Statements by Louis D. Brandeis), in **"The Social and Economic Views of Mr. Justice Brandeis"** (edited by Alfred Lief, 1930).

To Professor Alpheus Thomas Mason and the University of Pennsylvania Law Review for "Mr. Justice Brandeis and the Constitution," from 80 U. Pa. L. Rev. (1932).

To Mr. Justice Felix Frankfurter and the Harvard Law Review Association for "Mr. Justice Brandeis and the Constitution," from 45 Harv. L. Rev. (1931).

To Mr. Donald R. Richberg and the Columbia Law Review for "The Industrial Liberalism of Justice Brandeis," from 31 Col. L. Rev. (1931).

To Professor Paul A. Freund and the Washington University Law Quarterly for "Law and the Universities," from 1953 Wash. U. L. Q.

The editor is also indebted to Dean Frank R. Strong of The Ohio State University College of Law for his comments and criticism of the text; to Messrs. Kent F. Ozmun and Charles D. Hering, Jr., of the Ohio Bar, for their research assistance; and to Mrs. Nina Eastman for her assistance in typing the manuscript.

Printed in the U. S. A.

TABLE OF CONTENTS

TABLE OF CONTENTS (*Continued*)

FOREWORD

LOUIS D. BRANDEIS, PERFECTIONIST

"He was truly a ruthless man!"

The speaker was one of our most highly-respected jurists, who was discussing his lifelong friend and associate, Louis D. Brandeis. He went on to explain that he was using the word in a very special sense. Brandeis' phenomenal memory, his thirst to know everything about everything, his complete dedication to causes, his tremendous intellect and industry seemed perfectly normal to him. He assumed that any man had or could easily acquire the same qualities, that the importance of whatever project he was working on was so evident that friends should be willing to drop everything to help it along. His own life was so well-ordered, so completely devoted to the development of his mind and using it to the public good, that human frailty was as difficult for him to comprehend and accept as the slip-shod report or the badly-operated corporation.

Few men in our time have amassed so much knowledge and used it so wisely. His memory was almost photographic. His son-in-law recalls an illustration. During a discussion early in his association with the Justice, Brandeis cited Macaulay and quoted a long and complicated paragraph. At the earliest opportunity, he looked up the passage. Later he reported to his father-in-law that understandably doubting that anyone's memory could be so infallible, he had checked the source. "As nearly as I can recall your words this morning," he said, "you quoted Macaulay verbatim." "That's gratifying to hear," said the Justice, "since I last read that passage forty years ago."

Brandeis' masterly interpretation of the law as a living, everchanging organism was to revolutionize musty concepts and make the law more truly reflective of a changing society – man's servant, not his master. Proper Boston attorneys were first confused and later resentful when Brandeis sought out and weighed all of the data bearing on a case instead of limiting himself to that area which would benefit his client. This consuming passion to know all of the facts and to move in the direction they justified inevitably led to his participation in cases of broad public interest where he served as "people's attorney" without fee. "Private interests," he wrote in 1907, "will always be and should properly be active in presenting to legislators what they deem to be required for the protection of the enterprises they represent. But it is essential to just and safe legislation that the interests of the public should also be specifically and ably represented."

Brandeis never lost sight of the fact that the public is a collection of individuals. In the Boston gas-rate case he was representing every householder who used gas and ought not to pay exhorbitantly for it. In Muller vs. Oregon he was representing the right of every working-woman to reasonable hours. In establishing savings bank life insurance he was providing every thrifty working-man with the opportunity to obtain dependable insurance at low cost. But always he emphasized the duty of the individual to do the utmost for himself within the legal and social framework provided by his community. He agreed with Abraham Lincoln that "In all that the people can individually do as well for themselves, government ought not to interfere".

The privilege of living in a democracy carries with it the obligation on the part of every citizen to be independent, self-sustaining, and as wise as possible. "Democratic ideals cannot be attained by the mentally undeveloped," said Brandeis. "In a government where every one is part sovereign, every one should be competent, if not to govern at least to understand the problems of government; and to this end education is an essential."

To some who were confused, or pretended to be, by Brandeis' insistence on a literal interpretation of such words as freedom, liberty, justice, duty, and democracy, his liberal views seemed tinged by Socialism. Where such a suspicion could be nurtured and increased by vested interests to mask the real issues and discredit the man, this was done. Some of the damage still survives, but as a matter of record Socialism in this country was almost exactly what he wanted least. He honestly feared that the excesses of trusts and monopolies, and the wide gap between management and the workers who produced their profits were invitations to Socialism. He strove mightily to check the first and to correct the second. "What we want," Brandeis wrote during his fight for savings bank life insurance, "is to have the workingman free; not to have him the beneficiary of a benevolent employer or a benevolent state, and freedom demands a development in employees of that self-control which results in thrift and in adequate provisions for the future. What America needs is not that we do anything for these our fellow-citizens, but that we keep open the path of opportunity to enable them to do it for themselves."

It was this same confidence in do-it-yourself citizenship that led to the rift in 1921 between Brandeis and other disciples of Zionism. There were those who believed that money should be poured into Palestine indiscriminately, but he could not see the new Jewish homeland as an easy and immediate Utopia. The Justice made his view quite clear. "We cannot attain our objective of a manly self-supporting population unless the settlers are made to realize that they must, and unless they actually do incur, in some form, hardships equivalent to those incurred by hardy pioneers in other lands." His active devotion to Palestinian affairs continued all his life, even after the break with the Cleveland Convention. He organized support and outlined in hundreds of memoranda solid and constructive ideas. Here, as in everything he took part in his value rested in the sober, comprehensive, realistic analysis and planning that his brilliant mind was geared to. The extremes of some of the early Zionists were alien to his nature.

In closing, we should note Justice Brandeis' summation of an ad lib talk he gave in February, 1922, before a meeting of the Federal Council of Churches in America:

"Refuse to accept as inevitable any evil in business (e.g., irregularity of employment). Refuse to tolerate any immoral practice (e.g., espionage). But do not believe that you can find a universal remedy for evil conditions or immoral practices in effecting a fundamental change in society (as by State Socialism). And do not pin too much faith in legislation. Remedial institutions are apt to fall under the control of the enemy and to become instruments of oppression..

Seek for betterment within the broad lines of existing institutions. Do so by attacking evil in situ; and proceed from the individual to the general. Remember that progress is necessarily slow; that remedies are necessarily tentative; that because of varying conditions there must be much and constant enquiry into facts . . . and much experimentation; and that always and everywhere the intellectual, moral and spiritual development of those concerned will remain an essential—and the main factor—in real betterment.

"This development of the individual is, thus, both a necessary means and the end sought. For our objective is the making of men and women who shall be free, self-respecting members of a democracy—and who shall be worthy of respect. Improvement in material conditions of the worker and ease are the incidents of better conditions—valuable mainly as they may ever increase opportunities for development.

"The great developer is responsibility. Hence no remedy can be hopeful which does not devolve upon the workers participation in, responsibility for, the conduct of business; and their aim should be the eventual assumption of full responsibility—as in co-operative enterprises. This participation in, and eventual control of, industry is likewise an essential of obtaining justice in distributing the fruits of industry.

"But democracy in any sphere is a serious undertaking. It substitutes self-restraint for external restraint. It is more difficult to maintain than to achieve. It demands continuous sacrifice by the individual and more exigent obedience to the moral law than any other form of government. Success in any democratic undertaking must proceed from the individual. It is possible only where the process of perfecting the individual is pursued. His development is attained mainly in the process of common living. Hence the industrial struggle is essentially an affair of the Church and is its imperative task."

Yes, it is possible to see how a man who believes that, who has the ability to live in strict accordance with it and expects others to do so, might be called ruthless, but only in a fresh, healthy, and challenging sense of the word. All of Brandeis' writings and opinions clearly bear out this intensity of dedicated service.

FRANK L. WEIL, Chairman
Louis Dembitz Brandeis Centennial Commission
Brandeis University, Waltham, Massachusetts

INTRODUCTION

Our heroes and leaders, our men of eminence whose ideals and activities are the testaments of the ages are those who aspired toward a better life for humanity. In each period of civilization, a few individuals expressed such a yearning with unusual forcefulness, captured the spirit of the times and were singled out for their ability to articulate the strivings of the people.

Certainly, Louis D. Brandeis was such a man. He lived at a time when the United States was moving rapidly from the era of unrestricted individualism to one of greater social sensitivity. His philosophy and activities reflected this change, and he became one of its brilliant champions.

Louis Brandeis, a successful Boston attorney with a lucrative corporate practice, was not content to let the affairs of the world pass him by as he lived in quiet serenity and austere comfort. "I have only one life to live, and it's short enough," he told an interviewer. "Why waste it on things I don't want most. And I don't want money or property most. I want to be free." Thus, Brandeis became the "people's attorney."

It was the time of the populist movement; William Jennings Bryan was in the heyday of his popularity, espousing the cause of free silver; groups were voicing their concern with the encroachment of monopoly; Henry George's "Progress and Poverty," and Bellamy's "Looking Backward" were exciting people on behalf of social justice. Louis Brandeis became a part of this movement to protect people's rights.

His humanitarianism made him a spokesman for the underdog, and he worked tirelessly to ameliorate the social suffering of man. He supported the rights of employees to present their grievances when seeking an increase in wages. He favored civil service reform, incurring the enmity of traditional politicians. He lent his assistance to the pauper's home on Long Island but unhesitatingly reported that more interest should be shown in curing poverty than merely in helping people in need. "These people are not machines," he would say of those in distress; ". . . these people are human beings and each one of them, and all of them, can be raised and raised only by holding up before them that which is higher and that which is better than they."

With unusual foresight, he evolved a plan to regularize employment through reserves, a scheme which currently has the strikingly familiar overtones of guaranteed wages. Brandeis' savings bank insurance plan was adopted in Massachusetts and other states, providing "industrial" life insurance for workers at low cost. He described this program as his most significant undertaking.

When Congress was considering a tariff revenue increase during McKinley's administration, Brandeis appeared before the House Ways and Means Committee "in behalf," as he said, "of those . . . who form a larger part of the people in the United States. . . ." When private utilities sought to gain "absolute control" through franchises and charge the public what he considered exorbitant rates, he joined forces with others to oppose these activities.

During Wilson's administration, Brandeis became "the President's adviser-in-general." "A talk with Brandeis always sweeps the cobwebs out of one's mind," Wilson once observed. This close association and the high esteem in which he was held by the President led to his nomination to the United States Supreme Court upon the death of Justice Joseph R. Lamar.

Brandeis' nomination to the Supreme Court invoked furious opposition, for in his efforts on behalf of the many causes he championed, he had made numerous bitter enemies. The newspapers took up the fight against Brandeis' appointment, claiming he was "a man of furious partisanship, of violent antagonisms, and of irredeemable prejudices." But the attack failed and on June 1, 1916, Brandeis' nomination to the Supreme Court was confirmed by the Senate.

Brandeis brought to the Court, in the words of

Chief Justice Stone, "social conscience and vision, infinite patience, an extraordinary capacity for sustained intellectual effort, and serene confidence that truth revealed will ultimately prevail." Functioning within the framework of democratic law and with an abiding faith in the American principles of liberty, justice and equality of opportunity, his judicial decisions emphasized the social, political and economic considerations which bear a significant relationship to judicial judgment. His judicial opinions, therefore, again in the words of the Chief Justice, "Together . . . constitute one of the most important chapters of the history of this Court."

What then is the philosophy of Brandeis? Although he disavowed allegiance to any formal system of philosophy, being, as he stated, "too intent on concrete problems of practical justice," a study of his writings, opinions and activities unfolds a clear, symmetrical pattern of values.

In each significant area of social expression and human endeavor—civil rights, governmental powers, property rights, business and labor relations—Mr. Justice Brandeis moved with disarming astuteness and conscious consistency. To each social situation, he adapted the fundamental principle that individual freedom is the objective of civilized society.

It follows that the ultimate goal of the state is the guarantee of freedom to the ordinary individual, with maximum opportunity for him to develop his faculties, to realize his ambitions and to satisfy his desires. Thus, he stated, "The makers of our Constitution undertook to secure conditions favorable to the pursuit of happiness. They recognized the significance of man's spiritual nature, of his feelings and of his intellect. They knew that only a part of the pain, pleasure and satisfactions of life are to be found in material things. They sought to protect Americans in their beliefs, their thoughts, their emotions and their sensations. They conferred, as against the Government, the right to be let alone—the most comprehensive of rights and the right most valued by civilized men."

Since freedom is so precious, we must always be vigilant to oppose its invasion by rulers, whether well-meaning or corrupt, for concentration of power is a constant threat and danger to freedom. As a safeguard against governmental intrusions, he believed strongly in the principle of Federalism, hence the diffusion of political power. He endorsed the doctrine of states' rights, not as a limitation of governmental power but as a diffusion of political power, with its related dissemination of responsibility.

Brandeis realized that selfishness manifests itself readily when shielded by power. Therefore, in the exercise of governmental control, he firmly believed in the separation of powers, with its system of checks and balances, as a necessary safeguard against the abuse of autocratic rulers. Nor did the resulting inefficiency in governmental operations disturb him. As he asserted, the objective of the doctrine of the separation of powers was "not to promote efficiency, but to preclude the exercise of arbitrary power. The purpose was, not to avoid friction, but, by means of the inevitable friction incident to the distribution of the governmental powers among three departments, to save the people from autocracy."

On the question of civil rights, Brandeis believed that the deliberative powers of man should be given the widest range of expression, for to restrict speech and discussion is to deny political truth the essential nutriment for growth and development. But he refused, with his colleagues of the Supreme Court, to identify freedom of speech as an absolute right. Instead, he applied a rule of reason to this concept, allowing men of all convictions—including those who harbor dangerous ideas—freedom of expression so long as they are not used "in such circumstances and of such a nature as to create a clear and present danger" to the society which sustains freedom and gave it its life.

He distinguished between the rights of individuals, with their aspirations and desires, and the privileges of corporations, an artifice of an industrial society. This sharp distinction was drawn in his opinions involving freedom of speech and freedom of contract. The right to free and complete expression of personal opinion "has such value that only a positive case will justify its abridgment;" the right of free contract is limited to the confines of business usage and custom. Thus, he was not opposed to state interference in modifying the practices of industry to meet the needs of society. Such arrangements were deemed a thing apart from the deprivation of individual rights.

Brandeis placed clear limitations upon the function of the Supreme Court. Thus, he held that experimentation by legislatures to correct economic dislocation should not be interfered with by the courts when such action was considered necessary by the legislatures. To permit the economic biases of the judges to prevail under such circumstances "may be fraught with serious consequences to the Nation." Further, he thought that the legislatures were best suited to inquire into conflicting social issues, make empirical findings, evolve solutions, and revise and adapt remedies to meet social changes. While identifying these legislative responsibilities, he at the same time recognized the limited function of the courts, since they are confined necessarily to settling litigious disputes. Brandeis urged that in no sense should the process of judicial review by the Supreme Court be interpreted as "an exercise of the powers of a super-legislature."

His opposition to the concentration of economic power is in harmony with his general theory of diffusion of power. For years Brandeis opposed monopoly and concentration, defending competition and the preservation of small business. He attacked the inefficiencies and callousness of big business. He exhorted individual initiative and promoted opportunity for all as the soundest device to achieve social advancement.

In labor matters, Mr. Justice Brandeis espoused the idea that "Men must have industrial liberty as well as good wages." This concept assumed the most provocative form. "You cannot have true American citizenship, you cannot preserve political liberty, you cannot secure American standards of living unless some degree of industrial liberty accompanies it." This liberty for the employee can only be achieved—in his idealistic vision of a pure democratic state—by the worker's participation in the responsibilities of business management.

Of equal significance are his views on property rights. Although he subordinated property rights to human rights, Brandeis thought that social values should not be furthered to the utter disregard of property rights. Augmented by an incisive logic, he was consistent in his treatment of both civil and property matters, striking a balance between social needs and expectations and democratic tradition. "Property is subject to interference and destruction for good cause," but he would not countenance the unlimited exercise of governmental power over private property.

Mr. Justice Brandeis' contributions to humanity are too recent to bring them into proper focus, but this much is certain: through his selfless dedication to others, our social institutions are improved and are more stable; our values are finer and more attuned to man's requirements; our aspirations are nobler and more idealistic; and our faith in humanity is firmer and more resolute.

It is appropriate that this commemorative volume be published on the occasion of the 100th anniversary of Brandeis' birth, distilling from the writings and opinions of Mr. Justice Brandeis and those of his associates and eminent scholars his rich, practical philosophy—a philosophy which illumined American society in his day and remains as a guiding ideal of the present.

Ervin H. Pollack

Part I

LIFE AND WORK OF MR. JUSTICE BRANDEIS

The following account of the life of Mr. Justice Brandeis is reprinted from the Proceedings of the Bar of the Supreme Court of the United States and Meeting of the Court in Memory of Associate Justice Louis D. Brandeis, December 21, 1942 (Washington, 1942).

Louis Dembitz Brandeis was born in Louisville, Ky., November 13, 1856. His parents, Adolph and Fredericka Dembitz Brandeis, cultivated Bohemian Jews, and his scholarly uncle, Lewis Dembitz, had come to this country a few years before in quest of liberty. The son from his early youth was thus imbued with an active devotion to free institutions and to the processes of democracy as a means of enhancing the dignity and releasing the potentialities of the common man. After studying in the public schools of Louisville he went abroad, and for two years attended the Annen Realschule in Dresden. During this period there was some suggestion that he prepare for a medical or academic career in Europe, but he held to his resolve to return to America and study law.

Without a college degree he entered the Harvard Law School in 1875, at the age of eighteen. His father's fortune having been lost in the panic of 1873, Brandeis earned his way by tutoring fellow students. He made a preeminent scholastic record at the law school. Though not yet of the required age of twenty-one, he was given his LL.B. degree in 1877 by special vote of the Harvard Corporation. His intellectual distinction and prepossessing manner opened to him all gates in Boston and Cambridge. At this time he met Oliver Wendell Holmes. The acquaintanceship was destined to grow into an intimate and tender friendship through a long period of distinguished service of the two as colleagues on the Supreme Court of the United States.

After a further year of graduate study in Cambridge, Brandeis was admitted to the bar and practiced for some months in St. Louis, Mo. In 1879 he returned to Boston and entered into partnership with his classmate Samuel D. Warren under the firm name of Warren & Brandeis. Warren retired from practice in 1893, other partners were taken in, and in 1897 the name was changed to Brandeis, Dunbar & Nutter. Brandeis remained in this firm until 1916, when he was appointed to the bench.

In his early years of practice in Boston perhaps his major outside interest was in the growth and development of the Harvard Law School. He helped James Bradley Thayer collect materials for his notable course on constitutional law, and procured funds which enabled the School to appoint Holmes to the faculty. In 1882-83 Brandeis taught the course on evidence, but he declined an assistant professorship. In 1886 he was the prime mover in the formation of the Harvard Law School Association and for many years thereafter he served as its secretary. He rendered valuable assistance, financial and other, in the founding of the Harvard Law Review in 1886-87, the first of the academic periodicals which have become so lively and significant a part of legal education, not only for law students, but also for the bench and bar. His pioneering article on "The Right to Privacy" (as coauthor with his partner Warren) appeared in an early issue of the Review. In recognition of his services, Harvard University awarded him the honorary degree of Master of Arts in 1891.

Though not in chronological order, it is appropriate at this point to mention another educational interest with which he was much preoccupied in later years. In 1924 he formulated, and in succeeding years gave wise guidance to a broad-visioned program for the upbuilding of the law school and the general library of the University of Louisville, in the city of his birth. His thesis was that to become great "a university must express the people whom it serves, and must express the people and the community at their best." His generous gifts of money constituted the least important part of his contribution. He gave painstaking thought to the educational problems involved, laid the broad foundations, and sketched the lines of sound development. In the pamphlet "Mr. Justice Brandeis and the University of Louisville" Bernard Flexner tells the story of this great enterprise, which the Justice initiated and followed through with characteristic idealism, imagination, and scrupulous attention to detail. This project was all of a piece with one of his firmest convictions: that the strength of America lies in diversity, not uniformity; that local cultures and traditions should be preserved and fostered, a sense of local responsibility quickened, local leadership evoked and encouraged.

By 1890 Brandeis had built up a varied and lucrative practice and had established himself as one of the leaders of the Boston bar. He steadfastly maintained the independent standing of the profession and never hesitated to impress upon his clients the obligations that go with power. It was characteristic of him that whatever problem he dealt with, his concern went beyond the winning of a victory for his client. With intense concentration he mastered the facts, however intricate; then shrewdly appraised their social significance. and finally with technical skill, inventiveness, and imagination, and with objective consideration of diverse conflicting interests, he devised the means of long-range adjustment or solution.

In conscientious performance of his duty as a citizen, he found time more and more to devote his talents, without retainer, to various public causes. Thus he played a major part in the fight to preserve the Boston municipal subway system, in devising and establishing the Boston sliding-scale gas system, and in opposing the New Haven Railroad's monopoly of transportation in New England. His investigation of the abuses and tragic inadequacies of so-called industrial insurance led him to draft and procure the adoption by the Massachusetts Legislature of the savings bank life insurance plan which, under his watchful guidance, became established on a firm foundation. In these provocative activities he did not escape the shafts of criticism and personal abuse; notwithstanding this, he calmly held his ground, confident of ultimate vindication. He was sometimes called a crusader, and so he was. But he had qualities too often lacking in the crusader—a sure grasp of concrete fact, a constructive mind and, also, patience. He never tired of urging the steady improvement of society by "small reforms"—steps forward which were of intrinsic importance, but which did not alter the basic pattern of our institutions, nor overtax the capacities and imagination of men.

The country is vastly indebted to him for his creative work in the field of labor relations, in dispelling misunderstanding between management and labor, and in making collective bargaining an effective instrument for industrial peace. He successfully arbitrated or conciliated many labor disputes. In 1910 he was arbiter of a serious strike in the New York City garment trade. Not content with settling the immediate dispute, he devised the famous "protocol" for the permanent government of labor relations in the industry, with provision for the preferential union shop, for a Joint Board of Sanitary Control, and for a continuing Board of Arbitration composed of representatives of the public as well as of the employers and the union. The procedures thus developed and successfully tested served as a model in other industries. For several years he served as impartial chairman of this board of arbitration.

Recognizing his grasp of intricate economic problems, the Interstate Commerce Commission engaged him in 1913 as special counsel to develop the facts relevant to the application of the Eastern railroads for permission to put into effect a horizontal 5-percent increase of freight rates.

In a series of papers and public addresses he challenged the abuses of financial manipulation, and pointed out the dangers and diminishing efficiency of undue concentration of financial power. These, collected in the book "Other People's Money," exemplify extraordinary powers of analysis and lucid exposition, and state forcefully some of the dominant ideas of his life—ideas which, as intellectual working tools of great power, have had profound influence on thinking and on events. They are among the major contributions to American thought of the last half century, and have grown into our culture as the statement and fulfillment of some of its richest and most characteristic themes.

One of the most significant activities of his career at the bar was his advocacy of the constitutionality of state minimum wage and maximum hour legislation. With intelligent utilization of the doctrine of judicial notice, his unconventional type of legal brief went beyond the citation of legal precedent and set forth the social and economic background out of which the needs for the legislation arose, together with all relevant scientific material, expert opinion, and experience in other states and lands in dealing with comparable problems. Thus the "Brandeis brief," as it came to be called, lifted the issue of due process of law under the Fifth and Fourteenth Amendments out of the realm of the abstract and placed it in its proper setting of contemporary fact.

In 1914-16 Brandeis was chairman of the Provisional Committee for General Zionist Affairs, and thereafter remained in the forefront of the movement to develop the Jewish National Home in Palestine. In this great creative activity, he saw the fulfillment of a prophetic vision, the building of a haven of refuge against storms of intolerance and oppression, and the opportunity to realize his most cherished ideals of democracy and social justice. In the document known as the Zeeland Memorandum drafted by him in 1920 as a statement of proposed Zionist policy, there is exhibited in striking fashion his insight, his humanity, his practical idealism, his grasp of detail, his insistence upon sound financial management and efficient organization.

By appointment of President Wilson, Brandeis took his seat as Associate Justice of the Supreme Court on June 5, 1916. Its fortunate outcome is all that will be remembered of the long and bitter fight over his confirmation by the Senate. Though he was one of the few men who came to the Court without having previously held judicial or other public office, his career at the bar and experience in large affairs constituted a magnificent preparation for the tasks of judicial statecraft. In 528 opinions during twenty-three years of service, he found occasion to deal with all the issues, large and small, which come before the Court—problems of federalism, jurisdiction and venue, administrative law, patents and copyrights, bankruptcy, finance, public utilities, monopoly and restraint of trade, labor relations, civil rights, and the law of the public domain. The solid stuff of his opinions is set forth to advantage by a simple, straightforward, lucid style, without rhetorical flourish. Noteworthy illustration of his judicial work may be found in his opinions on the economic and constitutional problems of public utility valuation, and in his opinions on the rights of free speech and other civil liberties, in peace and in war, which have won high place among the best of our Anglo-American legal literature. To borrow the words of Chief Justice Hughes, Mr. Justice Brandeis was "the master of both microscope and telescope. Nothing of importance, however minute, escapes his microscopic examination of every problem, and, though his powerful telescopic lens, his mental vision embraces distant scenes ranging far beyond the familiar worlds of conventional thinking." How the future will regard his judicial work it is not for us to say, but this much is certain: from our contemporary viewpoint, Mr. Justice Brandeis stands with the half dozen giants of our law, wise, strong, and good.

In his own person, with the ready cooperation of his wife and children, Mr. Justice Brandeis practiced his austere preachment to others of "simple living, high thinking, and hard work." His marriage in 1891 to Alice Goldmark gave him warm intellectual comradeship and a happy home which sustained and fortified him throughout a long and vigorous career. The serenity of spirit which he achieved, and retained to the last, was the due reward of his dedication of great gifts to great purposes. His personal influence on young people was remarkable; in an age of cynicism and materialism they learned from him that life had not lost its spiritual meaning. Countless men and women, of all ages and walks of life, came to him as to a sage and counsellor and went away with lifted hearts and a new insight.

LOUIS DEMBITZ BRANDEIS (1856-1941)

Associate Justice, United States Supreme Court (1916-1939)

Edmond Cahn

This address by Professor Edmond Cahn was delivered on April 14, 1956, at centennial ceremonies in honor of Justice Brandeis, conducted by the American Jewish Congress as part of its biennial national convention, New York City. Professor Cahn is a professor of law at New York University. He is the author of *The Sense of Injustice* (1949) and *The Moral Decision* (1955); he edited and contributed to *Supreme Court and Supreme Law* (1954) and is the author of many legal and jurisprudential articles.

Let us begin by trying to evoke the living Brandeis. Many of you remember that tall, angular, wiry figure, which became slightly stooped as the years passed by. You recall that beautifully formed head of his with the hair that was always recalcitrant and unruly; in the last part of his life he allowed it to grow and wander as it would. Nobody who once saw those deeply set blue-gray eyes will ever forget how quick and brilliant they were. Perhaps his mouth was his most revealing feature, because even in old age the lips still remained sensitive and full as though to show his vitality and zestfulness — and yet at the corners the mouth would purse a bit, as though to admonish that reason and self-discipline were the constant masters of his spirit. If you knew him at all, you were not surprised that nature had given him a strong chin. In fact, you might wonder why it did not project farther.

In 1916 when Brandeis was sixty years of age President Woodrow Wilson appointed him to the United States Supreme Court. For four months a furious opposition raged from one end of the land to the other, centering in Boston, the city where Brandeis had spent his entire adult life practicing law. In the midst of the struggle over whether Brandeis should or should not be confirmed by the United States Senate, a public statement was issued by seven former presidents of the American Bar Association. It declared Louis Dembitz Brandeis unfit for the office to which he had been appointed. At the head of the list of seven appeared the signature of William Howard Taft, then ex-president of the United States. Never before or since has an appointment to the Supreme Court so infuriated the class of people who like to call themselves "respectable".

* * *

In the course of his practice, Brandeis had astonished and shocked many sincere lawyers of the old school. They had never seen anything quite like him before. To understand the bitterness, the heat, and the cruel injustice of that four-months ordeal, we have to see the man's career as it appeared to the leaders of his own day.

Brandeis was born in Louisville, Kentucky in 1856. As you may know, his home was cultivated, assimilated, non-religious. After he graduated from high school he was sent to study at the Annen-Realschule at Dresden, Germany. When he arrived there he went to see the rector, who told him that he could not be admitted without a birth certificate and a vaccination certificate. The youngster replied, "The fact that I'm here is proof of my birth, and you may look at my arm for evidence that I was vaccinated." This kind of reasoning would mean nothing to our modern bureaucrats; but in the 1870s there was still a modicum of common sense, even in Bismarck's Germany, and Louis was admitted to the school.

While he was there, he had an experience which was trivial enough in itself but rankled for decades in his memory. It seems that the authorities reproved him severely for daring to whistle at night. Apparently, he resolved then and there that he would devote his life to building the kind of society where an eighteen year old boy could feel free to whistle at night.

After two years of study in Dresden he omitted college entirely and entered the Harvard Law School. At the Law School his brilliance was noticed immediately. The students became convinced that Brandeis knew everything, that he was just about omniscient. One day a certain student misplaced his notebook on the law of agency. He searched and searched for it, but it was not to be found. "Ask Brandeis", his classmates said. "He knows everything." Sure enough, when he did ask Brandeis, the answer came forthwith. "Look on the window-sill in the west lecture room." And, of course, there it was!

At the age of twenty, Brandeis graduated from Harvard Law School with the highest average in its history, an average which has not been matched to this day. Perhaps his pre-eminence was due to habits acquired in Germany, or to his exceptional bent for mathematics, or to his extraordinarily methodical mind. Brandeis experienced a passionate joy in analysing social and economic data. For him there was fascination in balance sheets, earning statements and columns of statistics. Above all, he knew the magic that resides in long hours of hard work. As a lawyer, his day began with the dawn, around half past five, and when he became a Supreme Court Justice, he advanced the hour to five o'clock. As his body remained lean, trim, and wiry, so did his mind.

No wonder he made such a quick and brilliant success at the Bar! By the time he was thirty-five, around 1890, he was earning about $50,000 a year. Soon he was a self-made millionaire, in an era of few millionaires and no income taxes. What was the secret of this sensational success?

The secret was that in his professional practice Brandeis was making a new type of lawyer. At least his type appeared new and strange among the habits, customs and conventions of the Boston Brahmins of that epoch. It was not only that his mind was so brilliant and his judgment so sound, it was not only that he was so ingenious and bold in legal maneuvers. It was something more disturbing yet. Brandeis was different, he went about things in a different way.

For example, if a man who owned a shoe factory was having trouble with the wage demands of his labor and came to Brandeis for advice in resisting the demands, some very peculiar consequences would follow. Brandeis would proceed to make an intensive study of the entire business, would learn more about it than the client himself, would show the client how to run the business more efficiently and rationally, and would evolve a plan which actually paid the laborers what they were asking while leaving the owner with a larger net profit than ever before. Brandeis had the kind of mind which fairly leaped to understand, master, and control a problematic situation. If the problematic situation seemed too large and ramified for him to grasp, then he inferred that others could not understand it either. Consequently, he fought relentlessly against great concentrations of wealth and entrenched monopolies. In the industrial world, he felt bigness was a curse, not only because the giant corporation might crush the small businessman, not only because it might depersonalize human relationships, but specifically because bigness was often clumsy, unmanageable, wasteful, dropsical, and, therefore, stupid.

In those years, William James was preaching individualism and pluralism in philosophy, and was scandalizing the respectables. Freud's theories were embarrassing the respectables in psychology. These were bad enough. But Brandeis was defiling the ultimate holy of holies; if people listened to him, what would happen to the respectables in the great corporations and their friends in the bar associations?

Brandeis seemed incomprehensible. Here was a lawyer who would not take a case unless he was personally satisfied of its fairness! If a banker wanted him to conduct a reorganization of a railroad company, he could hardly believe his ears when Brandeis told him the plan of reorganization must first be changed. It must be made fair and equitable to all the interests concerned, if Brandeis was to submit it. Bankers weren't accustomed to hearing talk like that.

Moreover, with increasing frequency Brandeis would appear in a case and nobody seemed to know just whom he represented. Was he attorney for this interest or for that interest? Hadn't he begun by representing a single private group, say of investors, and here he was talking for the rights of the consumers and the laborers and the general public. How could a lawyer in a private negotiation concern himself with the interests of the general public? Yet this was exactly what Brandeis was doing, always speaking for the larger, more comprehensive interests. At times, when some puzzled lawyer would challenge him and demand to know just whose attorney he was, he would smile disarmingly and call himself "attorney for the situation"; but as years went on and his fame increased, the labor unions and liberal newspapers began to call him "attorney for the people."

Thus Brandeis became celebrated as an active reformer of the evils and injustices of industrial capitalism. He fought for democratic methods in industry. Sometimes he would go to Congress or the state legislature and lobby for more progressive laws. Sometimes he would invent his own solution when big business failed to satisfy the needs of the public. For example, it was he who inaugurated savings bank life insurance in Massachusetts, from which it has spread to New York and some other states. But most often it was in the commission hearings and collective negotiations and private conference rooms that Brandeis was seeking to bring justice and reason to capital, labor, and the general public.

At this stage in his career he invented the famous "Brandeis brief". In 1907 an Oregon statute was to be contested before the United States Supreme Court. The statute limited the working time of women in industry to ten hours a day. Brandeis was retained to defend its constitutionality. He submitted a brief to the Supreme Court containing two pages of legal argument and over one-hundred pages of evidence drawn from mountains of reports, both domestic and foreign, of committees, commissions, bureaus, and factory inspectors – all to show that long hours are in fact perilous to the health, safety and morals of women, and that shorter hours bring important social and economic advantages. He won his case, and he gave the mechanism of American law a shaking-up which it still feels today. The Brandeis brief was a truly inspired invention for the advocate's use.

Meanwhile, Brandeis grew into a close and confidential relation with Woodrow Wilson. Wilson had a profound respect not only for Brandeis' intellect but especially for his judgment and objectivity. He noticed what so many others had begun to notice: Brandeis never acted as an advocate without simultaneously acting as a judge. *This* was the unique and essential secret of his success at the bar.

It was also the reason why so many persons of great influence and power found him alien and infuriating, why they opposed his appointment to the Court. They raged and stormed during four ugly months, but in the end the Senate voted to confirm his nomination. This great and gifted advocate, who had dared so often to act the part of a private, unofficial judge, was now elevated to a seat on his country's highest judicial tribunal. The question was: What kind of public, official judge would Brandeis make?

II

To answer this question, we have to take the converse perspective. We have just concluded that the secret of Brandeis' success at the bar consisted in the fact that he never acted as an advocate without acting to some degree as a judge. Now it is time to recognize the secret of his superb success from 1916 to 1939 as an associate justice of the Supreme Court. The secret of this success was that he never acted as a judge without acting to some degree as an advocate. If we can visualize Brandeis as an advocate in the years 1916 to 1939, then we can really comprehend him as a judge.

What was Brandeis advocating during those years on the bench? Of course, being a justice of the Supreme Court, he could no longer engage actively in partisan politics or appear very often on public platforms. But while he showed due respect for the Court by keeping out of the limelight of political controversy, Brandeis could hardly be expected to strip himself of his life-long convictions. The Supreme Court is no monastery, nor had Brandeis taken a vow of silence. Through conference, correspondence, and personal interview, he remained throughout the years a regular powerhouse of social reform, stimulating here, generating there, lending the richness and depth of his experience to a distinguished series of liberal leaders from Woodrow Wilson to Franklin D. Roosevelt. He never grew complacent, never faltered in his efforts to combat the ills of American industrial life.

What kind of American society did he desire? What was his ideal? I think I can sum it all up this way: Brandeis preached the same diversity, experimentation, and mobility on the *legal and economic* levels that William James and Horace Kallen have preached on the *social and cultural* levels. Like these philosophers, Brandeis strove to build a society where a man would be able to find room and move around. His ideal is a society throbbing with novelty, improvisation, creative invention – a society in which, at any given moment, there are countless experiments under way to discover better and still better methods, not only to produce and sell goods but – what is more important – to adjust and harmonize human relations. It is not the kind of society in which any single method is ever designated as the final best, nor the kind of society in which government takes over problems which the citizens can handle. On the contrary, the government, in Brandeis' society, would be only one of the implements the community might use, if it saw fit, in order to regulate certain private experiments or to try industrial experiments of its own. Naturally, in this society of his, the citizens would never let themselves sink into a mire of complacency. Brandeis recognized that the one most important cosmic fact of the twentieth century is the acceleration in the rate of social change. In a world where change is so drastic and rapid, only the land of the vigilant, the daring, and the experimental would be found fit to survive.

Once you have this picture before you, it becomes almost superfluous to spell out Brandeis' doctrines of constitutional law. They all serve his ideal with admirable consistency.

For example, would he or would he not be inclined to hold a statute constitutional which embodied some new, experimental remedy for a social mischief? Evidently he would uphold it, because his deepest faith was in the efficacy of striving and experimentation. While, in all probability, Justice Holmes would likewise vote to sustain this type of law, *his* motivations would be entirely different. Holmes' economic views were quite conservative. Privately he thought most reform experiments were unwise and vain. Unwise and vain; but nevertheless constitutional. He said frankly, though of course quite elegantly, that if the imbeciles in Congress or the state legislature were resolved to attempt these futile measures, it was not the Supreme Court's function to protect them from their folly. In this perspective, Brandeis was the liberalism of expectant hope, while Holmes was the liberalism of skeptical detachment.

Let us take another example of Brandeis' constitutional doctrines. Given his ideal society, would he be favorable or unfavorable to the taxing and police powers of the 48 states? Within reason he would surely favor them. The authorities of government must not be permitted to coalesce in Washington. It was better that the states remain free to serve as separate economic laboratories. If a legislative experiment went wrong in a single state, it need not harm the whole country; if an experiment succeeded in a single state, the other states might see fit to emulate it. If a social problem was susceptible of being confined to a city or a state, it would be the very kind of problem that Brandeis – in his old days at the bar – had loved to attack, struggle with, and ultimately master.

What did he believe about the functioning of the Supreme Court? Would Brandeis, as a Supreme Court Justice, be satisfied for the Court to take and decide constitutional cases which it could avoid taking or deciding? To be concrete, suppose some lawyer appeared before the Court with no more definite client than Brandeis was wont to have in the days of his law practice; suppose the lawyer claimed that, although he couldn't say he represented any specified interest, he was acting as "attorney for the situation". Would Brandeis wish the Court to entertain such a case? As you can see, he would not. If a lawyer desired to be "attorney for the situation", let him serve that role in a conference room, on a public platform, or before a legislative committee. When he took his appeal into the Supreme Court, the Justices should not even hear him unless he represented some specific aggrieved party with an identified standing to raise the constitutional issue. Otherwise, as Brandeis thought, the Court would find itself deciding abstract questions and acting like a sort of "super-legislature". The judicial function under the Constitution ought to be limited strictly to genuine cases and controversies.

How then should we expect him to vote on questions of civil liberties? Here again, his answers follow directly from his economic and social premises. Brandeis was typically the jurist of a free and open society, a society unabashed by innovation and experiment. Imbued with this faith, Brandeis wrote what many scholars consider the most eloquent passage on free speech in the records of the United States Supreme Court. Let me read you part of his concurring opinion in Whitney v. California.

"Those who won our independence believed that the final end of the State was to make men free to develop their faculties; and that in its government the deliberative force should prevail over the arbitrary. They valued liberty both as an end and as a means. They believed liberty to be the secret of happiness and courage to be the secret of liberty. They believed that freedom to think as you will and to speak as you think are means indispensable to the discovery and spread of political truth; that without free speech and assembly discussion would be futile; that with them, discussion affords ordinarily adequate protection against the dissemination of noxious doctrine; that the greatest menace to freedom is an inert people; that public discussion is a political duty; and that this should be a fundamental principle of the American government. They recognized the risks to which all human institutions are subject. But they knew that order cannot be secured merely through fear of punishment for its infraction; that it is hazardous to discourage thought, hope and imagination; that fear breeds repression; that repression breeds hate; that hate menaces stable government; that the path of safety lies in the opportunity to discuss freely supposed grievances and proposed remedies; and that the fitting remedy for evil counsels is good ones. . .

"Those who won our independence by revolution were not cowards. They did not fear political change.

They did not exalt order at the cost of liberty. To courageous, self-reliant men, with confidence in the power of free and fearless reasoning applied through the processes of popular government, no danger flowing from speech can be deemed clear and present, unless the incidence of the evil apprehended is so imminent that it may befall before there is opportunity for full discussion. If there be time to expose through discussion the falsehood and fallacies, to avert the evil by the processes of education, the remedy to be applied is more speech, not enforced silence."

But there is much more to civil liberties than freedom of speech. Brandeis reached his moral zenith in cases where government officials had acted illegally, oppressively, unconscionably. He felt very strongly that every living person had a fundamental right to human dignity. Back in 1890, amid the pressures of a busy and prosperous law practice, Brandeis and his partner took time off to write a law review article, entitled "The Right of Privacy", which was destined to exert a pervasive influence on American jurisprudence. It foreshadowed how Brandeis would react when the famous Olmstead case came before the Supreme Court in the 1920s. Olmstead and others had been convicted of violating the Prohibition Act, and the evidence used against them included several incriminating telephone conversations which the government officials overheard by wire-tapping. Mr. Taft, who by this time had become Chief Justice, wrote the Court's opinion affirming the convictions. Brandeis filed a statement of magnificent dissent. Here are some of its lines:

"The makers of our Constitution undertook to secure conditions favorable to the pursuit of happiness. They recognized the significance of man's spiritual nature, of his feelings and of his intellect. They knew that only a part of the pain, pleasure and satisfactions of life are to be found in material things. They sought to protect Americans in their beliefs, their thoughts, their emotions and their sensations. They conferred, as against the Government, the right to be let alone — the most comprehensive of rights and the right most valued by civilized men. To protect that right, every unjustifiable intrusion by the Government upon the privacy of the individual, whatever the means employed, must be deemed a violation of the Fourth Amendment. And the use, as evidence in a criminal proceeding, of facts ascertained by such intrusion must be deemed a violation of the Fifth. . .

"Experience should teach us to be most on our guard to protect liberty when the Government's purposes are beneficent. Men born to freedom are naturally alert to repel invasion of their liberty by evil-minded rulers. The greatest dangers to liberty lurk in insidious encroachment by men of zeal, well-meaning but without understanding."

All in all, Justice Brandeis proved faithful and true to his vision of the good society. He did whatever lay within his power to provide his country with democracy in its industrial relations, experimental reform in its economic and social order, and dignity in the lives of its citizens.

* * *

III

If Louis D. Brandeis were with us here and now, what messages of counsel and guidance would he wish to convey? In all humility, I admit these are the thoughts he would declare in this, his centenary year:

To the lawyers of America he would say: First of all, learn "the logic of facts", not only the facts of this or that case but the facts of economic and social movement in your community and in the nation. As he used to say, "Knowledge of the decided cases and of the rules of logic cannot alone make a great lawyer." Second, it is not enough for a lawyer to devote his entire fidelity to any private interest without regard to the public interest. One must learn not only to practice law but also to practice justice.

To the Justices of the Supreme Court he would say: Stand firm against any and all attempts to abridge political advocacy and free speech. Even the vilest and most dangerous ideas must not be suppressed as long as there is "time to expose the falsehood and fallacy, and to avert the evil by the processes of education." Moreover, it is incumbent upon you to insist that state and federal officers uphold the basic liberties of individuals and the constitutional rights of minorities, for "our government is the potent, the omnipresent teacher."

To the American people he would say: Lift up your hearts in courage and your heads in thought. You are sitting back and letting problems attack you; in my day we were accustomed to attack problems. Put your own minds to work boldly, bravely, optimistically. Use legislation, litigation, and the rest of the apparatus of government to effectuate your social policy, but never surrender a policy wholly to the hands of government. Somewhere, somehow you will find many other implements to work with, if you will only consider and search. In the end, governments help those who help themselves.

These are the counsels Brandeis would give us, these the insights of his wisdom and experience. And he might see fit to conclude his advice in some such way as this: Listen, my friends, you who are believers and you who are doubters. In mankind's ancient book of Deuteronomy the radiant words are written, "Justice, justice shalt thou pursue!" There are two justices, each priceless and indispensable, and you will secure neither of them unless you seek for both. There is the justice of the government and the justice of the community. Standing alone, the justice of the government is not enough, it has never been enough, and it will never become enough. If your goal is a society of individual dignity and enterprise, then know this: The everlasting pursuit of justice is man's noblest enterprise on earth.

Part II

THE SOCIAL VIEWS OF MR. JUSTICE BRANDEIS

MR. JUSTICE BRANDEIS AND THE CONSTITUTION

Felix Frankfurter

This article was written by Mr. Justice Frankfurter when he was a professor of law at Harvard University. He has been an associate justice of the Supreme Court of the United States since January 30, 1939. Mr. Justice Frankfurter is the author of *The Commerce Clause Under Marshall, Taney and Waite* (1937), *Mr. Justice Holmes and the Supreme Court* (1938), *Mr. Justice Brandeis* (1932) and other books and articles. This article is reprinted from 45 Harvard Law Review 33, 38-44, 67-98, 104-105 (1931).

* * *

III

Never was there an easier transition from forum to bench than when Mr. Brandeis became Mr. Justice Brandeis. Since the significant cases before the Supreme Court always involve large public issues and are not just cases between two litigants, the general outlook of the Justices largely determines their views and votes in doubtful cases. Thus the divisions on the Court run not at all along party lines. They reflect not past political attachments, but the philosophy of the judges about government and our Government, their conception of the Constitution and of their own function as its interpreter.

Rich experience at the bar confirmed the teachings which Mr. Brandeis had received from James Bradley Thayer, the great master of constitutional law, that the Constitution had ample resources within itself to meet the changing needs of successive generations. The Constitution provided for the future partly by not forecasting it and partly by the generality of its language. The ambiguities and lacunae of the document left ample scope for the unfolding of life. If only the Court, aided by the bar, has access to the facts and heeds them, the Constitution, as he had shown, is flexible enough to respond to the demands of modern society. The work of Mr. Justice Brandeis is in the tradition of Marshall, for, underlying his opinions, is the realization "that it is a *constitution* we are expounding."[14] In essence, the Constitution is not a literary composition but a way of ordering society, adequate for imaginative statesmanship, if judges have imagination for statesmanship.

"But even if imprisonment at hard labor elsewhere than in a penitentiary had, in the past, been deemed an infamous punishment, it would not follow that confinement, or rather service, at a workhouse like Occoquan [the workhouse of the District of Columbia], under the conditions now prevailing should be deemed so. . . . The Constitution contains no reference to hard labor. The prohibition contained in the Fifth Amendment [against prosecution except by indictment] refers to infamous crimes—a term obviously inviting interpretation in harmony with conditions and opinion prevailing from time to time. And today commitment to Occoquan for a short term for non-support of minor children is certainly not an infamous punishment."[15]

"'We must never forget,' said Mr. Chief Justice Marshall in *McCulloch* v. *Maryland*, 4 Wheat, 316, 407, 'that it is a constitution we are expounding.' Since then, this Court has repeatedly sustained the exercise of power by Congress, under various clauses of that instrument, over objects of which the Fathers could not have dreamed. See *Pensacola Telegraph Co.* v. *Western Union Telegraph Co.*, 96 U. S. 1, 9; *Northern Pacific Ry. Co.* v. *North Dakota*, 250 U. S. 135; *Dakota Central Telephone Co.* v. *South Dakota*, 250 U. S. 163; *Brooks* v. *United States*, 267 U. S. 432. We have likewise held that general limitations on the powers of Government, like those embodied in the due process clauses of the Fifth and Fourteenth

Amendments, do not forbid the United States or the States from meeting modern conditions by regulations which 'a century ago, or even half a century ago, probably would have been rejected as arbitrary and oppressive.' *Village of Euclid* v. *Ambler Realty Co.*, 272 U. S. 365, 387; *Buck* v. *Bell*, 274 U. S. 200. Clauses guaranteeing to the individual protection against specific abuses of power, must have a similar capacity of adaptation to a changing world."[16]

This general point of view had led Mr. Justice Brandeis to give free play to the States and the Nation within their respective spheres.

For him, the Costitution affords the country, whether at war or at peace, the powers necessary to the life of a great nation. It is amply equipped for the conduct of war. It has the widest discretion in raising the fighting services; to strengthen these, it may also mobilize the social and moral forces of the nation. Whether to wage war or to enforce its revenue laws, the United States, like other nations, has all the rights on the high seas recognized by international law.

"Congress has the exclusive power to legislate concerning the Army and the Navy of the United States, and to determine, among other things, the conditions of enlistment. It has likewise exclusive power to declare war, to determine to what extent citizens shall aid in its prosecution and how effective aid may best be secured. Congress, which has power to raise an army and naval forces by conscription when public safety demands, may, to avert a clear and present danger, prohibit interference by persuasion with the process of either compulsory or voluntary enlistment. As an incident of its power to declare war it may, when the public safety demands, require from every citizen full suport, and may, to avert a clear and present danger, prohibit interference by persuasion with the giving of such support. But Congress might conclude that the most effective Army or Navy would be one composed wholly of men who had enlisted with full appreciation of the limitations and obligations which the service imposes, and in the face of efforts to discourage their doing so. It might conclude that the most effective Army would be one composed exclusively of men who are firmly convinced that war is sometimes necessary if honor is to be preserved, and also that the particular war in which they are engaged is a just one. Congress, legislating for a people justly proud of liberties theretofore enjoyed and suspicious or resentful of any interference with them, might conclude that even in times of grave danger, the most effective means of securing support from the great body of citizens is to accord to all full freedom to criticize the acts and administration of their country, although such freedom may be used by a few to urge upon their fellow-citizens not to aid the Government in carrying on a war, which reason or faith tells them is wrong and will, therefore, bring misery upon their country."[17]

"Plaintiff's argument is equivalent to saying that the war power of Congress to prohibit the manufacture and sale of intoxicating liquors does not extend to the adoption of such means to this end as in its judgment are necessary to the effective administration of the law. The contention appears to be, that since the power to prohibit the manufacture and sale of intoxicating liquors is not expressly granted to Congress, but is a power implied under §8 of Article I of the Constitution, which authorizes Congress 'to make all laws which shall be necessary and proper for carrying into execution' powers expressly enumerated, the power to prohibit non-intoxicants would be merely an incident of the power to prohibit intoxicants; and that it cannot be held to exist, because one implied power may not be grafted upon another implied power. This argument is a mere matter of words. The police power of a State over the liquor traffic is not limited to the power to prohibit the sale of intoxicating liquors supported by a separate implied power to prohibit kindred non-intoxicating liquors so far as necessary to make the prohibition of intoxicants effective; it is a single broad power to make such laws, by way of prohibition, as may be required to effectively suppress the traffic in intoxicating liquors. Likewise the implied war power over intoxicating liquors extends to the enactment of laws which will not merely prohibit the sale of intoxicating liquors but will effectually prevent their sale."[18]

"There is no limitation upon the right of the sovereign to seize without a warrant vessels registered under its laws, similar to that imposed by the common law and the Constitution upon the arrest of persons and upon the seizure of 'papers and effects.' See *Carroll* v. *United States,* 267 U. S. 132, 151-153. Smuggling is commonly attended by violation of the navigation laws. From the beginning of our Government officers of revenue cutters have, for the purpose of enforcing the custom laws, been expressly authorized to board and search inbound vessels on the high seas within twelve miles of our coast. It is not to be lightly assumed that Congress intended to deny to revenue cutters so engaged authority to seize American vessels found to be violating our navigation laws. Nor is it lightly to be assumed that Congress intended to deny to officers of revenue cutters engaged in enforcing other laws of the United States beyond the twelve-mile limit, the authority to seize American vessels found to be violating our navigation laws beyond those limits."[19]

Taxation has always been the most sensitive nerve of government. The enormous increase in the cost of society and the extent to which wealth is represented by intangibles, are putting public finance to its severest tests. To balance budgets, to pay for the cost of progressively civilized social standards, to safeguard the future and to divide these burdens with substantial fairness to the different interests in the community, strains to the utmost the ingenuity of statesmen. They must constantly explore new sources of revenue and find means to prevent the circumvention of their discovery. Subject as they are, in English-speaking countries, to popular control, they must be allowed the widest latitude of power. No finicky limitation upon their discretion nor jejune formula of equality should circumscribe the necessarily empirical process of tapping new revenue or stopping new devices for its evasion. To these needs Mr. Justice Brandeis has been especially alive. He has consistently refused to accentuate the fiscal difficulties of government by injecting into the Constitution his own notions of fiscal policy. In the "vague contours of the Fifth Amendment"[20] he reads no restriction upon historic methods of taxation. Nor has he found in the Constitution compulsion to grant additional immunity or benefit to taxpayers merely because they already hold tax-exempt securities.

"It [the Court] holds the Act void because the action of the law-making body is, in its opinion, unreasonable. Tested by the standard of reasonableness commonly adopted by man – use and wont – that action appears to be reasonable. Tested by a still higher standard to which all Americans must bow—long continued practice of Congress repeatedly sanctioned by this Court after full argument—its validity would have seemed unquestionable, but for views recently expressed. No other standard has been suggested.

"For more than half a century, it has been settled that a law of Congress imposing a tax may be retroactive in its operation. . . . Each of the fifteen income tax acts adopted from time to time during the last sixty-seven years has been retroactive, in that it applied to income earned, prior to the passage of the act, during the calendar year. . . .

"The Act with which we are here concerned had, however, a special justification for retroactive features. The gift tax was imposed largely to prevent evasion of the estate tax by gifts inter vivos, and evasion of the income tax by the splitting up of fortunes and the consequent diminution of surtaxes. If, as is thought by the Court, Congress intended the gift tax to apply to all gifts during the calendar year, its purpose may well have been to prevent evasion of the gift tax itself, by the making of gifts after its introduction and prior to its passage. Is Congress powerless to prevent such evasion by the vigilant and ingenious? This Court has often recognized that a measure may be valid as a necessary adjunct to a matter that lies within legislative power, even though, standing alone, its constitutionality might have been subject to doubt. *Purity Extract Co.* v. *Lynch,* 226 U. S. 192; *Ruppert* v. *Caffey,* 251 U. S. 264, 289; *Everard's Breweries* v. *Day,* 265 U. S. 545, 560. If the legislature may prohibit the sale of confessedly innocent articles in order to insure the effective prohibition of others, I see no reason why it may not spread a tax over a period in advance of its enactment sufficiently long to insure that the tax will not be evaded by anticipating the passage of the act. Compare *United States* v. *Doremus,* 249 U. S. 86, 94. In taxation, as well as in other matters, 'the law allows a penumbra to be embrased that goes beyond the outline of its object in order that the object may be secured.' See Mr. Justice Holmes, in *Schlesinger* v. *Wisconsin,* 270 U. S. 230, 241. Under the rule now applied, even a measure framed to prevent evasion of a tax from a date when it is practically certain that the act will become law, is deemed unreasonable and arbitrary. . . .

"The problem of preventing loss of revenue by transactions intervening between the date when legislation is introduced and its final enactment, is not a new one, nor is it one peculiar to gift tax. Other nations have met it by a method similar to that which the Court holds to be denied to Congress. England long ago adopted the practice of making customs and excise duties retroactive to the beginning of the fiscal year or to the date when the government's resolutions were agreed to by the House of Commons sitting as a Committee of Ways and Means. A similar practice prevails in Ireland, in all the self-governing Dominions, and to some extent in France and Italy. In the United States, retroactive operation of the tariff has been repeatedly recommended by the Tariff Commission and by the Secretary of Commerce. Legislation to that end was reported by the Committee on Ways and Means of the House of Representatives. No suggestion seems to have been made that such legislation would by its retroactive feature violate the due process clause."[21]

"The only factual basis for complaint by the Company is that, although a holder of tax-exempt bonds, it is, in respect to this particular tax, no better off than it would have been had it held only taxable bonds. Or, to put it in another way, the objection is not that the plaintiff is taxed on what is exempt, but that others, who do not hold tax-exempt securities, are not taxed more. But neither the Constitution nor any Act of Congress, nor any contract of the United States, provides that, in respect to this tax, a holder of tax-exempt bonds, shall be better off than if he held only taxable securities. Nowhere can the requirement be found that those who do not hold tax-exempt securities shall, in respect to every tax, be subjected to a heavier burden than the owners of tax-exempt bonds. . . .

"To hold that Congress may not legislate so that the tax upon an insurance company shall be the same whether it holds tax-exempt bonds or does not, would, in effect, be to read into the Constitution a provision that Congress must adapt its legislation so as to give to state securities, not merely tax exemption, but additional privileges; and to read into the contract of the United States with its own bond-holders a promise that it will, so long as the bonds are outstanding, so frame its system of taxation that its tax-exempt bonds shall, in respect to all taxes imposed entitle the holder to greater privileges than are enjoyed by holders of taxable bonds. But no rule is better settled than that provisions for tax exemption, constitutional or contractual, are to be strictly construed."[22]

* * *

VI

Thus far we have considered action by the States within their reserved spheres, limited merely by the negations of the Fourteenth Amendment and never in direct competition with the affirmative powers of the Federal Government. Where the States and Nation touch a field of legislation wherein both may move, fertile opportunities for conflict arise. The Commerce Clause gives controlling authority to the Nation. But how these conflicts are to be resolved—*when* the Commerce Clause becomes operative and the States have to stand aside, when the States are still free despite the Commerce Clause or because Congress has not seen fit to invoke its authority—depends ultimately upon the philosophy of the Justices regarding our federalism.

Mr. Justice Brandeis' regard for the States is no mere lip service. He is greatly tolerant of their powers because he believes intensely in the opportunities which they afford for decentralization. And he believes in decentralization not because of any persisting habit of political allegiance or through loyalty to an anachronistic theory of states' rights. His views are founded on deep convictions regarding the manageable size for the effective conduct of human affairs and the most favorable conditions for the exercise of wise judgment.

In the practical adjustments between national rule and local diversities, he is keenly mindful that the Nation spans a continent and that, despite the unifying forces of technology, the States for many purposes remain distinctive communities. As to matters not obviously of common national concern, thereby calling for a centralized system of control, the States have a localized knowledge of details, a concreteness of interest and varieties of social policy, which ought to be allowed tolerant scope.

And so he has closely scrutinized objections to state action based merely on remote or hypothetical encroachments upon that national uniformity which is the concern of the Commerce Clause. The ultimate organic nature of society is not a decree of constitutional centralization. Just because the national government will necessarily absorb more and more power, the States ought to be allowed to manage those activities which bear an essential state emphasis. Even though an enterprise is part of the concatenation that makes up interstate and foreign commerce, its local abuses should be removable by local remedies. The protection which states afford to industries within their borders may properly give rise to the states' taxing power, regardless of a nexus of that industry with interstate business.

"The statute is an exertion of the police power of the State. Its evident purpose is to prevent a particular species of fraud and imposition found to have been practiced in Pennsylvania upon persons of small means, unfamiliar with our language and institutions. Much of the immigration into the United States is effected by arrangements made here for remittance of the means of travel. The individual immigrant is often an advance guard. After gaining a foothold here, he has his wife and children, aged parents, brothers, sisters or other relatives follow. To this end he remits steamship tickets or orders for transportation. The purchase of the tickets involves trust in the dealer. This is so not only because of the nature of the transaction, but also because a purchaser when unable to pay the whole price at one time makes successive deposits on account, the ticket or order not being delivered until full payment is made. The facilities for remitting both cash and steamship tickets are commonly furnished by private bankers of the same nationality as the immigrant. It was natural that the supervision of persons engaged in the business of supplying steamship tickets should be committed by the statute to the Commissioner of Banking.

"Although the purchase made is of an ocean steamship ticket, the transaction regulated is wholly intrastate — as much so as if the purchase were of local real estate or of local theatre tickets. There is no purpose on the part of the State to regulate foreign commerce. The statute is not an obstruction to foreign commerce. It does not discriminate against foreign commerce. It places no direct burden upon such commerce. It does not affect the commerce except indirectly. Congress could, of course, deal with the subject, because it is connected with foreign commerce. But it has not done so. Nor has it legislated on any allied subject. Thus, there can be no contention that

Congress has occupied the field. And obviously, also, this is not a case in which the silence of Congress can be interpreted as a prohibition of state action — as a declaration that in the sale of ocean steamship tickets fraud may be practiced without let or hindrance. If Pennsylvania must submit to seeing its citizens defrauded, it is not because Congress has so willed, but because the Constitution so commands. I cannot believe that it does."[48]

"The business of the Narragansett Company is an intrastate one. The only electricity sold for use without the State is that agreed to be delivered to the Attleboro Company. That company takes less than 3 per cent. of the electricity produced and manufactured by the Narragansett, which has over 70,000 customers in Rhode Island. The problem is essentially local in character. The Commission found as a fact that continuance of the service to the Attleboro Company at the existing rate would prevent the Narragansett from performing its full duty towards its other customers and would be detrimental to the general public welfare. It issued the order specifically to prevent unjust discrimination and to prevent unjust increase in the price to other customers. The Narragansett, a public service corporation of Rhode Island, is subject to regulation by that State. The order complained of is clearly valid as an exercise of the police power, unless it violates the Commerce Clause.

"The power of the State to regulate the selling price of electricity produced and distributed by it within the State and to prevent discrimination is not affected by the fact that the supply is furnished under a long-term contract. *Union Dry Goods* v. *Georgia Public Service Corporation*, 248 U. S. 372. If the Commission lacks the power exercised, it is solely because the electricity is delivered for use in another State. That fact makes the transaction interstate commerce, and Congress has power to legislate on the subject. It has not done so, nor has it legislated on any allied subject, so there can be no contention that it has occupied the field. Nor is this a case in which it can be said that the silence of Congress is a command that the Rhode Island utility shall remain free from the public regulation — that it shall be free to discriminate against the citizens of the State by which it was incorporated and in which it does business. That State may not, of course, obstruct or directly burden interstate commerce. But to prevent discrimination in the price of electricity wherever used does not obstruct or place a direct burden upon interstate commerce."[49]

"From the multitude of cases this general rule may be reduced. The validity of a state tax under the commerce clause does not depend upon its character or classification. It is not void merely because it affects or burdens interstate commerce. The tax is void only if it directly burdens such commerce, or (where the burden is indirect) if the tax discriminates against or obstructs interstate commerce. In this case there is no claim that interstate commerce is discriminated against or obstructed. The contention is that the tax imposes a direct burden. Whether the burden should be deemed direct depends upon the character of plaintiff's occupation and its relation to interstate transactions. . . .

"The New Orleans tax is obviously not laid upon property moving in interstate commerce. Nor does it, like a gross-receipts tax, lay a burden upon every transaction. It is simply a tax upon one of the instrumentalities of interstate commerce. It is no more a direct burden, than is the tax on the other indispensable instrumentalities; upon the ship; upon the pilot boat, which she must employ; upon the wharf at which she must load and unload; upon the office which the owner would have to hire for his employees, if, instead of engaging the services of an independent contractor, he had preferred to perform those duties himself. The fact that, in this case, the services are performed by an independent contractor having his own established business, and the fact that the services rendered are not limited to soliciting, differentiate this case from *McCall* v. *California,* 136 U. S. 104. If these differences are deemed insufficient to distinguish that case from the one at bar, it should be frankly overruled as inconsistent with the general trend of later decisions."[50]

"The corporation maintains in Washington a branch office and a warehouse. There, it does a large intrastate business. Nearly one-half of the aggregate sales of $1,313,275.74 made within the State were local and were from broken packages. It is subjected to two taxes which are separate and distinct. The filing fee is payable only once and as laid was $545. The annual license fee is $580. The latter results in a charge of about one-tenth of one per cent on the intrastate business. The corporation's pay roll there is more than a hundred times as large. These small taxes are obviously not more than a fair contribution to the necessary expenses of the State government. They are the same for foreign corporations as for domestic. In my opinion both taxes are valid.

"If the statute sought to impose a tax on corporations engaged wholly in interstate commerce, or if the taxes laid a direct burden upon interstate commerce, or if they were laid upon property without the State, or if they were unjustly discriminatory, the fact that they are small in amount would, of course, be immaterial. *Sprout* v. *City of South Bend,* 277 U. S. 163, 171. But these taxes are not subject to any of those infirmities. The taxes are not laid upon interstate commerce. They are not measured by the amount of interstate commerce. They do not grow, or shrink, according to the volume of interstate commerce or of the capital used in it. They are not furtively directed against such commerce. The taxes would be precisely the same in amount if the corporation did in Washington no interstate business whatsoever. Nor are they taxes laid upon property without the State. Indeed, they are neither property taxes nor substitutes for property taxes. They are an excise, laid solely for the privilege of doing business as a corporation. An individual doing the same business would not be required to pay either these taxes or any substitute therefor.

"It would be unfortunate to hold that merely because a foreign corporation, doing a local business does also interstate business, the State may not lay upon it a reasonable, non-discriminatory excise, necessarily limited to a reasonable amount, to which all domestic corporations similarly situated are subjected and which can affect interstate commerce only indirectly, or at all."[51]

Similar issues are raised by the implied immunity from state taxation enjoyed by federal instrumentalities. The simple doctrine by which States and the Nation are forbidden to hamper one another's agencies of government has steadily been tortured beyond its original purpose. The practical result of inflating this doctrine has been the contraction of the allowable area of state taxation, without any compensating gain to the strength or resources of the Federal Government. Here again the influence of Mr. Justice Brandeis has been on the side of the States.

"The property taxed is lead and zinc ore in bins. The land from which the ore was extracted belongs to a Quapaw allottee under the Act of March 2, 1895, c. 188, 28 Stat. 876, 907. Restrictions on alienation of the land will not expire until 1946. Act of March 3, 1921, c. 119, § 26, 41 Stat. 1225, 1248. But the allottee may lease the land for mining and business purposes for ten years unless he is incompetent, in which case the power to lease is vested in the Secretary of the Interior. Act of June 7, 1897, c. 3, 30 Stat. 62, 72. The ore in question had been detached from the soil and is personal property. It is owned wholly by the Mining Company, a private Oklahoma corporation organized for profit. The ore is assessed under the general laws of the State which lays an ad valorem property tax on all property, real or personal, not exempt by law from taxation. Payment of the tax will not affect the financial return to the Indian under the lease. No state legislation exempts this property. There is no specific or general provision in any act of Congress which purports to do so. If an exemption exists, it arises directly from the Federal Constitution. Does ownership by an incompetent Indian of the land from which the ore was taken or ownership of the ore by an instrumentality of the Government create an exemption? . . .

"The rule that the property of a privately owned government agency is not exempt from state taxation rests fundamentally upon the principle that such a tax has only a remote relation to the capacity of such agencies efficiently to serve the Government. Such a tax, as distinguished from an occupation or privilege tax, does not impose a charge upon the privilege of acting as a government agent and thereby enable a State to control the power of the Federal Government to employ agents and the power of persons to accept such employment. The tax is levied as a charge by the State for rendering services relating to the protection of the property, which services are rendered alike to agents of the Government and of private persons. Such a tax cannot be deemed to be capable of deterring the entry of persons as agents into the employ of the Government. Conceivably an operating company might pay a higher royalty or bonus if it were assured that it would enjoy immunity from taxation for the small quantity of the year's output of the mine which might be in the ore bins on the day as of which property is assessed. Conceivably also, the cattle owner in *Thomas* v. *Gay, supra,* might have paid higher for the grazing rights if the cattle while on the reservation were immune from taxation. But, in either case, the effect of the immunity, if any, upon the Indian's financial return would be remote and indirect. If we are to regard realities we should treat it as negligible.

"The difference in the legal effect of acts which are remote causes and of those which are proximate pervades the law. The power of a State to tax property and its lack of power to tax the occupation in which it is used exist in other connections. In *Baltimore Shipbuilding Co.* v. *Baltimore,* 195 U. S. 375, 382, where the State had levied a tax upon property conveyed by the United States to the Shipbuilding Company on the condition that it construct a dry dock there for the use of the United States and that, if such dry dock were not kept in repair, the property should revert to the United States, this Court said: 'But, furthermore, it seems to us extravagant to say that an independent private corporation for gain, created by a State, is exempt from state taxation, either in its corporate person, or its property, because it is employed by the United States, even if the work for which it is employed is important and taxes much of its time.' "[52]

In the domain of interstate commerce, the States of course, must yield the field to Congress when Congress has occupied it. But these familiar phrases are, after all, figures of speech, and figures of speech are dangerous instruments for constitutional law. Whether Congress has occupied the field is not a problem in mensuration. Too often, it is an exercise of judgment about practical affairs; it calls for accommodation between state and national interests in the interacting areas of state and national power. Mr. Justice Brandeis, here also, eschews loose generalities and catchwords. He subjects federal enactment and its challenged state analogue to sharp, precise and comprehensive examination to ascertain whether both may survive or the national law alone can prevail.

"We are admonished also by another weighty consideration not to impute to Congress the will to deny to the States this power. The subject of compensation for accidents in industry is one peculiarly appropriate for state legislation. There must, necessarily, be great diversity in the conditions of living and in the needs of the injured and of his dependents, according to whether they reside in one or the other of our States and Territories, so widely extended. In a large majority of instances they reside in the State in which the accident occurs. Though the principle that compensation should be made, or relief given, is of universal application, the great diversity of conditions in the different sections of the United States may, in a wise application of the principle, call for differences between States, in the amount and method of compensation, the periods in which payment shall be made, and the methods and means by which the funds shall be raised and distributed. The field of compensation for injuries appears to be one in which uniformity is *not* desirable, or at least not essential to the public welfare.

"The contention that Congress has, by legislating on one branch of a subject relative to interstate commerce, preempted the whole field — has been made often in this court; and, as the cases above cited show, has been repeatedly rejected in case where the will of Congress to leave the balance of the field open to state action was far less clear than under the circumstances here considered. Tested by those decisions and by the rules which this court has framed for its guidance, I am of opinion, as was said in *Atlantic Coast Line R. R. Co.* v. *Georgia,* 234 U. S. 280, 294, that: 'The intent to supersede the exercise of the State's police power with respect to this subject cannot be inferred from the restricted action which thus far has been taken.' The field covered by Congress was a limited field of the carrier's liability for negligence, not the whole field of the carrier's obligation arising from accidents. I find no justification for imputing to Congress the will to deny to a large class of persons engaged in a necessarily hazardous occupation and otherwise unprovided for the protection afforded by beneficient statutes enacted in the long-deferred performance of an insistent duty and in a field peculiarly appropriate for state action."[53]

"The argument mainly urged by the States in support of the claim that Congress has not occupied the entire field, is that the federal and the state laws are aimed at distinct and different evils; that the federal regulation endeavors solely to prevent accidental injury in the operation of trains, whereas the state regulation endeavors to prevent sickness and disease due to excessive and unnecessary exposure; and that whether Congress has entered a field must be determined by the object sought through the legislation, rather than the physical elements affected by it. Did Congress intend that there might still be state regulation of locomotives, if the measure was directed primarily to the promotion of health and comfort and affected safety, if at all, only incidentally?

"The federal and the state statutes are directed to the same subject — the equipment of locomotives. They operate upon the same object. It is suggested that the power delegated to the Commission has been exerted only in respect to minor changes or additions. But this, if true, is not of legal significance. It is also urged that, even if the Commission has power to prescribe an automatic firebox door and a cab curtain, it has not done so; and that it has made no other requirement inconsistent with the state legislation. This, also, if true, is without legal significance. The fact that the Commission has not seen fit to exercise its authority to the full extent conferred, has no bearing upon the construction of the Act delegating the power. We hold that state legislation is precluded, because the Boiler Inspection Act, as we construe it, was intended to occupy the field. The broad scope of the authority conferred upon the Commission leads to that conclusion. Because the standard set by the Commission must prevail, requirements by the States are precluded, however commendable or however different their purpose."[54]

Safeguarding peculiar state interests is one thing; to discriminate against the common national interest is quite another. Through intimate acquaintance with the managerial and financial difficulties of railroads, Mr. Justice Brandeis is firm to check the imposition of gratuitous burdens. And behind the semblance of local regulation he is quick to detect a selfish attempt merely to obstruct interstate commerce.

"That the claims against interstate carriers for personal injuries and for loss and damage of freight are numerous; that the amounts demanded are large; that in many cases carriers deem it imperative, or advisable, to leave the determination of their liability to the courts; that litigation in States and jurisdictions remote from that in which the cause of action arose entails absence of employees from their customary occupations; and that this impairs efficiency in operation, and causes directly and indirectly, heavy expense to the carriers; these are matters of common knowledge. Facts, of which we, also, take judicial notice, indicate that the burden upon interstate carriers imposed specifically by the statute here assailed is a heavy one; and that the resulting obstruction to commerce must be serious. . . .

". . . orderly, effective administration of justice clearly does not require that a foreign carrier shall submit to a suit in a State in which the cause of action did not arise, in which the transaction giving rise to it was not entered upon, in which the carrier neither owns nor operates a railroad, and in which the plaintiff does not reside. The public and the carriers are alike interested in maintaining adequate, uninterrupted transportation service at reasonable cost. . . . Avoidance of waste, in interstate transportation, as well as maintenance of service, has become a direct concern of the public. With these ends the Minnesota statute, as here applied, unduly interferes. By requiring from interstate carriers general submission to suit, it unreasonably obstructs, and unduly burdens, interstate commerce."[55]

". . . It may be assumed that § 4 of the state statute is consistent with the Fourteenth Amendment; and also, that appropriate state regulations adopted primarily to promote safety upon the highways and conservation in their use are not obnoxious to the Commerce Clause, where the indirect burden imposed upon interstate commerce is not unreasonable. Compare *Michigan Public Utilities Commission* v. *Duke*, 266 U. S. 571. The provision here in question is of a different character. Its primary purpose is not regulation with a view to safety or to conservation of the highways, but the prohibition of competition. It determines not the manner of use, but the persons by whom the highways may be used. It prohibits such use to some persons while permitting it to others for the same purpose and in the same manner. Moreover, it determines whether the prohibition shall be applied by resort, through state officials, to a test which is peculiarly within the province of federal action — the existence of adequate facilities for conducting interstate commerce. The vice of the legislation is dramatically exposed by the fact that the State of Oregon had issued its certificate which may be deemed equivalent to a legislative declaration that, despite existing facilities, public convenience and necessity required the establishment by Buck of the auto stage line between Seattle and Portland. Thus, the provision of the Washington statute is a regulation, not of the use of its own highways, but of interstate commerce. Its effect upon such commerce is not merely to burden but to obstruct it. Such state action is forbidden by the Commerce Clause. It also defeats the purpose of Congress expressed in the legislation giving federal aid for the construction of interstate highways."[56]

"It appears that there was nothing in the new location which could in any wise affect injurously the health of the Railway's employees. The locations of the shops at West Tulsa and the vicinity in which employees may live are sanitary. The removal to West Tulsa had cost $150,000. It had resulted in a monthly saving of at least $33,500. It had effected a vast improvement of the interstate and other service. To restore the shops and division point to Sapulpa and make there the improvements essential to good service would require an outlay of $3,000,000, besides the expenditure of $300,000 for the shops; and it would entail in addition the operating expenses then being saved. Even with such large expenditures, restoration of the shops and division point to Sapulpa would inevitably impair interstate and other passenger and freight service. On these facts, which were established by affidavits filed in opposition to the motion to compel restitution, it must have seemed to the District Court at least probable that upon final hearing a permanent injunction would issue; and that to order restitution meanwhile would be, not merely an idle act, compare *Goltra* v. *Weeks*, 271 U. S. 536, 549, but one imposing unnecessary hardship on the Railway and the public."[57]

But whether state action unduly impinges upon interstate commerce depends more and more upon the particularities of fact in individual cases. If the

Court is to adhere to tradition in the administration of constitutional law and avoid hypothetical decisions or abstract pronouncements, the record must contain the details which control the application of general doctrine or the Court must secure their ascertainment.

"The contentions made in the briefs and arguments suggest, among other questions, the following: Where there is congestion of city streets sufficient to justify some limitation of the number of motor vehicles to be operated thereon as common carriers, or some prohibition of stops to load or unload passengers, may the limitation or prohibition be applied to some vehicles used wholly or partly in interstate commerce while, at the same time, vehicles of like character, including many that are engaged solely in local, or intrastate, commerce are not subjected thereto? Is the right in the premises to which interstate carriers would otherwise be entitled, affected by the fact that, prior to the establishment of the interstate lines, the City had granted to a local carrier, by contract or franchise, the unlimited right to use all the streets of the City, and that elimination of the interstate vehicles would put an end to the congestion experienced? May the City's right to limit the number of vehicles, and to prohibit stops to load or unload passengers, be exercised in such a way as to allocate streets on which motor traffic is more profitable exclusively to the local lines and to allocate streets on which the traffic is less profitable to the lines engaged wholly, or partly, in interstate commerce? Is limitation of the number of vehicles, or prohibition of stops to load or unload passengers, of carriers engaged wholly, or partly, in interstate commerce, justifiable, where the congestion could be obviated by denying to private carriers existing parking privileges or by curtailing those so enjoyed? Are the rights of the interstate carrier in the premises dependent, in any respect, upon the dates of the establishment of its lines, as compared with the dates of the establishment of the lines of the local carrier?

"These questions have not, so far as appears, been considered by either of the lower courts. The facts essential to their determination have not been found by either court. And the evidence in the record is not of such a character that findings could now be made with confidence. The answer denied many of the material allegations of the bill. The evidence consists of the pleadings and affidavits. The pleadings are confusing. The affidavits are silent as to some facts of legal significance; lack definiteness as to some matters; and present serious conflicts on issues of facts that may be decisive. For aught that appears, the lower courts may have differed in their decisions solely because they differed as to conclusions of fact. Before any of the questions suggested, which are both novel and of far reaching importance, are passed upon by this Court, the facts essential to their decision should be definitely found by the lower courts upon adequate evidence."[58]

VII

Marshall could draw with large and bold strokes the boundaries of state and national power; today most crucial issues involve the concrete application of settled, general doctrines. The fate of vast interests and hopeful reforms, the traditional contest between centralization and local rule, now turn on questions of more or less, on matters of degree, on drawing lines, sometimes very fine lines. Decisions therefore depend more and more on precise formulation of the issues imbedded in litigation, and on alertness regarding the exact scope of past decisions in the light of their present significance. The Court's conception of its own function and awareness of its processes in constitutional adjudication, determine the Constitution in action.

In his whole temperament, Mr. Justice Brandeis is poles apart from the attitude of the technically-minded lawyer. Yet no member of the Court invokes more rigorously the traditional limits of its jurisdiction.[59] In view of our federalism and the Court's peculiar function, questions of jurisdiction in constitutional adjudications imply questions of political power. The history of the Court and the nature of its business admonish against needless or premature decisions. It has no greater duty than the duty not to decide or not to decide beyond its circumscribed authority. And so Mr. Justice Brandeis will decide only if the record presents a *case* — a live, concrete, present controversy between litigants.

"When the bill was filed [to enjoin the construction of the Boulder Dam], the construction of the dam and reservoir had not been commenced. Years must elapse before the project is completed. If by operations at the dam any then perfected right of Arizona, or of those claiming under it, should hereafter be interfered with, appropriate remedies will be available. . . . The bill alleges, that plans have been drawn and permits granted for the taking of additional water in Arizona pursuit to its laws. But Wilbur threatens no physical interference with these projects; and the Act interposes no legal inhibitions on their execution. There is no occasion for determining now Arizona's rights to interstate or local waters which have not yet been, and which may never be appropriated. . . . This Court cannot issue declaratory decrees."[60]

When the record does present a case and judgment must be rendered, constitutional determination must be avoided if a non-constitutional ground disposes of the immediate litigation.

"If protection of the rights of The Chastleton Corporation and Hahn required us to pass upon the constitutionality of the District Rent Acts, I should agree, also the procedure directing the lower court to ascertain the facts. But in my opinion, it does not. For (on facts hereinafter stated which appear by the bill and which were, also, admitted at the bar) the order entered by the Commission is void as to them, even if the Rent Acts are valid. To express an opinion upon the constitutionality of the acts, or to sanction the enquiry directed, would, therefore, be contrary to a long-prevailing practice of the Court."[61]

Moreover, the duty to abstain from adjudicating, particularly in the field of public law, may arise from the restricted nature of the judicial process. The specific claim before the Court may be enmeshed in larger public issues beyond the Court's reach of investigation, or a suitable remedy may exceed judicial resources. Such a situation, even though formally disguised as a case, eludes adjudication. To forego judgment under such circumstances is not abdication of judicial power, but recognition of rational limits to its competence. Law is only partly in the keeping of courts; much must be left to legislation and administration. Nor does the absence of legislation create a vacuum to be occupied by judicial action.

"The rule for which the plaintiff contends would effect an important extension of property rights and a corresponding curtailment of the free use of knowledge and of ideas; and the facts of this case admonish us of the danger involved in recognizing such a property right in news, without imposing upon newsgatherers corresponding obligations. A large majority of the newspapers and perhaps half the newspaper readers of the United States are dependent for their news of general interest upon agencies other than the Associate Press. The channel through which about 400 of these papers received, as the plaintiff alleges, 'a large amount of news relating to the European war of the greatest importance and of intense interest to the newspaper reading public' was suddenly closed. The closing to the International News Service of these channels for foreign news (if they were closed) was due not to unwillingness on its part to pay the cost of collecting the news, but to the prohibitions imposed by foreign governments upon its securing news from their respective countries and from using cable or telegraph lines running therefrom. For aught that appears, this prohibition may have been wholly undeserved; and at all events the 400 papers and their readers may be assumed to have been innocent. For aught that appears, the International News Service may have sought then to secure temporarily by arrangement with the Associated Press the latter's foreign news service. For aught that appears, all of the 400 subscribers of the International News

Service would gladly have then become members of the Associated Press, if they could have secured election thereto. It is possible, also, that a large part of the readers of these papers were so situated that they could not secure prompt access to papers served by the Associated Press. The prohibition of the foreign governments might as well have been extended to the channels through which news was supplied to the more than a thousand other daily papers in the United States not served by the Associated Press; and a large part of their readers may also be so located that they can not procure prompt access to papers served by the Associated Press.

"A legislature, urged to enact a law by which one news agency or newspaper may prevent appropriation of the fruits of its labors by another, would consider such facts and possibilities and others which appropriate enquiry might disclose. . . .

"Courts are ill-equipped to make the investigations which should precede a determination of the limitations which should be set upon any property right in news or of the circumstances under which news gathered by a private agency should be deemed affected with a public interest. Courts would be powerless to prescribe the detailed regulations essential to full enjoyment of the rights conferred or to introduce the machinery required for enforcement of such regulations. Considerations such as these should lead us to decline to establish a new rule of law in the effort to redress a newly-disclosed wrong, although the propriety of some remedy appears to be clear."[62]

"The decisions to be made [regarding the allocations of West Virginia natural gas as between West Virginia consumers and those of other states] would be of the character which calls for the informed judgment of a board of experts. The tribunal would have to determine, among other things, whether inadequate service was due in the several States to inadequate supply or to improvident use by some consumers; whether to overcome inadequacy of supply new territory should be developed or more wells be sunk in old territory; whether, in view of prospective needs of the several communities, it would not be better that the reserves should be husbanded and that the uses to which gas may be put be curtailed. It would, thus, be called upon to review – and perhaps to control – the business judgment of those managing the companies. Pro rata distribution among all users of the gas from time to time available would obviously not result in equitable distribution. For domestic users, and also many industrial ones, would, if their gas supply were uncertain, find it necessary to assure themselves of an adequate supply for heating, cooking and power, of either oil or some other kind of fuel; and the expense of producing the necessary alternative appliances would be large. The tribunal would have to decide, also, many other serious questions of the character usually committed for determination to public utility commissions, and the difficulties involved in these decisions would be much enhanced by differences in the laws, rules and practices of the several States regarding the duties of natural gas companies to furnish adequate service.

"Clearly, this Court could not undertake such determinations. To make equitable distribution would be a task of such complexity and difficulty that even an interstate public service commission with broad powers, perfected administrative machinery, ample resources, practical experience and no other duties, might fail to perform it satisfactorily. As this Court would be powerless to frame a decree and provide machinery by means of which such equitable distribution of the available supply could be effected, it should, according to settled practice, refuse to entertain the suits."[63]

Even though the abstract conditions for judicial competence exist, the Supreme Court may not be the fittest tribunal for its exercise. When cases depend on subtle appreciation of complicated local arrangements or the interpretation of state enactments not yet interpreted by state courts nor yielding their meaning merely to a reading of English, original interpretations by the Supreme Court are likely to be *in vacuo*. The local court, whether state or federal, has judicial antennae for local situations seldom vouchsafed to the tribunal at Washington. The Supreme Court should draw on the experience and judgment of the local courts before giving ultimate judgment upon local law.

"If it be true that the Railway is not bound by the fare provisions, unless the City had power to bind itself in that respect, it is necessary to determine whether the City had that power and whether the parties did in fact contract as to the rate of fare. Whether the City had the power is, of course, a question of state law. In California, the constitution and the statutes leave the question in doubt. Counsel agree that there is no decision in any court of the State directly in point. They reason from policy and analogy. In support of their several contentions they cite, in the aggregate, 30 decisions of the California courts, 15 statutes of the State, besides 3 provisions of its code and 7 provisions of its constitution. The decisions referred to occupy 308 pages of the official reports; the sections of the constitution, code and statutes, 173 pages. Moreover, the 102 franchises here involved were granted at many different times between 1886 and 1927. And during that long period, there have been amendments both of relevant statutes and of the constitution. The City or the County may have had the power to contract as to the rate of fare at one time and not at another. If it is held that the City or the County ever had the power to contract as to rate of fare, it will be necessary to examine the 102 franchises to see whether the power was exercised. It may then be that some of the franchises contain valid fare contracts, while others do not. In that event, the relief to be granted will involve passing also on matters of detail.

"In my opinion, these questions of statutory construction, and all matters of detail, should, in the first instance, be decided by the trial court. To that end, the judgment of the District Court should be vacated and the case remanded for further proceedings, without costs to either party in this Court. Pending the decision of the trial court an interlocutory injunction should issue. Compare *City of Hammond* v. *Schappi Bus Line,* 275 U. S. 164; *City of Hammond* v. *Farine Bus Line & Transportation Co.,* 275 U. S. 173; *Ohio Oil Co.* v. *Conway,* 279 U. S. 813. It is a serious task for us to construe and apply the written law of California. Compare *Gilchrist* v. *Interborough Rapid Transit Co.,* 279 U. S. 159, 207-209. To 'one brought up within it, varying emphasis, tacit assumptions, unwritten practices, a thousand influences gained only from life, may give to the different parts wholly new values that logic and grammar never could have got from the books.' *Diaz* v. *Gonzales*, 261 U. S. 102, 106. This Court is not peculiarly fitted for that work. We may properly postpone the irksome burden of examining the many relevant state statutes and decisions until we shall have had the aid which would be afforded by a thorough consideration of them by the judges of the District Court, who are presumably more familiar with the law of California than we are. The practice is one frequently followed by this Court.

"In the case at bar, there are persuasive reasons for adopting the course suggested. The subject matter of this litigation is local to California. The parties are all citizens of that State and creatures of its legislature. Since the Railway denies that there ever was a valid contract governing the rate and asserts that if any such existed they have been abrogated, the contract clause of the Federal Constitution is not involved. The alleged existence of contracts concerning the rate of fare presents the fundamental issue of the case. Whether such contracts exist, or ever existed, depends wholly upon the construction to be given to laws of the State. Upon these questions, the decision of the Supreme Court of California would presumably have been accepted by this Court, if the case had come here on appeal from it. . . .

"The constitutional claim of confiscation gave jurisdiction to the District Court. We may be required, therefore, to pass, at some time, upon these questions of state law. And we may do so now. But the special province of this Court is the Federal law. The construction and application of the Constitution of the United States and of the legislation of Congress is its most important function. In order to give adequate consideration to the adjudication of great issues of government, it must, so far as possible, lessen the burden incident to the disposition of cases, which come here for review."[64]

And when, finally, a constitutional decision is rendered, not the language in explanation of it but the terms of the controversy which called it forth, alone determine the extent of its sway. This is merely the common-law lawyer's general disrespect for dicta; but in constitutional adjudications dicta are peculiarly pernicious usurpers. To let even accumulated dicta govern, is to give the future no hearing. And immortality does not inhere even in constitutional decisions. The Constitution owes its continuity to a continuous process of revivifying changes. "The Constitution can not make itself; some body made it, not at once but at several times. It is alterable; and by that draweth nearer Perfection; and without suiting itself to differing Times and Circumstances, it could not live. Its Life is prolonged by changing seasonably the several Parts of it at several times."[65] So wrote the shrewd Lord Halifax, and it is as true of our written Constitution as of that strange medley of imponderables which is the British Constitution. A ready and delicate sense of the need for alteration is perhaps the most precious talent required of the Supreme Court. Upon it depends the vitality of the Constitution as a vehicle for life.

"I suspect that my brethren would agree with me in sustaining this tax on ore in the bins but for *Gillespie* v. *Oklahoma*, 257 U. S. 501. The question there involved was different. Any language in the opinion which may seem opposite to the case at bar, should be disregarded as inconsistent with the earlier decisions. It is a peculiar virtue of our system of law that the process of inclusion and exclusion, so often employed in developing a rule, is to be allowed to end with its enunciation and that an expression in an opinion yields later to the impact of facts unforeseen.

The attitude of the Court in this respect has been especially helpful when called upon to adjust the respective powers of the States and the Nation in the field of taxation."[66]

"The recent legislation of Congress seeks, in a statesmanlike manner, to limit the practical scope and effect of our decisions in *Southern Pacific Co.* v. *Jensen,* 244 U. S. 205; *Knickerbocker Ice Co.* v. *Stewart,* 253 U. S. 149, and later cases, by making them hereafter applicable only to the relations of the ship to her master and crew. To hold that Congress can effect this result by sanctioning the application of state workmen's compensation laws to accidents to any other class of employees occurring on the navigable waters of the State would not, in my judgment, require us to overrule any of these cases. It would require merely that we should limit the application of the rule therein announced, and that we should declare that our disapproval of certain expressions used in the opinions. Such limitation of principles previously announced, and such express disapproval of *dicta,* are often necessary. It is an unavoidable incident of the search by courts of last resort for the true rule. The process of inclusion and exclusion, so often applied in developing a rule, cannot end with its first enunciation. The rule as announced must be deemed tentative. For the many and varying facts to which it will be applied cannot be foreseen. Modification implies growth. It is the life of the law.

"If the Court is of opinion that this act of Congress is in necessary conflict with its recent decisions, these cases should be frankly overruled. The reasons for doing so are persuasive. Our experience in attempting to apply the rule, and helpful discussions by friends of the Court, have made it clear that the rule declared is legally unsound; that it disturbs legal principles long established; and that if adhered to, it will make a serious addition to the classes of cases which this Court is required to review. Experience and discussion have also made apparent how unfortunate are the results, economically and socially. It has, in part, frustrated a promising attempt to alleviate some of the misery, and remove some of the injustice, incident to the conduct of industry and commerce. These far-reaching and unfortunate results of the rule declared in *Southern Pacific Co.* v. *Jensen* cannot have been foreseen when the decision was rendered. If it is adhered to, appropriate legislative provision, urgently needed, cannot be made until another amendment of the Constitution shall have been adopted. For no federal workmen's compensation law could satisfy the varying and peculiar economic and social needs incident to the diversity of conditions in the several States.

"The doctrine of *stare decisis* should not deter us from overruling that case and those which follow it. The decisions are recent ones. They have not been acquiesced in. They have not created a rule of property around which vested interests have clustered. They affect solely matters of a transitory nature. On the other hand, they affect seriously the lives of men, women and children, and the general welfare. *Stare decisis* is ordinarily a wise rule of action. But it is not a universal, inexorable command. The instances in which the Court has disregarded its admonition are many. The existing admiralty jurisdiction rests, in large part, upon like action of the Court in *The Genesee Chief,* 12 How. 443, 456. In that case the Court overruled *The Thomas Jefferson,* 10 Wheat. 428, and *The Steamboat Orleans* v. *Phoebus,* 11 Pet. 175; and a doctrine declared by Mr. Justice Story with the concurrence of Chief Justice Marshall, and approved by Chancellor Kent, was abandoned when found to be erroneous, although it had been acted on for twenty-six years."[67]

"It is usually more important that a rule of law be settled, than that it be settled right. Even where the error in declaring the rule is a matter of serious concern, it is ordinarily better to seek correction by legislation. Often this is true although the question is a constitutional one. The human experience embodied in the doctrine of *stare decisis* teaches us, also, that often it is better to follow a precedent, although it does not involve the declaration of a rule.

This is usually true so far as concerns a particular statute whether the error was made in construing it or in passing upon its validity. But the doctrine of *stare decisis* does not command that we err again when we have occasion to pass upon a different statute. In the search for truth through the slow process of inclusion and exclusion, involving trial and error, it behooves us to reject, as guides, the decisions upon such questions which prove to have been mistaken. This course seems to me imperative when, as here, the decision to be made involves the delicate adjustment of conflicting claims of the Federal Government and the States to regulate commerce. The many cases on the Commerce Clause in which this Court has overruled or explained away its earlier decisions show that the wisdom of this course has been heretofore recognized. In the case at bar, also, the logic of words should yield to the logic of realities."[68]

VIII

A philosophy of intellectual humility determines Mr. Justice Brandeis' conception of the Supreme Court's function: an instinct against the tyranny of dogma and scepticism regarding the perdurance of any man's wisdom, though he be judge. No one knows better than he how slender a reed is reason—how recent its emergence in man. how powerful the countervailing instincts and passions, how treacherous the whole rational process. But just because the efforts of reason are tenuous, a constant process of critical scrutiny of the tentative claims of reason is essential to the very progress of reason. Truth and knowledge can function and flourish only if error may freely be exposed. And error will go unchallenged if dogma, no matter how widely accepted or dearly held, may not be questioned. Man must be allowed to challenge it by speech or by pen, not merely by silent thought. Thought, like other instincts, will atrophy unless formally exercised. If men cannot speak or write freely, they will soon cease to think freely. Limits there are, of course, even to this essential condition of a free society. But they do not go beyond the minimum requirements of an imminent and substantial threat to the very society which makes individual freedom significant. Together with his colleagues, Mr. Justice Brandeis has refused to make freedom of speech an absolute. But the test of freedom of speech is readiness "to allow it to men whose opinions seem to you wrong and even dangerous."[69]

"The extent to which Congress may, under the Constitution, interfere with free speech was in *Schenck* v. *United States,* 249 U. S. 47, 52, declared by a unanimous court to be this: — 'The question in every case is whether the words used are used in such circumstances and are of such nature as to create a clear and present danger that they will bring about the substantive evils that Congress has a right to prevent. It is a question of proximity and degree.'

"This is a rule of reason. Correctly applied, it will preserve the right of free speech both from suppression by tyrannous, well-meaning majorities and from abuse by irresponsible, fanatical minorities. Like many other rules for human conduct, it can be applied correctly only by the exercise of good judgment; and to the exercise of good judgment; calmness is, in times of deep feeling and on subjects which excite passion, as essential as fearlessness and honesty. The question whether in a particular instance the words spoken or written fall within the permissible curtailment of free speech is, under the rule enunciated by this court, one of degree. And because it is a question of degree the field in which the jury may exercise its judgment is, necessarily, a wide one. But its field is not unlimited. The trial provided for is one by judge *and* jury; and the judge may not abdicate his function. If the words were of such a nature and were used under such circumstances that men, judging in calmness, could not reasonably say that they created a clear and present danger that they would bring about the evil which Congress sought and had a right to prevent, then it is the duty of the trial judge to withdraw the case from the consideration of the jury; and if he fails to do so, it is the duty of the appellate court to correct the error. In my opinion, no jury acting in calmness could reasonably say that any of the publications set forth in the indictment was of such a character or was made under such circumstances as to create a clear and present danger either that they would obstruct recruiting or that they would promote the success of the enemies of the United States."[70]

"A verdict should have been directed for the defendants on these counts also because the leaflet was not distributed under such circumstances, nor was it of such a nature, as to create a clear and present danger of causing either insubordination, disloyalty, mutiny or refusal of duty in the military or naval forces. The leaflet contains lurid and perhaps exaggerated pictures of the horrors of war. Its arguments as to the causes of this war may appear to us shallow and grossly unfair. The remedy proposed may seem to us worse than the evil which, it is argued, will be thereby removed. But the leaflet, far from counselling disobedience to law, points to the hopelessness of protest, under the existing system, pictures the irresistible power of the military arm of the Government, and indicates that acquiescence is a necessity. Insubordination, disloyalty, mutiny and refusal of duty in the military or naval forces are very serious crimes. It is not conceivable that any man of ordinary intelligence and normal judgment would be induced by anything in the leaflet to commit them and thereby risk the severe punishment prescribed for such offences. Certainly there was no clear and present danger that such would be the result. . . .

"The fundamental right of free men to strive for better conditions through new legislation and new institutions will not be preserved, if efforts to secure it by argument to fellow citizens may be construed as criminal incitement to disobey the existing law—merely, because the argument presented seems to those exercising judicial power to be unfair in its portrayal of existing evils, mistaken in its assumptions, unsound in reasoning or intemperate in language. No objections more serious than these can, in my opinion, reasonably be made to the arguments presented in 'The Price We Pay.'"[71]

"As the Minnesota statute is in my opinion invalid because it interferes with federal functions and with the right of a citizen of the United States to discuss them, I see no occasion to consider whether it violates also the Fourteenth Amendment. But I have difficulty in believing that the liberty guaranteed by the Constitution, which has been held to protect against state denial the right of an employer to discriminate against a workman because he is a member of a trade union, *Coppage* v. *Kansas,* 236 U. S. 1, the right of a business man to conduct a private employment agency, *Adams* v. *Tanner,* 244 U. S. 590, or to contract outside the State for insurance of his property, *Allgeyer* v. *Louisiana,* 165 U. S. 578, 589, although the legislature deems it inimical to the public welfare, does not include liberty to teach, either in the privacy of the home or publicly, the doctrine of pacifism; so long, at least, as Congress has not declared that the public safety demands its suppression. I cannot believe that the liberty guaranteed by the Fourteenth Amendment includes only liberty to acquire and to enjoy property."[72]

Freedom of speech and freedom of assembly are empty phrases if their exercise must yield to unreasonable fear. Great social convulsions like the Russian Revolution are bound to have their repercussions of panic among the timid and humorless, particularly panic stimulated by all the modern incitements to mass feeling. Such times present the decisive occasions for a stern enforcement of the right to air grievances, however baseless, and to propose remedies even more cruel than the grievances.

"This Court has not yet fixed the standard by which to determine when a danger shall be deemed clear; how remote the danger may be and yet be deemed present; and what degree of evil shall be deemed sufficiently substantial to justify resort to abridgment of free speech and assembly as the means of protection. To reach sound conclusions on these matters, we must bear in mind why a State is, ordinarily, denied the power to prohibit dissemination of social, economic and political doctrine which a vast majority of its citizens believes to be false and fraught with evil consequence.

"Those who won our independence believed that the final end of the State was to make men free to develop their facilities; and that in its government the deliberative forces should prevail over the arbitrary. They valued liberty both as an end and as a means. They believed liberty to be the secret of happiness and courage to be the secret of liberty. They believed that freedom to think as you will and to speak as you think are means indispensable to the discovery and spread of political truth; that without free speech and assembly discussion would be futile; that with them, discussion affords ordinarily adequate protection against the dissemination of noxious doctrine; that the greatest menace to freedom is an inert people, that public discussion is a political duty; and that this should be a fundamental principle of the American government. They recognized the risks to which all human institutions are subject. But they knew that order cannot be secured merely through fear of punishment for its infraction; that it is hazardous to discourage thought, hope and imagination; that fear breeds repression; that repression breeds hate; that hate menaces stable government; that the path of safety lies in the opportunity to discuss freely supposed grievances and proposed remedies; and that the fitting remedy for evil counsels is good ones. Believing in the power of reason as applied through public discussion, they eschewed silence coerced by law – the argument of force in its worst form. Recognizing the occasional tyrannies of governing majorities, they amended the Constitution so that free speech and assembly should be guaranteed.

"Fear of serious injury cannot alone justify suppression of free speech and assembly. Men feared witches and burnt women. It is the function of speech to free men from the bondage of irrational fears. To justify suppression of free speech there must be reasonable ground to fear that serious evil will result if free speech is practiced. There must be reasonable ground to believe that the danger apprehended is imminent. There must be reasonable ground to believe that the evil to be prevented is a serious one. Every denunciation of existing law tends in some measure to increase the probability that there will be violation of it. Condonation of a breach enhances the probability. Expressions of approval add to the probability. Propagation of the criminal state of mind by teaching syndicalism increases it. Advocacy of law-breaking heightens it still further. But even advocacy of violation, however reprehensible morally, is not a justification for denying free speech where the advocacy falls short of incitement and there is nothing to indicate that the advocacy would be immediately acted on. The wide difference between advocacy and incitement, between preparation and attempt, between assembling and conspiracy, must be borne in mind. In order to support a finding of clear and present danger it must be shown either that immediate serious violence was to be expected or was advocated, or that the past conduct furnished reason to believe that such advocacy was then contemplated.

"Those who won our independence by revolution were not cowards. They did not fear political change. They did not exalt order at the cost of liberty. To courageous, self-reliant men, with confidence in the power of free and fearless reasoning applied through the processes of popular government, no danger flowing from speech can be deemed clear and present, unless the incidence of the evil apprehended is so imminent that it may befall before there is opportunity for full discussion. If there be time to expose through discussion the falsehood and fallacies, to avert the evil by the processes of education, the remedy to be applied is more speech, not enforced silence. Only an emergency can justify repression. Such must be the rule if authority is to be reconciled with freedom. Such, in my opinion, is the command of the Constitution. It is therefore always open to Americans to challenge a law abridging free speech and assembly by showing that there was no emergency justifying it."[73]

Utterance also has responsibility. To misrepresent fact is to corrupt the source of opinion. No compensating social gain demands the right to such misrepresentation. But the free exchange of opinion upon complicated issues must not be turned into crime by treating the prevailing view as a fact and proscribing unpopular dissent.

"To prove the falsity of this statement the Government introduced the address made by the President to Congress on April 2, 1917, which preceded the adoption of the Joint Resolution of April 6, 1917, declaring that a state of war exists between the United States and the Imperial German Government (c. 1, 40 Stat. 1). This so-called statement of fact—which is alleged to be false — is merely a conclusion or a deduction from facts. True it is the kind of conclusion which courts call a conclusion of fact, as distinguished from a conclusion of law; and which is sometimes spoken of as a finding of ultimate fact as distinguished from an evidentiary fact. But, in its essence it is the expression of a judgment — like the statements of many so-called historical facts. . . .

"The cause of a war — as of most human action — is not single. War is ordinarily the result of many cooperating causes, many different conditions, acts and motives. Historians rarely agree in their judgment as to what was the determining factor in a particular war, even when they write under circumstances where detachment and the availability of evidence from all sources minimize both prejudice and other sources of error. For individuals, and classes of individuals, attach significance to those things which are significant to them. And as the contributing causes cannot be subjected, like a chemical combination in a test tube, to qualitative and quantitative analysis so as to weigh and value the various elements, the historians differ necessarily in their judgments. One finds the determining cause of war in a great man, another in an idea, a belief, an economic necessity, a trade advantage, a sinister machination, or an accident. It is for this reason largely that men seek to interpret anew in each age, and often with each new generation, the important events in the world's history."[74]

The press is the most important vehicle for the dissemination of opinion. The Constitution precludes its censorship. Equally inadmissible should be all oblique methods to censor the press. Particularly offensive is the coercive power of unregulated administrative control.

"This case arose during the World War; but it presents no legal question peculiar to war. It is important, because what we decide may determine in large measure whether in times of peace our press shall be free.

"The denial to a newspaper of entry as second-class mail, or the revocation of an entry previously made, does not deny to the paper admission to the mail; nor does it deprive the publisher of any mail facility. It merely deprives him of the very low postal rates, called second class, and compels him to pay postage for the same service at the rate called third class, which was, until recently, from eight to fifteen times as high as the second-class rate. Such is the nature and the only effect of an order denying or revoking entry.

"In conclusion I say again – because it cannot be stressed too strongly – that the power here claimed is not a war power. There is no question of its necessity to protect the country from insidious domestic foes. To that end Congress conferred upon the Postmaster General the enormous power contained in the Espionage Act of entirely excluding from the mails any letter, picture or publication which contained matter violating the broad terms of that act. But it did not confer – and the Postmaster General concedes that it did not confer – the vague and absolute authority practically to deny circulation to any publication which in his opinion is likely to violate in the future any postal law. The grant of that power is construed into a postal law. The grant of that power is construed into a postal rate statute passed forty years ago which has never before been suspected of containing such implication. I cannot believe that in establishing postal classifications in 1879 Congress intended to confer upon the Postmaster General authority to issue the order here complained of. If, under the Constitution, administrative officers may, as a mere incident of the peace time administration of their departments, be vested with the power to issue such orders as this, there is little of substance in our Bill of Rights and in every extension of governmental functions lurks a new danger to civil liberty."[75]

IX

His deep consciousness of the imperfections of reason leads Mr. Justice Brandeis to observe rigorously the conditions which alone assure the fair working of even disinterested judgment. Truth may be beyond mortals, but law should at least satisfy the requirements for truth-seeking. Laymen, and even lawyers who are not historically-minded, are too apt to identify procedure with obstructive technicalities.[76] But there are technicalities and technicalities. The fundamental aspects of judicial procedure have the support of enduring human interests.

English criminal justice rightly serves as a shining contrast to our own. Yet those features in our Bill of Rights which it is now fashionable to regard as unduly favorable to the accused, are even more securely embedded in the texture of English feeling than they are secured through the written words in our Constitution. Here the third degree is widely practised and too often condoned.[77] In England the suggestion that Scotland Yard applied the third degree aroused the condemnation of all parties in the House of Commons.[78] Mr. Justice Brandeis has been true to the civilized standards of the British tradition.

"The Court of Appeals appears to have held the prisoner's statements admissible on the ground that a confession made by one competent to act is to be deemed voluntary, as a matter of law, if it was not induced by a promise or a threat; and that here there was evidence sufficient to justify a finding of fact that these statements were not so induced. In the federal courts, the requisite of voluntariness is not satisfied by establishing merely that the confession was not induced by a promise or a threat. A confession is voluntarily in law if, and only if, it was in fact, voluntarily made. A confession may have been given voluntarily, although it was made to police officers, while in custody, and in answer to an examination conducted by them. But a confession obtained by compulsion, must be excluded whatever may have been the character of the compulsion, and whether the compulsion was applied in a judicial proceeding or otherwise. *Bram* v. *United States,* 168 U. S. 532. None of the five statements introduced by the Government as admissions or confessions was made until after Wan had been subjected for seven days to the interrogation. The testimony given by the superintendent of police, the three detectives and the chief medical officer left no room for a contention that the statements of the defendant were, in fact, voluntary. The undisputed facts showed that compulsion was applied. As to that matter there was no issue which the jury could properly have been required or permitted to pass. The alleged oral statements and the written confession should have been excluded."[79]

Anxiety over the deep shadows which crime casts upon the American scene should not tempt relaxation of the moral restraints which painful history has prescribed for law officers. Our own days furnish solemn reminders that police and prosecutors and occasionally even judges will, if allowed, employ illegality and yield to passion, with the same justification of furthering the public weal as their predecessors relied upon for the brutalities of the seventeenth and eighteenth centuries.

"Plaintiff's private papers were stolen. The thief, to further his own ends, delivered them to the law officer of the United States. He, knowing them to have been stolen, retains them for use against the plaintiff. Should the court permit him to do so?

"That the court would restore the papers to plaintiff if they were still in the thief's possession is not questioned. That it has power to control the disposition of these stolen papers, although they have passed into the possession of the law officer, is also not questioned. But it is said that no provision of the Constitution required their surrender and that the papers could have been subpoenaed. This may be true. Still I cannot believe that action of a public official is necessarily lawful, because it does not violate constitutional prohibitions and because the same result might have been attained by other and proper means. At the foundation of our civil liberty lies the principle which denies to government officials an exceptional position before the law and which subjects them to the same rules of conduct that are commands to the citizen. And in the development of our liberty insistence upon procedural regularity has been a large factor. Respect for law will not be advanced by resort, in its enforcement, to means which shock the common man's sense of decency and fair play."[80]

"I am aware that courts – mistaking relative social values and forgetting that a desirable end cannot justify foul means – have, in their zeal to punish, sanctioned the use of evidence obtained through criminal violation of property and personal rights or by other practices of detectives even more revolting. But the objection here is of a different nature. It does not rest merely upon the character of the evidence or upon the fact that the evidence was illegally obtained. The obstacle to the prosecution lies in the fact that the alleged crime was instigated by officers of the Government; that the act for which the Government seeks to punish the defendant is the fruit of their criminal conspiracy to induce its commission. The Government may set decoys to entrap criminals. But it may not provoke or create a crime and then punish the criminal, its creature."[81]

"Will this Court by sustaining the judgment below

sanction such conduct [wire-tapping] on the part of the Executive? The governing principle has long been settled. It is that a court will not redress a wrong when he who invokes its aid has unclean hands. The maxim of unclean hands comes from courts of equity. But the principle prevails also in courts of law. Its common application is in civil actions between private parties. Where the Government is the actor, the reasons for applying it are even more persuasive. Where the remedies invoked are those of the criminal law, the reasons are compelling. . . .

"Decency, security and liberty alike demand that government officials shall be subjected to the same rules of conduct that are commands to the citizen. In a government of laws, existence of the government will be imperilled if it fails to observe the law scrupulously. Our Government is the potent, the omnipresent teacher. For good or for ill, it teaches the whole people by its example. Crime is contagious. If the Government becomes a law-breaker, it breeds contempt for law; it invites every man to become a law unto himself; it invites anarchy. To declare that in the administration of the criminal law the end justifies the means – to declare that the Government may commit crimes in order to secure the conviction of a private criminal – would bring terrible retribution. Against that pernicious doctrine this Court should resolutely set its face."[82]

* * *

XI

To quote from Mr. Justice Brandeis' opinions is not to pick plums from a pudding but to pull threads from a pattern. He achieves not by epigrammatic thrust but through powerful exposition. His aim is not merely to articulate the grounds of his judgment, but to reach the mind even of the disappointed suitor, deeming it essential for defeated interests to know that their claims have adequately entered the judicial process. His opinions march step by step towards demonstration, with all the auxiliary reinforcement of detailed proof. The documentation of his opinions is one aspect of his reliance on reason. To sever text from accompanying footnotes is therefore to dismember an organic whole.[94]

The style of his opinions befits their aim. The dominant note is Doric simplicity. Occasionally, as in the terrible case of Ziang Sung Wan,[95] his restraint attains austerity. And sometimes the majesty of his theme stirs him to eloquence. When the issue is freedom of speech, he gives noble utterance to his faith and to the meaning of our institutions as the embodiment of that faith.

In truth, Mr. Justice Brandeis is a moral teacher, who follows Socrates in the belief that virtue is the pursuit of enlightened purpose. His long years of intimate connection with the history of the Harvard Law School symbolize his dominant impulse. Problems, for him, are never solved. Civilization is a sequence of new tasks. Hence his insistence on the extreme difficulty of government and its dependence on sustained interest and effort, on the need for constant alertness to the fact that the introduction of new forces is accompanied by new difficulties. This, in turn, makes him mindful of the limited range of human foresight, and leads him to practice humility in attempting to preclude the freedom of action of those who are to follow.

The Justice himself, while at the bar, disavowed allegiance to any general system of thought or hope. "I have no rigid social philosophy; I have been too intent on concrete problems of practical justice." Devotion to justice is widely professed. By Mr. Justice Brandeis it has been given concrete expression in a long effort towards making the life of the commonplace individual more significant. His zest for giving significance to life is not sentimentality; it arises from a keen sensitiveness to quality. He not only evokes the best qualities in others; he exacts the best in himself. Stern self-discipline of a mind preternaturally rich and deep has fashioned a judge who, by common consent, is a great and abiding figure of the world's most powerful court.

MR. JUSTICE BRANDEIS AND THE CONSTITUTION

ALPHEUS THOMAS MASON

Alpheus Thomas Mason is McCormick professor of jurisprudence at Princeton University. He has authored numerous books, among them are *Brandeis, A Free Man's Life* (1946), *Brandeis: Lawyer and Judge in the Modern State* (1953), *The Brandeis Way* (1938) and *American Constitutional Law* (1954). This article is reprinted from 80 University of Pennsylvania Law Review 799, 832--841 (1932).

* * *

The views of Mr. Justice Brandeis, so long propounded in dissent, are now coming into general acceptance. A few illustrations may be cited:

With regard to the limits of the constitutional function of judicial review, particularly in due process cases, his theory has recently been pronounced by him as spokesman for the Court in the *New Jersey Insurance* case. Herein he held that the presumption of constitutionality in favor of legislation, clearly within the police power, must prevail, "In the absence of some factual foundation of record for overthrowing the statute."[142] The burden of proof, therefore, is placed squarely on those who oppose the statute, not on the state that upholds it. This is reminiscent of the rule followed by the Court in the famous *Munn* case[143] more than fifty years earlier, — a rule, it may be added, from which the Court has departed in a number of important instances. By either placing the burden of proof upon the state[144] for the justification of social legislation, or by the Court's making an investigation of facts such as is proper only for the legislature and substituting its own findings for those of the legislature (as is the custom of the more conservative judges),[145] the Court has hitherto found it possible to set aside legislation of great social and economic significance.

In the *Railway Clerks'* case[146] the Supreme Court

went far toward accepting Mr. Justice Brandeis' view that a labor union is entitled to extend its operations beyond the bounds of a single enterprise. The Railway Clerks' Union, to preserve its integrity, had secured an injunction against the formation of a company union. A unanimous Court sustained that order. The case is also especially noteworthy in that it demonstrated for the first time, in a Supreme Court decision, the effectiveness with which the injunction can be used by labor *against* employers.

In the recent decision in the *Chain Store* case,[147] the claims of industrial liberty, the right of the independent merchant and manufacturer against the oppression of monopolistic combinations, triumphed and did so on the basis of the principles insisted upon by Mr. Justice Brandeis in the *Quaker City Cab* case.[148]

During the same term of Court, his conclusion, that "in frank expression of conflicting opinion lies the greatest promise of wisdom in governmental action; and in suppression lies ordinarily the greatest peril,"[149] prevailed in the *California Red Flag* case.[150]

In the public utility field, economic events have already confirmed the merit of his actual prudent investment theory of valuation, as against reproduction cost, which the Court has usually shown a tendency to favor. With characteristic insight into economic cause and effect Mr. Justice Brandeis wrote in 1923: "The present price level may fall to that of 1914 within a decade; and that, later, it may fall much lower."[151] With the fulfillment of this prophecy, another shift of position between the protagonists is in order, if the rule in the *Smyth* case is maintained, with the railroads and public utilities on the side of investment cost and the consumer favoring reproduction cost.[152]

Although usually coupled with Mr. Justice Holmes in any discussion of Supreme Court personnel, Mr. Justice Brandeis differs singularly in judicial technique and in approach to questions of social policy. Mr. Justice Holmes is generally called a liberal; although he himself has never, so far I know, pretended to be anything other than a constitutional skeptic.

Put in terms of political theory, Mr. Justice Holmes believes that the sovereign people, speaking through their authorized agent – the legislature – can, in general, embody their opinions in law; that there is nothing in the Constitution to prevent their doing so. Therein he follows Hobbes.[153] Mr. Justice Brandeis, however, believes that the legislature can embody opinion in law only when such enactments conform with certain standards of social justice. This recalls the "higher law" doctrine, and is somewhat reminiscent of the views of Sir Edward Coke, who antedates Hobbes. Therefore, to Mr. Justice Brandeis, judicial review of legislation involves "weighing public needs as against private desires"; and also "weighing relative social values." Consequently he claims for the judiciary a larger share in the exercise of sovereignty than Holmes seems disposed to allow. This, roughly, is the main divergence of their lines of thought.

It follows that Mr. Justice Holmes' brand of liberalism differs fundamentally from that of Mr. Justice Brandeis.[154] The latter becomes deeply concerned with economic and social maladjustments and the means of correction by legislative action, while Mr. Justice Holmes is likely to remain cold and unmoved toward legislative and other panaceas.[155] Mr. Justice Brandeis has demonstrated, both on and off the Bench, that he is a genuine liberal. He is an avowed partisan of the common man; his special concern is for those who are economically and financially dependent upon others for a livelihood; he prefers human welfare to property rights.[156] Highly sensitive to present-day economic and social ills, he could never remain aloof and indifferent as is the habit of Mr. Justice Holmes; he seeks the cause of abuses and examines the merit of proposed remedies.

Counsel frequently fail to make such presentation of the case as satisfies him. So as a member of the Supreme Court, Mr. Justice Brandeis resorts to fact-finding agencies on his own account. He feels called upon to make such investigation of the facts as enable him to decide whether the provision in question is "so clearly arbitrary or capricious that legislators acting reasonably could not have believed it to be necessary or appropriate for the public welfare."[157] Mr. Justice Holmes feels no such responsibility.[158] Not being addicted to the study of social and economic problems,[159] Mr. Justice Holmes is likely to be rather skeptical of social projects.[160] Exactly the reverse is true of Mr. Justice Brandeis. Whether he happens to be writing a brief or a judicial opinion, he is at heart a crusader.[161] Never has he seen social and economic life as logical fictions carefully built up by jurists. His reason for supporting any particular social enactment may be and usually is, as he himself admits "partly legal, partly sentimental and partly a recognition of economic rights and sound social policy.[162]

Another noteworthy characteristic of the judicial thinking of Mr. Justice Brandeis is the respect he pays legislative law, and his slight regard for a "jurisprudence of concepts" which would keep both society and the law in rigid and unchangeable form. The idea that law can be found but not made, forms no part of his juristic philosophy. Although reordering the law to bring it into accord with the ever-changing facts of life, is partly the work of the Courts, it is more truly the function of the legislature.[163] This makes him slow to question the wisdom of the legislature's judgment. Unlike his more conservative brethren, he has insisted that the law be made to look outside itself, if it is to cope adequately with problems raised by a rapidly changing civilization. Thus he brings to his consideration of the legislative product, not merely judicial precedents and decisions but committee reports, legislative debates and authoritative treatises of various sorts, all hitherto almost entirely neglected in judicial opinions.

It follows that law for Mr. Justice Brandeis is no mere embodiment of an arbitrary set of *a priori* abstractions existing in a vacuum; rather, law is essentially an instrument of social policy. Knowledge of it does not consist merely in the logical consistency of its rules. He emphasized time and again the truth of the old maxim of the civilians – *ex facto jus oritur.* "No law, written or unwritten, can be understood without a full knowledge of the facts out of which it arises, and to which it is to be applied."[164]

These words were written in 1916 shortly before he was appointed to the Supreme Court. It is not surprising, then, that as a member of the Court Mr. Justice Brandeis continues his investigations of underlying facts. His opinions are noteworthy and valuable if only for their references to secular literature.[165] No significant contribution, whether from a legal, social or economic point of view, escapes his attention. Elaborate documentation of all such material is made for the purpose of reaching a judicial solution of the problem in hand. His studies have exposed as fictions numerous "assumptions upon which many American judges and lawyers had rested comfortably."[166] His conviction that our individualistic philosophy of rights and property could no longer furnish an adequate basis for dealing with the problem of modern economic life has now become widespread. It is now generally recognized that society has to have protection against low wages, unemployment, industrial accidents, and other social and economic hardships, because society must ultimately bear the burden, financial and otherwise, which these entail. Thus out of the attempt to enforce individual justice, Mr. Brandeis lays the foundations of social justice.

Fundamentally Mr. Justice Brandeis is an idealist, not always entirely objective, seldom without liberal bias toward the social and economic questions that come before him. His vision is of an ideal state wherein tyranny, political and industrial, is abolished;[167] he longs "for a truer democracy."[168]

Although preeminently a factualist, a stickler for statistics, he never allows himself to be buried beneath the facts of modern industrial life. Particular emphasis should be given to the coherent and purposeful social-political philosophy which underlies his profound factual knowledge. Never is he forced "to improvise a theory, a philosophy, when confronted over night by the exigencies of the case before him."[169] With keen insight into the "universal element" involved in the case before him, his decisions are invariably quickened "with the inspiration of a principle."[170]

Judicial interpretation cannot eliminate the personal bias of the interpreter. All men are more or less partisan. Emotions, great and small, compel the judge to choose his side. When once that choice is made, historical events, social and economic facts, judicial precedents and philosophy, are marshalled and emphasized in such a way as to bolster up his viewpoint.[171] These observations are, I think, as applicable to Mr. Justice Brandeis as to any other judge.[172] Many years of study and of close contact with social and economic affairs have developed in him certain emotional preferences.[173] Noting the continuity of Mr. Justice Brandeis' views before and after his appointment, one is apt to feel that an ideal picture of society predetermines his position as to many of the Court's decisions.[174]

And yet his contention that he has "no rigid social philosophy," is logical and natural enough because he is essentially a social scientist, for whom problems are never solved but always in process of solution. New inventions, great emergencies and the like, give rise to new difficulties; a rule of law once settled may have to yield later on to the impact of facts unforeseen. "Modification implies growth. It is the life of the law."[175]

The Constitution itself does not block that growth except when interpreted by minds too rigid and in an age of change.[176] Then only does our fundamental law prevent legislation from achieving the social and economic ideal. Mr. Justice Brandeis understands that the Constitution must be given liberal construction, if it is, as John Marshall once said, "to endure for all ages to come, and, consequently, to be adapted to the various *crises* in human affairs."[177]

"Time works changes, brings into existence new conditions and purposes. Therefore a principle to be vital must be capable of wider application than the mischief which gave it birth. This is peculiarly true of constitutions. They are not ephemeral enactments, designed to meet passing occasions."[178]

". . . our social and industrial welfare demands that ample scope should be given for social as well as mechanical invention. It is a condition not only of progress but of conserving that which we have. Nothing could be more revolutionary than to close the door to social experimentation. . . . And surely the federal Constitution — itself perhaps the greatest of human experiments — does not prohibit [legislation reconciling] the existing industrial system with our striving for social justice and the preservation of the race."[179]

Thus limitations "like those embodied in the due process clauses of the Fifth and Fourteenth Amendments, do not forbid the United States or the states from meeting modern conditions by regulations which 'a century ago, or even half a century ago, probably would have been rejected as arbitrary and oppressive'.[180] Clauses guaranteeing the individual protection against specific abuses of power, must have a similar capacity of adaptation to a changing world."[181] "There must be power in the states, and in the nation to remould through experimentation our economic practises to meet changing social and economic needs."[182]

In considering Mr. Justice Brandeis' work on the Supreme Court, it is customary to lay special stress upon his mastery of figures and statistics.[183] But such analysis may lose sight of the fact that Mr. Justice Brandeis is a social and political philosopher as well as a technician. He sees, as have few of his generation, the social and economic perils of the industrial revolution; he understands that the development of the machine and of the business corporation, are threats to liberty and to the general welfare. To him this means that we have "passed to a subtler civilization"; and therefore he urges "the law must still protect a man from things that rob him of his freedom, whether the oppressing force be physical or of a subtler kind".[184] The Justice emphasized the need for social intelligence. But he did more: he studied some of the outstanding social and economic ills from which society increasingly suffers. In these novel and creative activities Mr. Justice Brandeis has been dominated by a philosophy, an ideal, the vision of a social and political structure within which the individual may best develop a creative personality.

As a member of the Supreme Court, Mr. Justice Brandeis has been and is significant because certain preeminent qualities of mind enable him to bring the law into vital relationship with the social possibilities of industry in our own day. He sees beyond the daily facts of economics and statistics to their basic social and economic consequences, to their philosophic implication for the future.[185] Methods of legal technique are not idols but tools, tools serving the art of juristic philosophy and statesmanship. Vast learning in the social sciences and a well-nigh unique mastery of current data are used merely as instruments of juristic thought.[186] Thus it is that Mr. Justice Brandeis builds deep foundations for our law of days to come.

THE RIGHT TO PRIVACY

Louis D. Brandeis and
Samuel D. Warren

Mr. Justice Brandeis, with his law partner, wrote this article in 1890 when he was in private practice. It is a classic in legal literature, having had a direct influence on the development of a new legal concept, the right to privacy, by the courts. It is reprinted from 4 Harvard Law Review 193-220 (1890).

That the individual shall have full protection in person and in property is a principle as old as the common law; but it has been found necessary from time to time to define anew the exact nature and extent of such protection. Political, social and economic changes entail the recognition of new rights, and the common law, in its eternal youth, grows to meet the demands of society. Thus, in very early times, the law gave a remedy only for physical interference with life and property, for trespasses *vi et armis*. Then the "right to life" served only to protect the subject from battery in its various forms; liberty meant freedom from actual restraint; and the right to property secured to the individual his lands and his cattle. Latter, there came a recognition of man's spiritual nature, of his feelings and his intellect. Gradually the scope of these legal rights broadened; and now the right to life has come to mean the right to enjoy life,—the right to be let alone; the right to liberty secures the exercise of extensive civil privileges; and the term "property" has grown to comprise every form of possession—intangible, as well as tangible.

Thus, with the recognition of the legal value of sensations, the protection against actual bodily injury was extended to prohibit mere attempts to do such injury; that is, the putting another in fear of such injury. From the action of battery grew that of assault.[1] Much later there came a qualified protection of the individual against offensive noises and odors, against dust and smoke, and excessive vibration. The law of nuisance was developed.[2] So regard for human emotions soon extended the scope of personal immunity beyond the body of the individual. His reputation, the standing among his fellow-men, was considered, and the law of slander and libel arose.[3] Man's family relations became a part of the legal conception of his life, and the alienation of a wife's affections was held remediable.[4] Occasionally the law halted,—as in its refusal to recognize the intrusion by seduction upon the honor of the family. But even here the demands of society were met. A mean fiction, the action *per quod servitium amisit*, was resorted to, and by allowing damages for injury to the parents' feelings, an adequate remedy was ordinarily afforded.[5] Similar to the expansion of the right to life was the growth of the legal conception of property. From corporeal property arose the incorporeal rights issuing out of it; and then there opened the wide realm of intangible property, in the products and processes of the mind,[6] as works of literature and art,[7] goodwill,[8] trade secrets, and trademarks.[9]

This development of the law was inevitable. The intense intellectual and emotional life, and the heightening of sensations which came with the advance of civilization, made it clear to men that only a part of the pain, pleasure, and profit of life lay in physical things. Thoughts, emotions, and sensations demanded legal recognition, and the beautiful capacity for growth which characterizes the common law enabled the judges to afford the requisite protection, without the interposition of the legislature.

Recent inventions and business methods call attention to the next step which must be taken for the protection of the person, and for securing to the individual what Judge Cooley calls the right "to be let alone."[10] Instantaneous photographs and newspaper enterprise have invaded the sacred precincts of private and domestic life; and numerous mechanical devices threaten to make good the prediction that "what is whispered in the closet shall be proclaimed from the house-tops." For years there has been a feeling that the law must afford some remedy for the unauthorized circulation of portraits of private persons;[11] and the evil of the invasion of privacy by the newspapers, long keenly felt, has been but recently discussed by an able writer.[12] The alleged facts of a somewhat notorious case brought before an inferior tribunal in New York a few months ago,[13] directly involved the consideration of the right of circulating portraits; and the question whether our law will recognize and protect the right to privacy in this and in other respects must soon come before our courts for consideration.

Of the desirability—indeed of the necessity—of some such protection, there can, it is believed, be no doubt. The press is overstepping in every direction the obvious bounds of propriety and of decency. Gossip is no longer the resource of the idle and of the vicious, but has become a trade, which is pursued with industry as well as effrontery. To satisfy a prurient taste the details of sexual relations are spread broadcast in the columns of the daily papers. To occupy the indolent, column upon column is filled with idle gossip, which can only be procured by intrusion upon the domestic circle. The intensity and complexity of life, attendant upon advancing civilization, have rendered necessary some retreat from the world, and man, under the refining influence of culture, has become more sensitive to publicity, so that solitude and privacy have become more essential to the individual; but modern enterprise and invention have, through invasions upon his privacy, subjected him to mental pain and distress, far greater than could be inflicted by mere bodily injury. Nor is the harm wrought by such invasions confined to the suffering of those who may be made the subjects of journalistic or other enterprise. In this, as in other branches of commerce, the supply creates the demand. Each crop of unseemly gossip, thus harvested, becomes the seed of more, and, in direct proportion to its circulation, results in a lowering of social standards and of morality. Even gossip apparently harmless, when widely and persistently circulated, is potent for evil. It both belittles and perverts. It belittles by inverting the relative importance of things, thus dwarfing the thoughts and aspirations of a people. When personal gossip attains the dignity of print, and crowds the space available for matters of real interest to the community, what wonder that the ignorant and thoughtless mistake its relative importance. Easy of comprehension, appealing to that weak side of human nature which is never wholly cast down by the misfortunes and frailties of our neighbors, no one can be surprised that it usurps the place of interest in brains capable of other things. Triviality destroys at once robustness of thought and delicacy of feeling. No enthusiasm can flourish, no generous impulse can survive under its blighting influence.

It is our purpose to consider whether the existing

law affords a principle which can properly be invoked to protect the privacy of the individual; and, if it does, what the nature and extent of such protection is.

Owing to the nature of the instruments by which privacy is invaded, the injury inflicted bears a superficial resemblance to the wrongs dealt with by the law of slander and of libel, while a legal remedy for such injury seems to involve the treatment of mere wounded feelings, as a substantive cause of action. The principle on which the law of defamation rests, covers, however, a radically different class of effects from those for which attention is now asked. It deals only with damage to reputation, with the injury done to the individual in his external relations to the community, by lowering him in the estimation of his fellows. The matter published of him, however widely circulated, and however unsuited to publicity, must, in order to be actionable, have a direct tendency to injury him in his intercourse with others, and even if in writing or in print, must subject him to the hatred, ridicule, or contempt of his fellowmen,—the effect of the publication upon his estimate of himself and upon his own feelings not forming an essential element in the cause of action. In short, the wrongs and correlative rights recognized by the law of slander and libel are in their nature material rather than spiritual. That branch of the law simply extends the protection surrounding physical property to certain of the conditions necessary or helpful to worldly prosperity. On the other hand, our law recognizes no principle upon which compensation can be granted for mere injury to the feelings. However painful the mental effects upon another of an act, though purely wanton or even malicious, yet if the act itself is otherwise lawful, the suffering inflicted is *damnum absque injuria.* Injury of feelings may indeed be taken account of in ascertaining the amount of damages when attending what is recognized as a legal injury;[14] but our system, unlike the Roman law, does not afford a remedy even for mental suffering which results from mere contumely and insult, from an intentional and unwarranted violation of the "honor" of another.[15]

It is not however necessary, in order to sustain the view that the common law recognizes and upholds a principle applicable to cases of invasion of privacy, to invoke the analogy, which is but superficial, to injuries sustained, either by an attack upon reputation or by what the civilians called a violation of honor; for the legal doctrines relating to infractions of what is ordinarily termed the common-law right to intellectual and artistic property are, it is believed, but instances and applications of a general right to privacy, which properly understood afford a remedy for the evils under consideration.

The common law secures to each individual the right of determining, ordinarily, to what extent his thoughts, sentiments, and emotions shall be communicated to others.[16] Under our system of government, he can never be compelled to express them (except when upon the witness-stand); and even if he has chosen to give them expression, he generally retains the power to fix the limits of the publicity which shall be given them. The existence of this right does not depend upon the particular method of expression adopted. It is immaterial whether it be by word[17] or by signs,[18] in painting,[19] by sculpture, or in music.[20] Neither does the existence of the right depend upon the nature or value of the thought or emotion, nor upon the excellence of the means of expression.[21] The same protection is accorded to a casual letter or an entry in a diary and to the most valuable poem or essay, to a botch or daub and to a masterpiece. In every such case the individual is entitled to decide whether that which is his shall be given to the public.[22] No other has the right to publish his productions in any form, without his consent. This right is wholly independent of the material on which, or the means by which, the thought, sentiment, or emotion is expressed. It may exist independently of any corporeal being, as in words spoken, a song sung, a drama acted. Or if expressed on any material, as a poem in writing, the author may have parted with the paper, without forfeiting any proprietary right in the composition itself. The right is lost only when the author himself communicates his production to the public – in other words, publishes it.[23] It is entirely independent of the copyright laws, and their extension into the domain of art. The aim of those statutes is to secure to the author, composer, or artist the entire profits arising from publication; but the common-law protection enables him to control absolutely the act of publication, and in the exercise of his own discretion, to decide whether there shall be any publication at all.[24] The statutory right is of no value, *unless* there is a publication; the common-law right is lost *as soon as* there is a publication.

What is the nature, the basis, of this right to prevent the publication of manuscripts or works of art? It is stated to be the enforcement of a right of property;[25] and no difficulty arises in accepting this view, so long as we have only to deal with the reproduction of literary and artistic compositions. They certainly possess many of the attributes of ordinary property: they are transferable; they have a value; and publication or reproduction is a use by which that value is realized. But where the value of the production is found not in the right to take the profits arising from publication, but in the peace of mind or the relief afforded by the ability to prevent any publication at all, it is difficult to regard the right as one of property, in the common acceptation of that term. A man records in a letter to his son, or in his diary, that he did not dine with his wife on a certain day. No one into whose hands those papers fall could publish them to the world, even if possession of the documents had been obtained rightfully; and the prohibition would not be confined to the publication of a copy of the letter itself, or of the diary entry; the restraint extends also to a publication of the contents. What is the thing which is protected? Surely, not the intellectual act of recording the fact that the husband did not dine with his wife, but that fact itself. It is not the intellectual product, but the domestic occurrence. A man writes a dozen letters to different people. No person would be permitted to publish a list of the letters written. If the letters or the contents of the diary were protected as literary compositions, the scope of the protection afforded should be the same secured to a published writing under the copyright law. But the copyright law would not prevent an enumeration of the letters, or the publication of some of the facts contained therein. The copyright of a series of paintings or etchings would prevent a reproduction of the paintings as pictures; but it would not prevent a publication of a list or even a description of them.[26] Yet in the famous case of *Prince Albert v. Strange,* the court held that the common-law rule prohibited not merely the reproduction of the etchings which the plaintiff and Queen Victoria had made for their own pleasure, but also "the publishing (at least by printing or writing), though not by copy or resemblance, a description of them, whether more or less limited or summary, whether in the form of a catalogue or otherwise."[27] Likewise, an unpublished collection of news possessing no element of a literary nature is protected from piracy.[28]

That this protection cannot rest upon the right to literary or artistic property in any exact sense, appears the more clearly when the subject-matter for which protection is invoked is not even in the form of intellectual property, but has the attributes of ordinary tangible property. Suppose a man has a collection of gems or curiosities which he keeps private: it would hardly be contended that any person could publish a catalogue of them, and yet the articles enumerated are certainly not intellectual property in the legal sense, any more than a collection of stoves or of chairs.[89]

The belief that the idea of property in its narrow sense was the basis of the protection of unpublished manuscripts led an able court to refuse, in several cases, injunctions against the publication of private letters, on the ground that "letters not possessing the attributes of literary compositions are not properly entitled to protection;" and that it was "evident the plaintiff could not have considered the letters as of any value whatever as literary productions, for a letter cannot be considered of value to the author which he never would consent to have published."[30] But these decisions have not been followed,[31] and it may now be considered settled that the protection afforded by the common law to the author of any writing is entirely independent of its pecuniary value, its intrinsic merits, or of any intention to publish the same, and, of course, also, wholly independent of the material, if any, upon which, or the mode in which, the thought or sentiment was expressed.

Although the courts have asserted that they rested their decisions on the narrow grounds of protection to property, yet there are recognitions of a more liberal doctrine. Thus in the case of *Prince Albert* v. *Strange*, already referred to, the opinions both of the Vice-Chancellor and of the Lord Chancellor, on appeal, show a more or less clearly defined perception of a principle broader than those which were mainly discussed, and on which they both placed their chief reliance. Vice-Chancellor Knight Bruce referred to publishing of a man that he had "written to particular persons or on particular subjects" as an instance of possibly injurious disclosures as to private matters, that the courts would in a proper case prevent; yet it is difficult to perceive how, in such a case, any right of property, in the narrow sense, would be drawn in question, or why, if such a publication would be restrained when it threatened to expose the victim not merely to sarcasm, but to ruin, it should not equally be enjoined, if it threatened to embitter his life. To deprive a man of the potential profits to be realized by publishing a catalogue of his gems cannot *per se* be a wrong to him. The possibility of future profits is not a right of property which the law ordinarily recognizes; it must, therefore, be an infraction of other rights which constitutes the wrongful act, and that infraction is equally wrongful, whether its results are to forestall the profits that the individual himself might secure by giving the matter a publicity obnoxious to him, or to gain an advantage at the expense of his mental pain and suffering. If the fiction of property in a narrow sense must be preserved, it is still true that the end accomplished by the gossip-monger is attained by the use of that which is another's, the facts relating to his private life, which he has seen fit to keep private. Lord Cottenham stated that a man "is entitled to be protected in the exclusive use and enjoyment of that which is exclusively his," and cited with approval the opinion of Lord Eldon, as reported in a manuscript note of the case of *Wyatt v. Wilson,* in 1820, respecting an engraving of George the Third during his illness, to the effect that "if one of the late king's physicians had kept a diary of what he heard and saw, the court would not, in the king's lifetime, have permitted him to print and publish it;" and Lord Cottenham declared, in respect to the acts of the defendants in the case before him, that "privacy is the right invaded." But if privacy is once recognized as a right entitled to legal protection, the interposition of the courts cannot depend on the particular nature of the injuries resulting.

These considerations lead to the conclusion that the protection afforded to thoughts, sentiments, and emotions, expressed through the medium of writing or of the arts, so far as it consists in preventing publication, is merely an instance of the enforcement of the more general right of the individual to be let alone. It is like the right not to be assaulted or beaten, the right not to be imprisoned, the right not to be maliciously prosecuted, the right not to be defamed. In each of these rights, as indeed in all other rights recognized by the law, there inheres the quality of being owned or possessed—and (as that is the distinguishing attribute of property) there may be some propriety in speaking of those rights as property. But, obviously, they bear little resemblance to what is ordinarily comprehended under that term. The principle which protects personal writings and all other personal productions, not against theft and physical appropriation, but against publication in any form, is in reality not the principle of private property, but that of an inviolate personality.[31]

If we are correct in this conclusion, the existing law affords a principle which may be invoked to protect the privacy of the individual from invasion either by the too enterprising press, the photographer, or the possessor of any other modern device for recording or reproducing scenes or sounds. For the protection afforded is not confined by the authorities to those cases where any particular medium or form of expression has been adopted, nor to products of the intellect. The same protection is afforded to emotions and sensations expressed in a musical composition or other work of art as to a literary composition; and words spoken, a pantomine acted, a sonata performed, is no less entitled to protection than if each had been reduced to writing. The circumstance that a thought or emotion has been recorded in a permanent form renders its identification easier, and hence may be important from the point of view of evidence, but it has no significance as a matter of substantive right. If, then, the decisions indicate a general right to privacy for thoughts, emotions, and sensations, these should receive the same protection, whether expressed in writing, or in conduct, in conversation, in attitudes, or in facial expression.

It may be urged that a distinction should be taken between the deliberate expression of thoughts and emotions in literary or artistic compositions and the casual and often involuntary expression given to them in the ordinary conduct of life. In other words, it may be contended that the protection afforded is granted to the conscious products of labor, perhaps as an encouragement to effort.[33] This contention, however plausible, has, in fact, little to recommend it. If the amount of labor involved be adopted as the test, we might well find that the effort to conduct one's self properly in business and in domestic relations had been far greater than that involved in painting a picture or writing a book; one would find that it was far easier to express lofty sentiments in a diary than in the conduct of a noble life. If the test of deliberateness of the act be adopted, much casual correspondence which is now accorded full protection would be excluded from the beneficient operation of existing rules. After the decisions denying the distinction attempted to be made between those literary productions which it was intended to publish and those which it was not, all considerations of the amount of labor involved, the degree of deliberation, the value of the product, and the intention of publishing must be abandoned, and no basis is discerned upon which the right to restrain publication and reproduction of such so-called literary and artistic works can be rested, except the right to privacy, as a part of the more general right to the immunity of the person,—the right to one's personality.

It should be stated that, in some instances where protection has been afforded against wrongful publication, the jurisdiction has been asserted, not on the ground of property, or at least not wholly on that ground, but upon the ground of an alleged breach of an implied contract or of a trust or confidence.

Thus, in *Abernethy* v. *Hutchinson,* 3 L. J. Ch. 209 (1825), where the plaintiff, a distinguished surgeon, sought to restrain the publication in the "Lancet" of unpublished lectures which he had delivered at St. Bartholomew's Hospital in London, Lord Eldon doubted whether there could be property in lectures which had not been reduced to writing, but granted the injunction on the ground of breach of confidence, holding "that when persons were admitted as pupils or otherwise, to hear these lectures, although they were orally delivered, and although the parties might go to the extent, if they were able to do so, of putting down the whole by means of short-hand, yet they could do that only for the purpose of their own information, and could not publish, for profit, that which they had not obtained the right of selling."

In *Prince Albert* v. *Strange,* 1 McN. & G. 25 (1849), Lord Cottenham, on appeal, while recognizing a right of property in the etchings which of itself would justify the issuance of the injunction, stated, after discussing the evidence, that he was bound to assume that the possession of the etchings by the defendant had "its foundation in a breach of trust, confidence, or contract," and that upon such ground also the plaintiff's title to the injunction was fully sustained.

In *Tuck* v. *Priester,* 19 Q.B.D. 639 (1887), the plaintiffs were owners of a picture, and employed the defendant to make a certain number of copies. He did so, and made also a number of other copies for himself, and offered them for sale in England at a lower price. Subsequently, the plaintiffs registered their copyright in the picture, and then brought suit for an injunction and damages. The Lords Justices differed as to the application of the copyright acts to the case, but held unanimously that independently of those acts, the plaintiffs were entitled to an injunction and damages for breach of contract.

In *Pollard v. Photographic Co.*, 40 Ch. Div. 345 (1888), a photographer who had taken a lady's photograph under the ordinary circumstances was restrained from exhibiting it, and also from selling copies of it, on the ground that it was a breach of an implied term in the contract, and also that it was a breach of confidence. Mr. Justice North interjected in the argument of the plaintiff's counsel the inquiry: "Do you dispute that if the negative likeness were taken on the sly, the person who took it might exhibit copies?" and counsel for the plaintiff answered: "In that case there would be no trust or consideration to support a contract." Later, the defendant's counsel argued that "a person has no property in his own features; short of doing what is libellous or otherwise illegal, there is no restriction on the photographer's using his negative." But the court, while expressly finding a breach of contract and of trust sufficient to justify its interposition, still seems to have felt the necessity of resting the decision also upon a right of property,[34] in order to bring it within the line of those cases which were relied upon as precedents.[35]

This process of implying a term in a contract, or of implying a trust (particularly where the contract is written, and where there is no established usage or custom), is nothing more nor less than a judicial declaration that public morality, private justice, and general convenience demand the recognition of such a rule, and that the publication under similar circumstances would be considered an intolerable abuse. So long as these circumstances happen to present a contract upon which such a term can be engrafted by the judicial mind, or to supply relations upon which a trust or confidence can be erected, there may be no objection to working out the desired protection through the doctrines of contract or of trust. But the court can hardly stop there. The narrower doctrine may have satisfied the demands of society at a time when the abuse to be guarded against could rarely have arisen without violating a contract or a special confidence; but now that modern devices afford abundant opportunities for the perpetration of such wrongs without any participation by the injured party, the protection granted by the law must be placed upon a broader foundation. While, for instance, the state of the photographic art was such that one's picture could seldom be taken without his consciously "sitting" for the purpose, the law of contract or of trust might afford the prudent man sufficient safeguards against the improper circulation of his portrait; but since the latest advances in photographic art have rendered it possible to take pictures surreptitiously, the doctrines of contract and of trust are inadequate to support the required protection, and the law of tort must be resorted to. The right of property in its widest sense, including all possession, including all rights and privileges, and hence embracing the right to an inviolate personality, affords alone that broad basis upon which the protection which the individual demands can be rested.

Thus, the courts, in searching for some principle upon which the publication of private letters could be enjoined, naturally came upon the ideas of a breach of confidence, and of an implied contract; but it required little consideration to discern that this doctrine could not afford all the protection required, since it would not support the court in granting a remedy against a stranger; and so the theory of property in the contents of letters was adopted.[36] Indeed, it is difficult to conceive on what theory of the law the casual recipient of a letter, who proceeds to publish it, is guilty of a breach of contract, express or implied, or of any breach of trust, in the ordinary acceptation of that term. Suppose a letter has been addressed to him without his solicitation. He opens it, and reads. Surely, he has not made any contract; he has not accepted any trust. He cannot, by opening and reading the letter, have come under any obligation save what the law declares; and, however expressed, that obligation is simply to observe the legal right of the sender, whatever it may be, and whether it be called his right of property in the contents of the letter, or his right to privacy.[37]

A similar groping for the principle upon which a wrongful publication can be enjoined is found in the law of trade secrets. There, injunctions have generally been granted on the theory of a breach of contract, or of an abuse of confidence.[38] It would, of course, rarely happen that any one would be in the possession of a secret unless confidence had been reposed in him. But can it be supposed that the court would hesitate to grant relief against one who had obtained his knowledge by an ordinary trespass,—for instance, by wrongfully looking into a book in which the secret was recorded, or by eavesdropping? Indeed, in *Yovatt v. Winyard,* 1 J. & W. 394 (1820), where an injunction was granted against making any use of or communicating certain recipes for veterinary medicine, it appeared that the defendant, while in the plaintiff's employ, had surreptitiously got access to his book of recipes, and copied them. Lord Eldon "granted the injunction, upon the ground of there having been a breach of trust and confidence;" but it would seem to be difficult to draw any sound legal distinction between such a case and one where a mere stranger wrongfully obtained access to the book.[39]

We must therefore conclude that the rights, so protected, whatever their exact nature, are not rights arising from contract or from special trust, but are rights as against the world; and, as above stated, the principle which has been applied to protect these rights is in reality not the principle of private property, unless that word be used in an extended and unusual sense. The principle which protects personal writings and any other productions of the intellect or of the emotions, is the right to privacy, and the law has no new principle to formulate when it extends this protection to the personal appearance, sayings, acts, and to personal relation, domestic or otherwise.[40]

If the invasion of privacy constitutes a legal *injuria*, the elements for demanding redress exist, since already the value of mental suffering, caused by an act wrongful in itself, is recognized as a basis for compensation.

The right of one who has remained a private individual, to prevent his public portraiture, presents the simplest case for such extension; the right to protect one's self from pen portraiture, from a discussion by the press of one's private affairs, would be a more important and far-reaching one. If casual and unimportant statements in a letter, if handiwork, however inartistic and valueless, if possessions of all sorts are protected not only against reproduction, but against description and enumeration, how much more should the acts and sayings of a man in his social and domestic relations be guarded from ruthless publicity. If you may not reproduce a woman's face photographically without her consent, how much less should be tolerated the reproduction of her face, her form, and her actions, by graphic descriptions colored to suit a gross and depraved imagination.

The right to privacy, limited as such right must necessarily be, has already found expression in the law of France.[41]

It remains to consider what are the limitations of this right to privacy, and what remedies may be granted for the enforcement of the right. To determine in advance of experience the exact line at which the dignity and convenience of the individual must yield to the demands of the public welfare or of private justice would be a difficult task; but the more general rules are furnished by the legal analogies already developed in the law of slander and libel, and in the law of literary and artistic property.

1. The right to privacy does not prohibit any publication of matter which is of public or general interest.

In determining the scope of this rule, aid would be afforded by the analogy, in the law of libel and slander, of cases which deal with the qualified privilege of comment and criticism on matters of public and general interest.[42] There are of course difficulties in applying such a rule; but they are inherent in the subject-matter, and are certainly no greater than those which exist in many other branches of the law,—for instance, in that large class of cases in which the reasonableness or unreasonableness of an act is made the test of liability. The design of the law must be to protect those persons with whose affairs the community has no legitimate concern, from being dragged into an undesirable and undesired publicity and to protect all persons, whatsoever; their position or station, from having matters which they may properly prefer to keep private, made public against their will. It is the unwarranted invasion of individual privacy which is reprehended, and to be, so far as possible, prevented. The distinction, however, noted in the above statement is obvious and fundamental. There are persons who may reasonably claim as a right, protection from the notoriety entailed by being made the victims of journalistic enterprise. There are others who, in varying degrees, have renounced the right to live their lives screened from public observation. Matters which men of the first class may justly contend, concern themselves alone, may in those of the second be the subject of legitimate interest to their fellow-citizens. Peculiarities of manner and person, which in the ordinary individual should be free from comment, may acquire a public importance, if found in a candidate for political office. Some further discrimination is necessary, therefore, than to class facts or deeds as public or private according to a standard to be applied to the fact or deed *per se*. To publish of a modest and retiring individual that he suffers from an impediment in his speech or that he cannot spell correctly, is an unwarranted, if not an unexampled, infringement of his rights, while to state and comment on the same characteristics found in a would-be congressman could not be regarded as beyond the pale of propriety.

The general object in view is to protect the privacy of private life, and to whatever degree and in whatever connection a man's life has ceased to be private, before the publication under consideration has been made, to that extent the protection is to be withdrawn.[43] Since, then, the propriety of publishing the very same facts may depend wholly upon the person concerning whom they are published, no fixed formula can be used to prohibit obnoxious publications. Any rule of liability adopted must have in it an elasticity which shall take account of the varying circumstances of each case,—a necessity which unfortunately renders such a doctrine not only more difficult of application, but also to a certain extent uncertain in its operation and easily rendered abortive. Besides, it is only the more flagrant breaches of decency and propriety that could in practice be reached, and it is not perhaps desirable even to attempt to repress everything which the nicest taste and keenest sense of the respect due to private life would condemn.

In general, then, the matters of which the publication should be repressed may be described as those which concern the private life, habits, acts, and relations of an individual, and have no legitimate connection with his fitness for a public office which he seeks or for which he is suggested, or for any public or quasi public position which he seeks or for which he is suggested, and have no legitimate relation to or bearing upon any act done by him in a public or quasi public capacity. The foregoing is not designed as a wholly accurate or exhaustive definition, since that which must ultimately in a vast number of cases become a question of individual judgment and opinion is incapable of such definition; but it is an attempt to indicate broadly the class of matters referred to. Some things all men alike are entitled to keep from popular curiosity, whether in public life or not, while others are only private because the persons concerned have not assumed a position which makes their doings legitimate matters of public investigation.[44]

2. The right to privacy does not prohibit the communication of any matter, though in its nature private, when the publication is made under circumstances which would render it a privileged communication according to the law of slander and libel.

Under this rule, the right to privacy is not invaded by any publication made in a court of justice, in legislative bodies, or the committees of those bodies; in municipal assemblies, or the committees of such assemblies, or practically by any communication made in any other public body, municipal or parochial, or in any body quasi public, like the large voluntary associations formed for almost every purpose of benevolence, business, or other general interest; and (at least in many jurisdictions) reports of any such proceedings would in some measure be accorded a like privilege.[45] Nor would the rule prohibit any publication made by one in the discharge of some public or private duty, whether legal or moral, or in conduct of one's own affairs, in matters where his own interest is concerned.[46]

3. The law would probably not grant any redress for the invasion of privacy by oral publication in the absence of special damage.

The same reasons exist for distinguishing between oral and written publication of private matters, as is afforded in the law of defamation by the restricted liability for slander as compared with the liability for libel.[47] The injury resulting from such oral communications would ordinarily be so trifling that the law might well, in the interest of free speech, disregard it altogether.[48]

4. The right to privacy ceases upon the publication of the facts by the individual, or with his consent.

This is but another application of the rule which

has become familiar in the law of literary and artistic property. The cases there decided established also what should be deemed a publication,—the important principle in this connection being that a private communication of circulation for a registered purpose is not a publication within the meaning of the law.[49]

5. The truth of the matter published does not afford a defence. Obviously this branch of the law should have no concern with the truth of falsehood of the matters published. It is not for injury to the individual's character that redress or prevention is sought, but for injury to the right of privacy. For the former, the law of slander and libel provides perhaps a sufficient safeguard. The latter implies the right not merely to prevent inaccurate portrayal of private life, but to prevent its being depicted at all.[50]

6. The absence of "malice" in the publisher does not afford a defence.

Personal ill-will is not an ingredient of the offence, any more than in an ordinary case of trespass to person or to property. Such malice is never necessary to be shown in an action for libel or slander at common law, except in rebuttal of some defence, *e.g.*, that the occasion rendered the communication privileged, or, under the statutes in this State and elsewhere, that the statement complained of was true. The invasion of the privacy that is to be protected is equally complete and equally injurious, whether the motives by which the speaker or writer was actuated are, taken by themselves, culpable or not; just as the damage to character, and to some extent the tendency to provoke a breach of the peace, is equally the result of defamation without regard to the motives leading to its publication. Viewed as a wrong to the individual, this rule is the same pervading the whole law of torts, by which one is held responsible for his intentional acts, even though they are committed with no sinister intent; and viewed as a wrong to society, it is the same principle adopted in a large category of statutory offences.

The remedies for an invasion of the right of privacy are also suggested by those administered in the law of defamation, and in the law of literary and artistic property, namely:—

1. An action of tort for damages in all cases.[51] Even in the absence of special damages, substantial compensation could be allowed for injury to feelings as in the action of slander and libel.

2. An injunction, in perhaps a very limited class of cases.[52]

It would doubtless be desirable that the privacy of the individual should receive the added protection of the criminal law, but for this, legislation would be required.[53] Perhaps it would be deemed proper to bring the criminal liability for such publication within narrower limits; but that the community has an interest in preventing such invasions of privacy, sufficiently strong to justify the introduction of such a remedy, cannot be doubted. Still, the protection of society must come mainly through a recognition of the rights of the individual. Each man is responsible for his own acts and omissions only. If he condones what he reprobates, with a weapon at hand equal to his defence, he is responsible for the results. If he resists, public opinion will rally to his support. Has he then such a weapon? It is believed that the common law provides him with one, forged in the slow fire of the centuries, and to-day fitly tempered to his hand. The common law has always recognized a man's house as his castle, impregnable, often, even to its own officers engaged in the execution of its commands. Shall the courts thus close the front entrance to constituted authority, and open wide the back door to idle or prurient curiosity?

Footnotes to

MR. JUSTICE BRANDEIS AND THE CONSTITUTION, BY FELIX FRANKFURTER

* * *

14. McCulloch v. Maryland, 4 Wheat. 315, 407 (1819).

15. United States v. Moreland, 258 U. S. 433, 451 (1922) (dissent).

16. Olmstead v. United States, 277 U. S. 438, 472 (1928) (dissent)

17. Gilbert v. Minnesota, 254 U. S. 325, 336-37 (1920) (dissent).

18. Jacob Ruppert v. Caffey, 251 U. S. 264, 299-300 (1920).

19. Maul v. United States, 274 U. S. 501, 524-27 (1927) (concurrence).

20. Mr. Justice Holmes, dissenting, in Adkins v. Childrens' Hospital, 261 U. S. 525, 568 (1923).

Judge Learned Hand has also put the matter in telling language. The provisions of the Fifth Amendment "represent a mood rather than a command, the sense of moderation, of fair play, of mutual forebearance, without which states become the prey of faction. They are not the rules of a game; their meaning is lost when they are treated as though they were." Daniel Reeves, Inc. v. Anderson, 43 F. (2d) 679, 682 (C. C. A. 2d, 1930).

21. Untermeyer v. Anderson, 276 U. S. 440, 447, 450-51, 451-52 (1928) (dissent).

22. National Life Ins. Co. v. United States, 277 U. S. 508, 527-28, 533 (1928) (dissent).

* * *

48. Di Santo v. Pennsylvania, 273 U. S. 34, 37-39 (1927) (dissent).

49. Public Utility Comm. v. Attleboro Co., 273 U. S. 83, 91-92 (1927) (dissent).

50. Texas Transport & Terminal Co. v. New Orleans, 264 U. S. 150, 155, 157 (1924) (dissent).

51. Cudahy Packing Co. v. Hinkle, 278 U. S. 460, 467-68, 470 (1929) (dissent).

52. Jaybird Mining Co. v. Weir, 271 U. S. 609, 615, 617-19 (1926) (dissent).

53. N. Y. Cent. R. R. v. Winfield, 244 U. S. 147, 617-70 (1917) (dissent).

54. Napier v. Atlantic Coast Line R. R., 272 U. S. 605, 612-13 (1926).

55. Davis v. Farmers' Cooperative Co., 262 U. S. 312, 315-16, 317 (1923).

56. Buck v. Kuykendall, 267 U. S. 307, 315-16 (1924).

57. Lawrence v. St. Louis-San Francisco Ry., 278 U. S. 228, 233-34 (1929).

58. Hammond v. Schapi Bus Line, 275 U. S. 164, 171-72 (1927).

59. The following criteria have guided him: "It [the Court] has no jurisdiction to pronounce any statute, either of a State or of the United States, void, because irreconciliable with the Constitution, except as it is called upon to adjudge the legal rights of litigants in actual controversies. In the exercise of that jurisdiction, it is bound by two rules, to which it has rigidly adhered, one, never to anticipate a question of constitutional law in advance of the necessity of deciding it; the other never to formulate a rule of constitutional law broader than is required by the precise facts to which it is to be applied. These rules are safe guides to sound judgment. It is the dictate of wisdom to follow them closely and carefully." Steamship Co. v. Emigration Commissioners, 113 U. S. 33, 39 (1885).

"Whenever, in pursuance of an honest and actual antagonistic assertion of rights by one individual against another, there is presented a question involving the validity of any act of any legislature, State or Federal, and the decision necessarily rests on the competency of the legislature to so enact, the court must, in the exercise of its solemn duties, determine whether the act be constitutional or not; but such an exercise of power is the ultimate and supreme function of courts. It is legitimate only in the last resort, and as a necessity in the determination of real, earnest and vital controversy between individuals." Chicago etc. Ry. v. Wellman, 143 U. S. 339, 345 (1892).

60. Arizona v. California, 283 U. S. 423, 463-64 (1931). See also Swift Co. v. Hocking Valley Ry. 243 U. S. 281 (1917); Bilby v. Stewart, 246 U. S. 255 (1918); Sugarman v. United States, 249 U. S. 182 (1919); Barbour v. Georgia, 249 U. S. 454 (1919); Collins v. Miller, 252 U. S. 364 (1920); Terrace v. Thompson, 263 U. S. 197 (1923); Oliver Co. v. Mexico, 264 U. S. 440 (1924); Willing v. Chicago Auditorium, 277 U. S. 274 (1928).

61. Chastleton Corp. v. Sinclair, 264 U. S. 543, 549 (1924) (concurring in part).

62. International News Service v. Associated Press, 248 U. S. 215, 263-64, 267 (1918) (dissent).

63. Pennsylvania v. West Virginia, 262 U. S. 553, 621-23 (1923) (dissent).

64. Railroad Comm. v. Los Angeles, 280 U. S. 145, 163-66 (1929) (dissent). As to his general desire to confine the volume of the Supreme Court's business to limits consonant with excellence of judicial output, see King Mfg. Co. v. Augusta, 277 U. S. 100, 115 (1928) (dissent).

65. The WORKS OF GEORGE SAVILLE, FIRST MARQUESS OF HALIFAX (Raleigh ed. 1912) 211.

66. Jaybird Mining Co. v. Weir, 271 U. S. 609, 619 (1926) (dissent).

67. Washington v. Dawson & Co., 264 U. S. 219, 235-39 (1924) (dissent).

68. Di Santo v. Pennsylvania, 273 U. S. 34, 42-43 (1927).

69. Scrutton, L. J., in Rex v. Secretary of State for Home Affairs, [1923] 2 K. B. 361, 382.

70. Schaefer v. United States, 251 U. S. 466, 482-83 (1920) (dissent).

71. Pierce v. United States, 252 U. S. 239, 272-73 (1920) (dissent).

72. Gilbert v. Minnesota, 254 U. S. 325, 343 (1920) (dissent).

73. Whitney v. California, 274 U. S. 357, 374-77 (1927) (concurring).

74. Pierce v. United States, 252 U. S. 239, 266-67 (1920) (dissent).

75. Milwaukee Pub. Co. v. Burleson, 255 U. S. 407, 417, 436 (1921) (dissent).

76. "The judge may enlighten the understanding of the jury aund thereby influence their judgment; but he may not use undue influence. He may advise; he may persuade; but he may not command or coerce. He does coerce when without convincing the judgment he overcomes the will by the weight of his authority. . . .

"It is said that if the defendant suffered any wrong it was purely formal. . . . Whether a defendant is found guilty by a jury or is declared to be so by a judge is not, under the Federal Constitution, a mere formality. . . . The offence here in question is punishable by imprisonment. Congress would have been powerless to provide for imposing the punishment except upon the verdict of the jury." Horning v. District of Columbia, 254 U. S. 135, 139-40 (1920).

77. See *Report on the Third Degree* by Chafee, Pollock and Stern in IV Reports, NATIONAL COMMISSION ON LAW OBSERVANCE AND ENFORCEMENT (1931) 13.

78. See 220 HAS. DEB. (Commons) col. 5, 805 *et seq.* (July 20, 1928); Inquiry in regard to the Interrogation by the Police of Miss Savidge (1928, Cmd. 3147).

79. Wan v. United States, 266 U. S. 1, 14-17 (1924).

80. Burdeau v. McDowell, 256 U. S. 465, 476-77 (1921) (dissent).

81. Casey v. United States, 276 U. S. 413, 423 (1928) (dissent).

82. Olmstead v. United States, 277 U. S. 438, 483-84, 485 (1928) (dissent).

* * *

94. Exigencies of space have enforced omission of footnotes from the quoted opinions. See, among others, the following cases in which the heavily documented footnotes in the opinions of Mr. Justice Brandeis are largely the result of his independent research: Truax v. Corrigan, 257 U. S. 312 (1921) (dissent); Southwestern Bell Tel. & Co. v. Public Serv. Comm., 262 U. S. 276 (1923) (dissent); Jay Burns Baking Co. v. Bryan, 264 U. S. 504 (1924) (dissent); Myers v. United States, 272 U. S. 52 (1926) (dissent); Frost v. Corp. Comm., 278 U. S. 515 (1929) (dissent); St. Louis & O'Fallon Ry. v. United States, 279 U. S. 461 (1929) (dissent).

95. Wan v. United States, 266 U. S. 1 (1924).

Footnotes to

MR. JUSTICE BRANDEIS AND THE CONSTITUTION, BY ALPHEUS T. MASON.

* * *

142. O'Gorman & Young v. Hartford Ins. Co., 282 U. S. 251 at 258, 51 Sup. Ct. 130 at 132 (1931).

The same position is taken by Chief Justice Hughes in Corporation Commission of Okla. v. Lowe, *supra* note 122, at 438, 50 Sup. Ct. at 399:

"It was incumbent upon the appellee in invoking the protection of the Fourteenth Amendment to show with convincing clarity that the law of the State created against him the discrimination of which he complained. An infraction of the constitutional provision is not to be assumed. On the contrary, it is to be presumed that the State in enforcing its local policies will conform its requirements to the Federal guarantees. Doubts on this point are to be resolved in favor of, and not against, the State." Compare with Mr. Justice Hughes' opinion in Price v. Illinois, 238 U. S. 446, 452, 35 Sup. Ct. 892, 895 (1915).

143. "For our purposes we must assume that, if a state of facts could exist that would justify such legislation, it actually did exist when the statute under consideration was passed. For us the question is one of power, not of expediency." Munn v. Illinois, *supra* note 76, at 132. As to the reasonableness of the rate the court declared: "For protection against abuses by legislatures the people must resort to the polls, not to the courts." At 135.

". . . as it does not appear upon the face of the statute, or from any facts of which the court must take judicial cognizance, that it infringes rights secured by the fundamental law, the legislative determination of those questions is conclusive upon the courts. It is not a part of their functions to conduct investigations of facts entering into questions of public policy merely, and to sustain or frustrate the legislative will, embodied in statutes, as they may happen to approve or disapprove its determination of such questions." Mr. Justice Harlan in Powell v. Pennsylvania, 127 U. S. 678, 685, 8 Sup. Ct. 992 at 996 (1888). See also Atkins v. Kansas, 191 U. S. 207, 222, 24 Sup. Ct. 124, 128 (1903).

144. As Mr. Justice Sutherland held in Adkins v. Children's Hospital, 261 U. S. 525, 43 Sup. Ct. 394 (1923): ". . . freedom of contract is . . . the general rule and restraint the exception, and the exercise of legislative authority . . . can be justified only by the existence of exceptional circumstances. Whether these circumstances exist in the present case constitutes the question to be answered." At 546, 43 Sup. Ct. at 397.

Continuing he wrote:

"The feature of this statute which, perhaps more than any others, puts upon it the stamp of invalidity is that it exacts from the employer an arbitrary payment for a purpose upon a basis having no casual connection with his business, or the contract, or the work the employee engages to do." At 558, 43 Sup. Ct. at 401.

Thus such facts as Mr. Frankfurter presented were, in Mr. Justice Sutherland's opinion, entirely irrelevant. He said of them: "A mass of reports, opinions of special observers and students of the subject, and the like, has been brought before us in support of this statement, [that great benefit had resulted from the operation of minimum wage legislation] all of which we have found interesting but only mildly persuasive. . . .

"These are all proper enough for the consideration of law-making bodies, since their tendency is to establish the desirability or undesirability of the legislation; but they reflect no legitimate light upon the question of its validity; and that is what we are called upon to decide. The elucidation of that question cannot be aided by counting heads." At 560, 43 Sup. Ct. at 402.

145. As in Mr. Justice Butler's opinion in Jay Burns Baking Co. v. Bryan, *supra* note 8.

146. Texas and N. O. Ry. v. Brotherhood of Railway & Steamship Clerks, supra note 17.

147. State Board of Tax Commissioners v. Jackson, 283 U. S. 527, 51 Sup. Ct. 540 (1931).

148. Quaker City Cab Co. v. Pensylvania, *supra* note 127.

149. Gilbert v. Minnesota, *supra* note 112, at 338, 41 Sup. Ct. at 129.

150. Stromberg v. California, 283 U. S. 359, 51 Sup. Ct. 532

(1931). Delivering the opinion of the Court, Chief Justice Hughes wrote:

"The maintenance of the opportunity for free political discussion to the end that government may be responsive to the will of the people and that changes may be obtained by lawful means, an opportunity essential to the security of the Republic, is a fundamental principle of our constitutional system. At 369, 51 Sup. Ct. at 536.

Ten years earlier Mr. Justice Brandeis had used much the same language in dissent:

"Like the course of the heavenly bodies, harmony in national life is a resultant of the struggle between contending forces. In frank expression of conflicting opinion lies the greatest promise of wisdom in governmental action; and in suppression lies ordinarily the greatest peril." Gilbert v. Minnesota, *supra* note 112, at 338, 41 Sup. Ct. at 129.

151. Southwestern & Bell Tel. Co. v. Public Serv. Co., *supra* note 85, at 303, 43 Sup. Ct. 551, n. 16.

See also Near v. Minnesota, 283 U. S. 697, 51 Sup. Ct. 625 (1931) where the Court in a five to four decision held unconstitutional the Minnesota "Gag Law" which made possible the enjoining of any publication which, in the opinion of a single judge, was contrary to public morals.

152. Such a change of front is already in evidence. At the recent hearings in Washington before the House Committee on Interstate and Foreign Commerce, there were intimations that some of the railway managers may once more look with favor on the theory of "original investment". New York Times, Feb. 28, 1932.

153. For evidence of Hobbes' influence, see Mr. Justice Holmes' references to THE LEVIATHAN in Heard v. Sturgis, 146 Mass. 545, 548-549, 16 N. E. 437, 441 (1888); In re Opinion of the Justices, 160 Mass. 586 at 595, 36 N. E. 488 at 492 (1894); Kawanahakoa v. Polyblank, 205 U. S. 340 at 353, 27 Sup. Ct. 526 at 527 (1907). See also the very pertinent observations of Elizabeth S. Sargeant, *Justice Touched with Fire*, reprinted in FRANKFURTER, MR. JUSTICE HOLMES (1931) 186.

154. A good illustration of the divergent viewpoints of the two justices is the case of Pennsylvania Coal Co. v. Mahon, 260 U. S. 393, 43 Sup. Ct. 158 (1922) where Mr. Justice Holmes delivered the opinion of the Court and Mr. Justice Brandeis wrote a dissenting opinion.

When the legislatures of Nebraska and Iowa prohibited teaching German in the public schools, Holmes' brand of liberalism, his willingness to allow the state to experiment even though he did not agree, prompted him to uphold the legislation; Brandeis, on the other hand, believing in liberty as an end as well as a means of achieving that which is most valuable in human life, voted with the Court to overthrow the statute. Meyer v. Nebraska, 262 U. S. 390, 43 Sup. Ct. 625 (1923);

Bartels v. Iowa, 262 U. S. 404, 43 Sup. Ct. 628 (1923). In the Nebraska case Holmes' dissenting opinion was concurred in by Mr. Justice Sutherland—a strange judicial bedfellow for one reputed to be a genuine liberal! Perhaps the best illustration of the dissimilar methods and viewpoints of the two justices is Truax v. Corrigan, *supra* note 48. After reviewing at considerable length the application of the common law to the struggle between employers and employees in England and the United States, and after full "consideration of the contemporary conditions, social, industrial and political, of the community to be affected", Mr. Justice Brandeis reaches the conclusion that the Arizona statute limiting the remedy of injunction in disputes between capital and labor, is necessary and expedient as well as constitutional.

Mr. Justice Holmes, in a much briefer opinion, and with no consideration of the points stressed by Mr. Justice Brandeis, stated his reaction to the ruling of the Court by saying:

"There is nothing that I more deprecate than the use of the Fourteenth Amendment beyond the absolute compulsion of its words to prevent the making of social experiments that an important part of the community desires, in the insulated chambers afforded by the several states, even though the experiments may seem futile or even noxious to me and to those whose judgment I most respect." At 344, 42 Sup. Ct. at 134.

155. The following is a typical statement of Holmes' position: "I am far from saying that I think this particular law a wise and rational provision. That is not my affair. But if the people of the State of New York speaking by their authorized voice say that they want it, I see nothing in the Constitution of the United States to prevent their having their will." Mr. Justice Holmes dissenting in Tyson & Brothers v. Banton, 272 U. S. 418 at 447, 47 Sup. Ct. 426 at 434 (1927). Dissenting in Lochner v. New York, 198 U. S. 45 at 76, 25 Sup. Ct. 539 at 546 (1905) Mr. Justice Holmes wrote: "I strongly believe that my agreement or disagreement [with any particular economic theory] has nothing to do with the right of a majority to embody their opinions in law."

For similar utterances, see his opinion in Noble Bank v. Haskell, 219 U. S. 104, 31 Sup. Ct. 186 (1911); Missouri, Kans. & Tex. Ry. v. May, 194 U. S. 267 at 270, 24 Sup. Ct. 638 at 639 (1904); Block v. Hirsch, 256 U. S. 135 at 155, 41 Sup. Ct. 458 at 459 (1921); Otis v. Parker, 187 U. S. 606 at 609, 23 Sup. Ct. 168 at 169 (1903); Louisville & Nashville R. R. v. Barber Asphalt Paving Co., 197 U. S. 430 at 435, 25 Sup. Ct. 466 at 467 (1905).

The position taken by Justice Holmes in these cases, regarding the leeway that should be allowed the legislature, is entirely in accord with his earlier views:

"The first requirement of a sound body of law is that it should correspond with actual feelings and demands of the community, whether right or wrong." HOLMES, THE COMMON LAW (1881) 41.

"What proximate test of excellence [of good government] can be found except correspondence to the actual equilibrium of force in the community—that is, conformity to the wishes of the dominant power? Of course, such conformity may lead to destruction, and it is desirable that the dominant power should be wise. But wise or not, the proximate test of a good government is that the dominant power have its way." HOLMES, COLLECTED LEGAL PAPERS (1920) 258.

His position is further elaborated in the following: "I do not expect or think it desirable that the judges should undertake to renovate the law . . . But I think it most important to remember whenever a doubtful case arises, that what is really before us is a conflict between two social desires, . . . the . . . question is which desire is strongest at the point of conflict. . . . Where there is doubt the simple tool of logic does not suffice, and even if it is disguised and unconscious, the judges are called on to exercise the sovereign prerogative of choice." *Law in Science and Science in Law* (1899) 12 HARV. L. REV. 443, 460-461. Reprinted in HOLMES, COLLECTED LEGAL PAPERS 210.

156. His protest against the tendency of the Court to accord property greater protection than liberty is pithily expressed as follows: "I have difficulty in believing that the liberty guaranteed by the Constitution, which has been held to protect against state denial, the right of an employer to discriminate against a workman because he is a member of a trade union [Coppage v. Kansas, *supra* note 16]; the right of a business man to conduct a private employment agency [Adams v. Tanner, *supra* note 1]; or to contract outside the state for insurance of his property [Allgeyer v. Louisiana, 165 U. S. 578, 589, 17 Sup. Ct. 427, 430 (1897)], although the legislature deems it inimical to the public welfare, does not include liberty to teach, either in the privacy of the home or publicly, the doctrine of pacifism; so long, at least, as Congress has not declared that public safety demands its supression." Gilbert v. Minnesota, *supra* note 112. See also his dissenting opinion in the Bedford Cut Stone case, *supra* note 30.

157. Jay Burns Baking Co. v. Bryan, *supra* note 8, at 520, 44 Sup. Ct. at 416.

158. "It may or may not be that if facts were called to our attention in a proper way the objection would prove to be real. But even if, when called to our attention, the facts should be taken notice of judicially, whether because they are only the premise for a general proposition of law [citing cases] or for any other reason, still there are many things that courts would notice if brought before them that beforehand they do not know. *It rests with counsel to take the proper steps, and if they deliberately omit them, we do not feel called upon to institute inquiries on our own account.*" Mr. Justice Holmes, speaking for the Court in Quong Wing v. Kirkendall, 223 U. S.

59 at 64, 32 Sup. Ct. 192 at 193 (1912). The italics are the writer's. Yet in 1899, Mr. Holmes himself had written: "The true science of the law does not consist mainly in a theological working out of dogma or a logical development as in mathematics, or only in a study of it as an anthropological document from the outside; an even more important part consists in the establishment of its postulates from within upon accurately measured social desires instead of tradition." HOLMES, COLLECTED LEGAL PAPERS 225-226.

A point of view more in keeping with the earlier statement of Mr. Holmes is illustrated in the following quotation from a dissenting opinion of Mr. Justice Brandeis: "Much evidence referred to by me is not in the record. Nor could it have been included. It is the history of the experience gained under similar legislation, and the result of scientific experiments made, since the entry of the judgment below. Of such events in our history, whether occurring before or after the enactment of the statute or of the entry of the judgment, the Court should acquire knowledge, and must, in my opinion, take judicial notice, whenever required to perform the delicate judicial task here involved." Jay Burns Baking Co. v. Bryan, *supra* note 8, at 533, 44 Sup. Ct. at 421.

159. Soon after taking his seat on the Supreme Court, Mr. Justice Brandeis impressed his new associate, Mr. Justice Holmes, with the idea that " 'A study of statistics would be good for him'." Justice Holmes was then leaving for his summer home at Beverly Farms and so instructed Mr. Brandeis to " 'pick out the right books and send them up'." The box of books arrived in due course. An examination of the titles revealed a formidable array of monographs and books on the eight-hour day, the textile industry, the employment of women, employers' liability and so on. Gazing at the box in unaffected dismay, Mr. Justice Holmes is said to have instructed a servant: " 'Nail it up and send it back to him'." And then with a sigh of relief the Justice imersed himself in Plato. (Related by Silas Bent in his recent volume, JUSTICE OLIVER WENDELL HOLMES (1932) 280-281).

160. "The social reformers of today seem to me so far to forget the we . . . can [not] get something for nothing by legislation . . . . Probably I am too skeptical as to our ability to do more than shift disagreeable burdens from the shoulders of the stronger to those of the weaker. . . . The notion that with socialized property we should have women free and a piano for everybody seems to me an empty humbug. . . . But it is a pleasure to see more faith and enthusiasm in the young men; and I thought that one of them made a good answer to some of my skeptical talk when he said, "You would base legislation upon regrets rather than upon hopes.' " HOLMES, COLLECTED LEGAL PAPERS 305-307.

161. After discussing informally with Mr. Justice Brandeis the constitutional issues involved in the California Criminal

Synlicalism Statute of 1919, Mr. Justice Holmes said to have remarked to his Secretary: "'I am afraid Brandeis has the crusading spirit. He talks like one of those upward-and-onward fellows'." Related by Bent, *loc. cit. supra* note 159.

162. Statement before the Commission on Industrial Relations, *supra* note 65, at 7681.

163. ". . . with the increasing complexity of society, the public interest tends to become omnipresent; and the problems presented by new demands for justice cease to be simple. Then the creation or recognition by courts of a new private right may work serious injury to the general public, unless the boundaries of the right are definitely established and wisely guarded. In order to reconcile the new private right with the public interest, it may be necessary to prescribe limitations and rules for its enjoyment; and also to provide administrative machinery for enforcing the rules. It is largely for this reason that, in the effort to meet the many new demands for justice incident to a rapidly changing civilization, resort to legislation has latterly been had with increasing frequency." International News Serv. v. Associated Press, 248 U. S. 215 at 262, 39 Sup. Ct. 68 at 81 (1918).

"The fundamental right of free men to strive for better conditions through new legislation and new instiutions will not be preserved, if efforts to secure it by argument to fellow citizens may be construed as criminal incitement to disobey the existing law—merely because the argument presented seems to those exercising judicial power to be unfair in its portrayal of existing evils, mistaken in its assumptions, unsound in reasoning or intemperate in language." Pierce v. United States, 252 U. S. 239 at 273, 40 Sup. Ct. 205 at 217 (1920).

See, in this connection, the excellent article by J. M. Landis, *The Study of Legislation in the Law Schools,* THE HARVARD GRADUATE MAGAZINE, June, 1931.

164. Brandeis, *The Living Law* (1916) 10 ILL. L. REV. 461 at 467.

165. See especially his opinions in the following cases: Adams v. Tanner, *supra* note 1; Truax v. Corrigan, *supra* note 48; Southwestern Bell Tel. Co. v. Public Serv. Comm., *supra* note 85; New York Central R. R. v. Winfield, 244 U. S. 147, 37 Sup. Ct. 546 (1917); United Railways & Electric Co. v. West, *supra* note 99; Jay Burns Baking Co. v. Bryan, *supra* note 8; St. Louis & O'Fallon Ry. v. United States, *supra* note 128.

166. New York Central R. R. v. Winfield, *supra* note 165 at 165, 37 Sup. Ct. at 547.

167. These conclusions, in part, are confirmed in the recently published recollections of William G. McAdoo:

"Brandeis is a humanitarian; an idealist, but not a dreamer, for no man living has a firmer grasp of business or of economic actualities. He has an unusual capacity for looking at civilization objectively, as if he were not a part of it and reducing its activities and results to a common denominator of human welfare." MC ADOO, CROWDED YEARS (1931) 182.

168. Brandeis, *loc. cit. supra* note 113.

169. CARDOZO, THE GROWTH OF THE LAW (1924) 102.

170. *Ibid.*

171. "The scrutiny and dissection of social facts may supply us with the data upon which the creative spirit broods, but in the process of creation something is given out in excess of what is taken in." CARDOZO, THE GROWTH OF THE LAW (1924) 90.

172. He has usually shown himself unable to regard constitutional-social issues with that cool detachment which is the unique characteristic of Mr. Justice Holmes.

173. Nor is there any reason for concluding that this is not as it should be.

"Deep below consciousness are . . . the likes and the dislikes, the predilections and the prejudices, the complex of instincts and emotions and habits and convictions, which make the man, whether he be litigant or judge. . . . The great tides and currents which engulf the rest of men, do not turn aside in their course, and pass the judges by." CARDOZO, THE NATURE OF THE JUDICIAL PROCESS (1928) 167, and 167-180 generally.

174. A striking illustration of Mr. Justice Brandeis' sympathy with the viewpoint of labor is the case of Wolff Packing Co. v. Court of Industrial Relations, 267 U. S. 552, 45 Sup. Ct. 441 (1925), wherein the court set aside certain sections of the Kansas Court of Industrial Relations Act. Strenuously opposed by labor, Mr. Justice Brandeis joined in the opinion of Chief Justice Taft in overturning the act—an opinion which embodiies one of the most conservative utterances that has issued from the Court in recent years.

175. Washington v. Dawson & Co., *supra* note 47.

176. Such obstacles as there are exist not in the Constitution, but in the minds of those who expound it:

"It [the Constitution] has not lost its capacity for expansion to meet new conditions, unless it be interpreted by rigid minds which have no such capacity." Poole, *op. cit. supra* note 123, at 493.

What Mr. Brandeis said in 1915 with particular reference to minimum wage legislation is applicable to social legislation generally. See Brandeis, *supra* note 9, at 524.

177. McCulloch v. Maryland, 4 Wheat. 316 at 415 (U. S. 1819).

178. Olmstead v. United States, *supra* note 110, at 472, 48 Sup. Ct. at 570 (quoted from Weems v. United States, 217 U. S. 349 at 373, 30 Sup. Ct. 544 at 551 (1910)).

179. Brandeis, *loc. cit. supra* note 176. This point of view

is reiterated in his most recent judicial utterance (New State Ice Co. v. Liebmann, decided March 21, 1932.

The main point of his disagreement with the Court is on its construction of the Fourteenth Amendment so as to restrict the states in their efforts to deal with free competition and other problems of economies in "an emergency more serious than war".

"Economists are searching for the causes of this disorder and are re-examining the bases of our industrial structure. Businessmen are seeking possible remedies. Most of them realize that failure to distribute widely the profits of industry has been a prime cause of our present plight. But, rightly or wrongly, many persons think that one of the major contributing causes has been unbridled competition. Increasingly, doubt is expressed as to whether it is economically wise, or morally right, that men should be permitted to add to the producing facilities of an industry which is already suffering from overcapacity. . . .

"All agree that irregularity in employment—the greatest of our evils—cannot be overcome unless production and consumption are more nearly balanced. Many insist there must be some form of economic control. . . .

"I cannot believe that the framers of the Fourteenth Amendment, or the states which ratified it, intended to leave us helpless to correct the evils of technological unemployment and excess productive capacity, which the march of invention and discovery have entailed.

"To stay experimentation within the law in things social and economic is a grave responsibility. Denial of the right to such experimentation may be fraught with serious consequences to the nation. It is one of the happy incidents of the Federal system that a single courageous state may, if its citizens choose, serve as a laboratory, and try novel social and economic experiments without risk to the rest of the country. This court has the power to stay such experimentation. We may strike down the statute embodying it on the ground that in our opinion, it is arbitrary, capricious or unreasonable; for the due process clause has been held applicable to matters of substantive law as well as to matters of procedure. But in the exercise of this power, we should be ever on our guard, lest we erect our prejudices into legal principles. If we would guide by the light of reason, we must let our minds be bold." —New York Herald-Tribune, March 22, 1932.

180. Olmstead v. United States, *supra* note 110, at 472, 48 Sup. Ct. at 570 (citing Euclid v. Ambler Realty Co., 272 U. S. 365 at 387, 47 Sup. Ct. 114 at 118 (1926); Buck v. Bell, 274 U. S. 200, 47 Sup. Ct. 584 (1927)).

181. *Ibid.*

182. New State Ice Co. v. Liebmann, *supra* note 179.

183. One writer, for example, in appraising the work of the Justice, found the following observation of Mr. Justice Holmes

especially applicable to Mr. Justice Brandeis: "For the rational study of the law the black-letter man may be the man of the present, but the man of the future is the man of statistics and the master of economics." Bikle, *op. cit. supra* note 131, at 32, quoting HOLMES, COLLECTED LEGAL PAPERS 187.

Norman Hapgood, also, in his preface to BRANDEIS, OTHER PEOPLE'S MONEY (1914), attributes Mr. Brandeis' success in various fields largely to his mastery of figures and of the technical details of accounting.

184. Recorded by Ernest Poole in his interview with Mr. Brandeis, *supra* note 123, at 492.

185. Mr. Justice Brandeis possessed to an unusual degree that peculiar quality of mind which, in the opinion of Justice Cardozo judges so frequently lack:

"The judge is often left to improvise . . . a theory, a philosophy, when confronted over night by the exigencies of the case before him. Often he fumbles about, feeling in a vague way that some such problem is involved, but missing the universal element which would have quickened his decision with the inspiration of a principle. If he lacks an adequate philosophy, he either goes astray altogether, or at best does not rise above the empiricism that pronounces upon particulars." CARDOZO, THE GROWTH OF THE LAW (1925) 102. "An avalanche of decisions by tribunals great and small is producing a situation where citation of precedent is tending to count for more. . . .We shall be caught in the tentacles of the web, unless some superintending mind imparts the secret of the structure, lifting us to a height where the unity of the circle will be visible as it lies below." *Ibid.* 5-6. In an address on December 17, 1931, Judge Cardozo again made a strong plea for a "new philosophy in law that will guide the thought of our successors when those of us in place today shall have vanished from the scene." *New York Times*, Dec. 18, 1931.

Mr. Justice Holmes has emphasized the same point:

"Theory is the most important part of the dogma of the law, as the architect is the most important man who takes part in the building of a house. The most important improvements of the last twenty-five years are improvements in theory. It is not to be feared as impracticable, for, to the competent it simply means going to the bottom of the subject." HOLMES, COLLECTED LEGAL PAPERS 200. See also Holmes' introduction to THE CONTINENTAL LEGAL HISTORY SERIES (1911) xlvi.

186. "The man of science in the law is not merely a bookworm. To a microscopic eye for detail he must unite an insight which tells him what details are significant. Not every maker of exact investigation counts, but only he who directs his investigation to a crucial point." HOLMES, COLLECTED LEGAL PAPERS 224.

Footnotes to

THE RIGHT TO PRIVACY

BY LOUIS D. BRANDEIS AND SAMUEL D. WARREN

1. Year Book, Lib. Ass., folio 99, pl. 60 (1348 or 1349), appears to be the first reported case where damages were recovered for a civil assault.

2. These nuisances are technically injuries to property; but the recognition of the right to have property free from interference by such nuisances involves also a recognition of the value of human sensations.

3. Year Book, Lib. Ass., folio 177, pl. 19 (1356), (2 Finl. Reeves Eng. Law, 395) seems to be the earliest reported case of an action for slander.

4. Winsmore v. Greenbank, Willes, 577 (1745).

5. Loss of service is the gist of the action; but it has been said that "we are not aware of any reported case brought by a parent where the value of such services was held to be the measure of damages." Cassoday, J., in Lavery v. Crooke, 52 Wis. 612, 623 (1881). First the fiction of constructive service was invented; Martin v. Payne, 9 John. 387 (1812). Then the feelings of the parent, the dishonor to himself and his family, were accepted as the most important element of damage. Bedford v. McKowl, 3 Esp. 119 (1800); Andrews v. Askey, 8 C. & P. 7 (1837); Phillips v. Hoyle, 4 Gray, 568 (1855); Phelin v. Kenderdine, 20 Pa. St. 354 (1853). The allowance of these damages would seem to be a recognition that the invasion upon the honor of the family is an injury to the parent's person, for ordinarily mere injury to parental feelings is not an element of damage, *e.g.*, the suffering of the parent in case of physical injury to the child. Flemington v. Smithers, 2 C. & P. 292 (1827); Black v. Carrolton R. R. Co., 10 La. Ann. 33 (1855); Covington Street Ry. Co. v. Packer, 9 Bush, 455 (1872).

6. "The notion of Mr. Justice Yates that nothing is property which cannot be earmarked and recovered in detinue or trover, may be true in an early stage of society, when property is in its simple form, and the remedies for violation of it also simple, but is not true in a more civilized state, when the relations of life and the interests arising therefrom are complicated." Erle, J., in Jefferys v. Boosey, 4 H. L. C. 815, 869 (1854).

7. Copyright apears to have been first recognized as a species of private property in England in 1558. DRONE ON COPYRIGHT, 54, 61.

8. Gibblett v. Read, 9 Mod. 459 (1743), is probably the first recognition of goodwill as property.

9. Hogg v. Kirby, 8 Ves. 215 (1803). As late as 1742 Lord

Hardwicke refused to treat a trade-mark as property for infringement upon which an injunction could be granted. Blanchard v. Hill, 2 Atk. 484.

10. COOLEY ON TORTS, 2d ed. p. 29.

11. 8 AMER. LAW REG. N. S. 1 (1869); 12 WASH. LAW REP. 353 (1884); 24 SOL. J. & REP. 4 (1879).

12. SCRIBNER'S MAGAZINE, July, 1890. "The Right of the Citizen. To his Reputation." by E. L. Godkin, Esq., pp. 65, 67.

13. Marion Manola v. Stevens & Myers, N. Y. Supreme Court, "NEW YORK TIMES" of June 15, 18, 21, 1890. There the complainant alleged that while she was playing in the Broadway Theatre, in a role which required her appearance in tights, she was, by means of a flash light, photographed surreptitiously and without her consent, from one of the boxes by defendant Stevens, the manager of the "Castle in the Air" company, and defendant Myers, a photographer, and prayed that the defendants might be restrained from making use of the photograph taken. A preliminary injunction issued *ex parte,* and a time was set for argument of the motion that the injunction should be made permanent, but no one then appeared in opposition.

14. Though the legal value of "feelings" is now generally recognized, distinctions have been drawn between the several classes of cases in which compensation may or may not be recovered. Thus, the fright occasioned by an assault constitutes a cause of action, but fright occasioned by negligence does not. So fright coupled with bodily injury affords a foundation for enhanced damages; but, ordinarily, fright unattended by bodily injury cannot be relied upon as an element of damages, even where a valid cause of action exists, as in trespass *quare clausum fregit.* Wyman v. Leavitt, 71 Me. 227; Canning v. Williamstown 1 Cush. 451. The allowance of damages for injury to the parents' feelings, in case of seduction, abduction of child (Stowe v. Heywood, 7 All. 118), or removal of the corpse of child from a burial-ground (Meagher v. Driscoll, 99 Mass. 281), are said to be exceptions to a general rule. On the other hand, injury to feelings is a recognized element of damages in actions of slander and libel, and of malicious prosecution. These distinctions between the cases, where injury to feelings does not constitute a cause of action or legal element of damages, are not logical, but doubtless serve well as practical rules. It will, it is believed, be found, upon examination of the authorities, that wherever substantial mental suffering would be the natural and probable result of the act, there compensation for injury to feelings has been allowed, and that where no mental suffering would ordinarily result, or if resulting, would naturally be but trifling, and, being unaccompanied by visible signs of injury, would afford a wide scope for imaginative ills, there damages have been disallowed. The

decisions on this subject illustrate well the subjection in our law of logic to common-sense.

15. "Injuria, in the narrower sense, is every intentional and illegal violation of honour, *i.e.,* the whole personality of another." "Now an outrage is committed not only when a man shall be struck with the fist, say, or with a club, or even flogged, but also if abusive language has been used to one." SALKOWSKI, ROMAN LAW, p. 668 and p. 669, n. 2.

16. "It is certain every man has a right to keep his own sentiments, if he pleases. He has certainly a right to judge whether he will make them public, or commit them only to the sight of his friends." Yates, J., in Millar v. Taylor, 4 Burr. 2303, 2379 (1769).

17. Nicols v. Pitman, 26 Ch. D. 374 (1884).

18. Lee v. Simpson, 3 C. B. 871, 881; Daly v. Palmer, 6 Blatchf. 256.

19. Turner v. Robinson, 10 Ir. Ch. 121; s.c. ib. 510.

20. DRONE ON COPYRIGHT, 102.

21. "Assuming the law to be so, what is its foundation in this respect? It is not, I conceive, referable to any consideration peculiarly literary. Those with whom our common law originated had not probably among their many merits that of being patrons of letters; but they knew the duty and necessity of protecting property, and with that general object laid down rules providently expansive, — rules capable of adapting themselves to the various forms and modes of property which peace and cultivation might discover and introduce.

"The produce of mental labor, thoughts and sentiments, recorded and preserved by writing, became, as knowledge went onward and spread, and the culture of man's understanding advanced, a kind of property impossible to disregard, and the interference of modern legislation upon the subject, by the stat. 8 Anne, professing by its title to be 'For the encouragement of learning,' and using the words 'taken the liberty,' in the preamble, whether it operated in augmentation or diminution of the private rights of authors, having left them to some extent untouched, it was found that the common law, in providing for the protection of property, provided for their security, at least before general publication by the writer's consent." Knight Bruce, V. C., in Prince Albert v. Strange, 2 DeGex & Sm. 652, 695 (1849).

22. "The question, however, does not turn upon the form or amount of mischief or advantage, loss or gain. The author of manuscripts, whether he is famous or obscure, low or high, has a right to say of them, if innocent, that whether interesting or dull, light or heavy, saleable or unsaleable, they shall not, without his consent, be published." Knight Bruce, V. C., in Prince Albert v. Strange, 2 DeGex & Sm. 652, 694.

23. Duke of Queensberry v. Shebbeare, 2 Eden, 329 (1758); Bartlett v. Crittenden, 5 McLean, 32, 41 (1849).

24. DRONE ON COPYRIGHT, pp. 102, 104; Parton v. Prang, 3 Clifford, 537, 548 (1872); Jefferys v. Boosey, 4 H. L. C. 815, 867, 962 (1854).

25. "The question will be whether the bill has stated facts of which the court can take notice, as a case of civil property, which it is bound to protect. The injunction cannot be maintained on any principle of this sort, that if a letter has been written in the way of friendship, either the continuance or the discontinuance of the friendship affords a reason for the interference of the court." Lord Eldon in Gee v. Pritchard, 2 Swanst. 402, 413 (1818).

"Upon the principle, therefore, of protecting property, it is that the common law, in cases not aided or prejudiced by statute, shelters the privacy and seclusion of thought and sentiments committed to writing, and desired by the author to remain not generally known." Knight Bruce, V. C., in Prince Albert v. Strange, 2 deGex & Sm. 652, 695.

"It being conceded that reasons of expediency and public policy can never be made the sole basis of civil jurisdiction, the question, whether upon any ground the plaintiff can be entitled to the relief which he claims, remains to be answered; and it appears to us that there is only one ground upon which his title to claim, and our jurisdiction to grant, the relief, can be placed. We must be satisfied, that the publication of private letters, without the consent of the writer, is an invasion of an exclusive right of property which remains in the writer, even when the letters have been sent to, and are still in the possession of his correspondent." Duer, J., in Woolsey v. Judd, 4 Duer, 379, 384 (1855).

26. "A work lawfully published, in the popular sense of the term, stands in this respect, I conceive, differently from a work which has never been in that situation. The former may be liable to be translated, abridged, analyzed, exhibited in morsels, compliment, and otherwise treated, in a manner that the latter is not.

"Suppose, however,—instead of a translation, an abridgment, or a review,—the case of a catalogue,—suppose a man to have composed a variety of literary works ('innocent,' to use Lord Eldon's expression), which he has never printed or published, or lost the right to prohibit from being published,—suppose a knowledge of them unduly obtained by some unscrupulous person, who prints with a view to circulation a descriptive catalogue, or even a mere list of the manuscripts, without authority or consent, does the law allow this? I hope and believe not. The same principles that prevent more candid piracy must, I conceive, govern such a case also.

"By publishing of a man that he has written to particular persons, or on particular subjects, he may be exposed, not merely to sarcasm, he may be ruined. There may be in his possession returned letters that he had written to former correspondents, with whom to have had relations, however harmlessly, may not in after life be a recommendation; or his writings may be otherwise of a kind squaring in no sort with his outward habits and worldly position. There are callings even now in which to be convicted of literature, is dangerous, though the danger is sometimes escaped.

"Again, the manuscripts may be those of a man on account of whose name alone a mere list would be matter of general curiosity. How many persons could be mentioned, a catalogue of whose unpublished writings would, during their lives or afterwards, command a ready sale!" Knight Bruce, V. C., in Prince Albert v. Strange, 2 DeGex & Sm. 652, 693.

27. "A copy or impression of the etchings would only be a means of communicating knowledge and information of the original, and does not a list and description of the same? The means are different, but the object and effect are similar; for in both, the object and effect is to make known to the public more or less of the unpublished work and composition of the author, which he is entitled to keep wholly for his private use and pleasure, and to withhold altogether, or so far as he may please, from the knowledge of others. Cases upon abridgments, translations, extracts, and criticisms of published works have no reference whatever to the present question; they all depend upon the extent of right under the acts respecting copyright, and have no analogy to the exclusive rights in the author of unpublished compositions which depend entirely upon the common-law right of property." Lord Cottenham in Prince Albert v. Strange, 1 McN. & G. 23, 43 (1849). "Mr. Justice Yates, in Mallar v. Taylor, said, that an author's case was exactly similar to that of an inventor of a new mechanical machine; that both original inventions stood upon the same footing in point of property, whether the case were mechanical or literary, whether an epic poem or an orrery; that the immorality of pirating another man's invention was as great as that of purloining his ideas. Property in mechanical works or works of art, executed by a man for his own amusement, instruction, or use, is allowed to subsist, certainly, and may, before publication by him, be invaded, not merely by copying, but by description or by catalogue, as it appears to me. A catalogue of such works may in itself be valuable. It may also as effectually show the bent and turn of the mind, the feelings and taste of the artist, especially if not professional, as a list of his papers. The portfolio or the studio may declare as much as the writing-table. A man may employ himself in private in a manner very harmless, but which, disclosed to society, may destroy the comfort of his life, or even his success in it. Every one, however, has a right, I apprehend, to say that the produce of his private hours is not more liable to publication without his consent, because the publication must be creditable or advantageous to him, than it would be in opposite circumstances."

"I think, therefore, not only that the defendant here is unlawfully invading the plaintiff's rights, but also that the invasion is of such a kind and affects such property as to entitle the plaintiff to the preventive remedy of an injunction; and if not the more, yet, certainly, not the less, because it is an intrusion,—an unbecoming and unseemly intrusion,—an intrusion not alone in breach of conventional rules, but offensive to that inbred sense of propriety natural to every man,—if intrusion, indeed, fitly describes a sordid spying into the privacy of domestic life,—into the home (a word hitherto sacred among us), the home of a family whose life and conduct form an acknowledged title, though not their only unquestionable title, to the most marked respect in this country." Knight Bruce, V. C., in Prince Albert v. Strange, 2 DeGex & Sm. 652, 696, 697.

28. Kiernan v. Manhattan Quotation Co., 50 How. Pr. 194 (1876).

29. "The defendants' counsel say, that a man acquiring a knowledge of another's property without his consent is not by any rule or principle which a court of justice can apply (however secretly he may have kept or endeavored to keep it) forbidden without his consent to communicate and publish that knowledge to the world, to inform the world what the property is, or to describe it publicly, whether orally, or in print or writing.

"I claim, however, leave to doubt whether, as to property of a private nature, which the owner, without infringing on the right of any other, may and does retain in a state of privacy, it is certain that a person who, without the owner's consent, express or implied, acquires a knowledge of it, can lawfully avail himself of the knowledge so acquired to publish without his consent a description of the property.

"It is probably true that such a publication may be in a manner or relate to property of a kind rendering a question concerning the lawfulness of the act too slight to deserve attention. I can conceive cases, however, in which an act of the sort may be so circumstanced or relate to property such, that the matter may weightily affect the owner's interest or feelings, or both. For instance, the nature and intention of an unfinished work of an artist; prematurely made known to the world, may be painful and deeply prejudicial against him; nor would it be difficult to suggest other examples. . . .

"It was suggested that, to publish a catalogue of a collector's gems, coins, antiquities, or other such curiosities, for instance, without his consent, would be to make use of his property without his consent; and it is true, certainly, that a proceeding of that kind may not only as much embitter one collector's life as it would flatter another,—may be not only an ideal calamity,—but may do the owner damage in the most vulgar sense. Such catalogues, even when not descriptive, are often sought after, and sometimes obtain very substantial prices.

These, therefore, and the like instances, are not necessarily examples merely of pain inflicted in point of sentiment or imagination; they may be that, and something else beside." Knight Bruce, V. C., in Prince Albert v. Strange, 2 DeGex & Sm. 652, 689, 690.

30. Hoyt v. Mackenzie, 3 Barb. Ch. 320, 324 (1848); Wetmore v. Scovell, 3 Edw. Ch. 515 (1842). See Sir Thomas Plumer in 2 Ves. & B. 19 (1813).

31. Woolsey v. Judd, 4 Duer, 379, 404 (1855). "It has been decided, fortunately for the welfare of society, that the writer of letters, though written without any purpose of profit, or any idea of literary property, possesses such a right of property in them, that they cannot be published without his consent, unless the purposes of justice, civil or criminal, require the publication." Sir Samuel Romilly, *arg.*, in Gee v. Pritchard, 2 Swanst. 402, 418 (1818). But see HIGH ON INJUNCTIONS, 3d ed. § 1012, *contra.*

32. "But a doubt has been suggested, whether mere private letters, not intended as literary compositions, are entitled to the protection of an injunction in the same manner as compositions of a literary character. This doubt has probably arisen from the habit of not discriminating between the different rights of property which belong to an unpublished manuscript, and those which belong to a published book. The latter, as I have intimated in another connection, is a right to take the profits of publication. The former is a right to control the act of publication, and to decide whether there shall be any publication at all. It has been called a right of property; an expression perhaps not quite satisfactory, but on the other hand sufficiently descriptive of a right which, however incorporeal, involves many of the essential elements of property, and is at least positive and definite. This expression can leave us in no doubt as to the meaning of the learned judges who have used it, when they have applied it to cases of unpublished manuscripts. They obviously intended to use it in no other sense, than in contradistinction to the mere interests of feeling, and to describe a substantial right of legal interest." CURTIS ON COPYRIGHT, pp. 93, 94.

The resemblance of the right to prevent publication of an unpublished manuscript to the well-recognized rights of personal immunity is found in the treatment of it in connection with the rights of creditors. The right to prevent such publication and the right of action for its infringement, like the cause of action for an assault, battery, defamation, or malicious prosecution, are not assets available to creditors.

"There is no law which can compel an author to publish. No one can determine this essential matter of publication but the author. His manuscripts, however valuable, cannot, without his consent, be seized by his creditors as property." McLean, J., in Bartlett v. Crittenden, 5 McLean, 32, 37 (1849).

It has also been held that even where the sender's rights are not asserted, the receiver of a letter has not such property in it as passes to his executor or administrator as a salable asset. Eyre v. Higbee, 22 How. Pr. (N. Y.) 198 (1861).

"The very meaning of the word 'property' in its legal sense is 'that which is peculiar or proper to any person; that which belongs exclusively to one.' The first meaning of the word from which it is derived—*proprius—is* 'one's own.'" DRONE ON COPYRIGHT, p. 6.

It is clear that a thing must be capable of identification in order to be the subject of exclusive ownership. But when its identity can be determined so that individual ownership may be asserted, it matters not whether it be corporeal or incorporeal.

33. "Such then being, as I believe, the nature and the foundation of the common law as to manuscripts independently of Parliamentary additions and subtractions, its operation cannot of necessity be confined to literary subjects. That would be to limit the rule by the example. Wherever the produce of labor is liable to invasion in an analogous manner, there must, I suppose, be a title to analogous protection or redress." Knight Bruce, V. C., in Prince Albert v. Strange, 2 DeGex & Sm. 652, 696.

34. "The question, therefore, is whether a photographer who has been employed by a customer to take his or her portrait is justified in striking off copies of such photograph for his own use, and selling and disposing of them, or publicly exhibiting them by way of advertisement or otherwise, without the authority of such customer, either express or implied. I say 'express or implied,' because a photographer is frequently allowed, on his own request, to take a photograph of a person under circumstances in which a subsequent sale by him must have been in the contemplation of both parties, though not actually mentioned. To the question thus put, my answer is in the negative, that the photographer is not justified in so doing. Where a person obtains information in the course of a confidential employment, the law does not permit him to make any improper use of the information so obtained; and an injunction is granted, if necessary, to restrain such use; as, for instance, to restrain a clerk from disclosing his master's accounts, or an attorney from making known his client's affairs, learned in the course of such employment. Again, the law is clear that a breach of contract, whether express or implied, can be restrained by injunction. In my opinion the case of the photographer comes within the principles upon which both these classes of cases depend. The object for which he is employed and paid is to supply his customer with the required number of printed photographs of a given subject. For this purpose the negative is taken by the photographer on glass; and from this negative copies can be printed in much larger numbers than are generally required by the customer. The customer who sits for the negative thus puts the power of

reproducing the object in the hands of the photographer; and in my opinion the photographer who uses the negative to produce other copies for his own use, without authority, is abusing the power confidentially placed in his hands merely for the purpose of supplying the customer; and further, I hold that the bargain between the customer and the photographer includes, by implication, an agreement that the prints taken from the negative are to be appropriated to the use of the customer only." Referring to the opinions delivered in Tuck v. Priester, 19 Q. B. D. 639, the learned justice continued: "Then Lord Justice Lindley says: 'I will deal first with the injunction, which stands, or may stand, on a totally different footing from either the penalties or the damages. It appears to me that the relation between the plaintiffs and the defendant was such that, whether the plaintiffs had any copyright or not, the defendant has done that which renders him liable to an injunction. He was employed by the plaintiffs to make a certain number of copies of the picture, and that employment carried with it the necessary implication that the defendant was not to make more copies for himself, or to sell the additional copies in this country in competition with his employer. Such conduct on his part is a gross breach of contract and a gross breach of faith, and, in my judgment, clearly entitles the plaintiffs to an injunction, whether they have a copyright in the picture or not.' That case is the more noticeable, as the contract was in writing; and yet it was held to be an implied condition that the defendant should not make any copies for himself. The phrase 'a gross breach of faith' used by Lord Justice Lindley in that case applies with equal force to the present, when a lady's feelings are shocked by finding that the photographer she has employed to take her likeness for her own use is publicly exhibiting and selling copies thereof." North, J., in Pollard v. Photographic Co., 40 Ch. D. 345, 349-352 (1888).

"It may be said also that the cases to which I have referred are all cases in which there was some right of property infringed, based upon the recognition by the law of protection being due for the products of a man's own skill or mental labor; whereas in the present case the person photographed has done nothing to merit such protection, which is meant to prevent legal wrongs, and not mere sentimental grievances. But a person whose photograph is taken by a photographer is not thus deserted by the law; for the Act of 25 and 26 Vict., c. 68, s. 1, provides that when the negative of any photograph is made or executed for or on behalf of another person for a good or valuable consideration, the person making or executing the same shall not retain the copyright thereof, unless it is expressly reserved to him by agreement in writing signed by the person for or on whose behalf the same is so made or executed; but the copyright shall belong to the person for or on whose behalf the same is so made or executed; but the copyright shall belong to the person for or on whose behalf the same shall have been made or executed.

"The result is that in the present case the copyright in the photograph is in one of the plaintiffs. It is true, no doubt, that sect. 4 of the same act provides that no proprietor of copyright shall be entitled to the benefit of the act until registration, and no action shall be sustained in respect of anything done before registration; and it was, I presume, because the photograph of the female plaintiff has not been registered that this act was not referred to by counsel in the course of the argument. But, although the protection against the world in general conferred by the act cannot be enforced until after registration, this does not deprive the plaintiffs of their common-law right of action against the defendant for his breach of contract and breach of faith. This is quite clear from the cases of Morison v. Moat [9 Hare, 241] and Tuck v. Priester [19 Q. B. D. 629] already referred to, in which latter case the same act of Parliament was in question." Per North, J., ibid. p. 352.

This language suggests that the property right in photographs or portraits may be one created by statute, which would not exist in the absence of registration; but it is submitted that it must eventually be held here, as it has been in the similar cases, that the statute provision becomes applicable only when there is a publication, and that before the act of registering there is property in the thing upon which the statute is to operate.

35. Duke of Queensberry v. Shebbeare, 2 Eden, 329; Murray v. Heath, 1 B. & Ad. 804; Tuck v. Priester, 19 Q. B. D. 629.

36. See Mr. Justice Story in Folsom v. Marsh, 2 Story, 100, 111 (1841):

"If he [the recipient of a letter] attempt to publish such letter or letters on other occasions, not justifiable, a court of equity will prevent the publication by an injunction, as a breach of private confidence or contract, or of the rights of the author; and *a fortiori,* if he attempt to publish them for profit; for then it is not a mere breach of confidence or contract, but it is a violation of the exclusive copyright of the writer. . . . The general property, and the general rights incident to property, belong to the writer, whether the letters are literary compositions, or familiar letters, or details of facts, or letters of business. The general property in the manuscripts remains in the writer and his representatives, as well as the general copyright. *A fortiori,* third persons, standing in no privity with either party, are not entitled to publish them, to subserve their own private purposes of interest, or curiosity, or passion."

37. "The receiver of a letter is not a bailee, nor does he stand in a character analogous to that of a bailee. There is no right to possession, present or future, in the writer. The only right to be enforced against the holder is a right to prevent publication, not to require the manuscript from the holder

in order to a publication of himself." Per Hon. Joel Parker, quoted in Grigsby v. Breckenridge, 2 Bush. 480, 489 (1867).

38. In Morison v. Moat, 9 Hare, 241, 255 (1851), a suit for an injunction to restrain the use of a secret medical compound, Sir George James Turner, V. C., said: "That the court has exercised jurisdiction in cases of this nature does not, I think, admit of any question. Different grounds have indeed been assigned for the exercise of that jurisdiction. In some cases it has been referred to property, in others to contract, and in others, again, it has been treated as founded upon trust or confidence,—meaning, as I conceive, that the court fastens the obligation on the conscience of the party, and enforces it against him in the same manner as it enforces against a party to whom a benefit is given, the obligation of performing a promise on the faith of which the benefit has been conferred; but upon whatever grounds the jurisdiction is founded, the authorities leave no doubt as to the exercise of it."

39. A similar growth of the law showing the development of contractual rights into rights of property is found in the law of goodwill. There are indications, as early as the Year Books, of traders endeavoring to secure to themselves by contract the advantages now designated by the term "goodwill," but it was not until 1743 that goodwill received legal recognition as property apart from the personal covenants of the traders. See ALLAN ON GOODWILL, pp. 2, 3.

40. The application of an existing principle to a new state of facts is not judicial legislation. To call it such is to assert that the existing body of law consists practically of the statutes and decided cases, and to deny that the principles (of which these cases are ordinarily said to be evidence) exist at all. It is not the application of an existing principle to new cases, but the introduction of a new principle, which is properly termed judicial legislation.

But even the fact that a certain decision would involve judicial legislation should not be taken as conclusive against the propriety of making it. This power has been constantly exercised by our judges, when applying to a new subject principles of private justice, moral fitness, and public convenience. Indeed, the elasticity of our law, its adaptability to new conditions, the capacity for growth, which has enabled it to meet the wants of an ever changing society and to apply immediate relief for every recognized wrong, have been its greatest boast.

"I cannot understand how any person who has considered the subject can suppose that society could possibly have gone on if judges had not legislated, or that there is any danger whatever in allowing them that power which they have in fact exercised, to make up for the negligence or the incapacity of the avowed legislator. That part of the law of every country which was made by judges has been far better made than that part which consists of statutes enacted by the legislature." 1 AUSTIN'S JURISPRUDENCE, p. 224.

The cases referred to above show that the common law has for a century and a half protected privacy in certain cases, and to grant the further protection now suggested would be merely another application of an existing rule.

41. Loe Relative á la Presse. 11 Mai 1868.

"II. Toute publication dans un écrit periodique relative á un fait de la vie priveé constitue une contravention punie d'un amende de cinq cent francs.

"La poursuite ne pourra être exercée que sur la plainte de la partie interessée." Rivière, Codes Français et Lois Usuelles. App. Code Pen., p. 20.

42. See Campbell v. Spottiswoode, 3 B. & S. 769, 776; Henwood v. Harrison, L. R. 7 C. P. 606; Gott v. Pulsifer, 122 Mass. 235.

43. "Nos moeurs n'admettent pas la prétention d'enlever aux investigations de la publicité les actes qui relèvent de la vie publique, et ce dernier mot ne doit pas être restreint á la vie officielle ou á celle du fonctionnaire. Tout homme qui appelle sur lui l'attention ou les regard du publique, soit par une mission qu'il a reçue ou qu'il se donne, soit par le rôle qu'il s'attribue dans l'industrie, les arts, le theâtre, etc., ne peut plus invoquer contre la critique ou l'exposé de sa conduite d'autre protection que les lois qui repriment a diffamation et l'injure." Circ. Mins. Just., 4 Juin, 1868. Rivière Codes Français et Lois Usuelles, App. Code Pen. 20 n (b).

44. "Celui-la seul a droit au silence absolu qui n'a pas expressément ou indirectment provoqué ou authorisé l'attention, l'approbation ou le blâme." Circ. Mins. Just., 4 Juin, 1868. Rivière Codes Français et Lois Usuelles, App. Code Pen. 20 n (b).

The principle thus expressed evidently is designed to exclude the wholesale investigations into the past of prominent public men with which the American public is too familiar, and also, unhappily, too well pleased; while not entitled to the "silence absolu" which less prominent men may claim as their due, they may still demand that all the details of private life in its most limited sense shall not be laid bare for inspection.

45. Wason v. Walters, L. R. 4 Q. B. 73; Smith v. Higgins, 16 Gray, 251; Barrows v. Bell, 7 Gray, 331.

46. This limitation upon the right to prevent the publication of private letters was recognized early:

"But, consistently with this right [of the writer of letters], the persons to whom they are addressed may have, nay must, by implication, possess, the right to publish any letter or letters addressed to them, upon such occasions, as require, or justify, the publication or public use of them; but this right is strictly limited to such occasions. Thus, a person may justifiably use and publish, in a suit at law or in equity, such letter or letters as are necessary and proper, to establish his right to maintain the suit, or defend the same. So, if he be aspersed or misrepresented by the writer, or accused of improper conduct, in a public manner, he may publish such parts of such letter or letters, but no more, as may be necessary to vindicate his character and reputation, or free him from unjust obloquy and reproach." Story, J., in Folsom v. Marsh, 2 Story, 100, 110, 111 (1841).

The existence of any right in the recipient of letters to publish the same has been strenuously denied by Mr. Drone; but the reasoning upon which his denial rests does not seem satisfactory. DRONE ON COPYRIGHT, pp. 136-139.

47. TOWNSHEND ON SLANDER AND LIBEL, 4th ed., § 18; ODGERS ON LIBEL AND SLANDER, 2d ed., p. 3.

48. "But as long as gossip was oral, it spread, as regards any one individual, over a very small area, and was confined to the immediate circle of his acquaintances. It did not reach, or but rarely reached, those who knew nothing of him. It did not make his name, or his walk, or his conversation familiar to strangers. And what is more to the purpose, it spared him the pain and mortification of knowing that he was gossipped about. A man seldom heard of oral gossip about him which simply made him ridiculous, or trespassed on his lawful privacy, but made no positive attack upon his reputation. His peace and comfort were, therefore, but slightly affected by it." E. L. Godkin, "The Rights of the Citizen: To his Reputation." SCRIBNER'S MAGAZINE, July, 1890, p. 66.

Vice-Chancellor Knight Bruce suggested in Prince Albert v. Strange, 2 DeGex & Sm. 652, 694, that a distinction would be made as to the right to privacy of works of art between an oral and a written description or catalogue.

49. See DRONE ON COPYRIGHT, pp. 121, 289, 290.

50. Compare the French law.

"En prohibant l'envahissement de la vie privée, sans qu'il soit nêcessaire d'établir l'intention criminelle, la lois a entendue interdire toute discussion de la part de la défense sur la vérité des faits. Le remède eut été pire que le mal, si un débat avait pu s'engager sur ce terrain." Circ. Mins. Just., 4 Juin, 1868. Rivière Code Français et Lois Usuelles, App. Code Pen. 20 n (a).

51. Comp. DRONE ON COPYRIGHT, p. 107.

52. Comp. HIGH ON INJUNCTIONS, 3d ed., § 1015; TOWNSHEND ON LIBEL AND SLANDER, 4th ed., §§ 417a-417d.

53. The following draft of a bill has been prepared by William H. Dunbar, Esq., of the Boston bar, as a suggestion for possible legislation:

"SECTION I. Whoever publishes in any newspaper, journal, magazine, or other periodical publication any statement concerning the private life or affairs of another, after being requested in writing by such other person not to publish such statement or any statement concerning him, shall be punished by imprisonment in the State prison not exceeding five years, or by imprisonment in the jail not exceeding two years, or by fine not exceeding one thousand dollars; provided, that no statement concerning the conduct of any person in, or the qualifications of any person for, a public office or position which such person holds, has held, or is seeking to obtain, for which such person is at the time of such publication a candidate, or for which he or she is then suggested as a candidate, and no statement of or concerning the acts of any person in his or her business, profession, or calling, and no statement concerning any person in relation to a position, profession, business, or calling, bringing such person prominently before the public, or in relation to the qualifications for such a position, business, profession, or calling of any person prominent or seeking prominence before the public, and no statement relating to any act done by any person in a public place, nor any other statement of matter which is of public and general interest, shall be deemed a statement concerning the private life or affairs of such person within the meaning of this act.

"SECT. 2. It shall not be a defence to any criminal prosecution brought under section I of this act that the statement complained of is true, or that such statement was published without a malicious intention; but no person shall be liable to punishment for any statement published under such circumstances that if it were defamatory the publication thereof would be privileged."

Part III

THE POLITICAL VIEWS OF MR. JUSTICE BRANDEIS

MR. JUSTICE BRANDEIS AND THE CONSTITUTION

FELIX FRANKFURTER

This is a reprint of a portion of the article which relates to Brandeis' vieiws on the separation of powers, from 45 Harvard Law Review 33, 97-98 (1931).

* * *

The possession of political power assumes subtler forms of temptation than its vulgar abuse. The love of power grows by what it feeds on. To Mr. Justice Brandeis, as to Lincoln, concentration of power is a standing threat to liberty; and to him liberty is a greater good than efficiency. So it was to the Age of Reason, and the Constitution is a product of that Age. It is in the light of his prejudice for liberty that Mr. Justice Brandeis construes the Constitution.

"The separation of the powers of government did not make each branch completely autonomous. It left each, in some measure, dependent upon the others, as it left to each power to exercise, in some respects, functions in their nature executive, legislative and judicial. Obviously the President cannot secure full execution of the laws, if Congress denies to him adequate means of doing so. Full execution may be defeated because Congress declines to create offices indispensable for that purpose. Or, because Congress, having created the office, declines to make the indispensable appropriation. Or, because, Congress, having both created the office and made the appropriation, prevents, by restrictions which it imposes, the appointment of officials who in quality and character are indispensable to the efficient execution of the law. If, in any such way, adequate means are denied to the President, the fault will lie with Congress. The President performs his full constitutional duty, if, with the means and instruments provided by Congress within the limitations prescribed by it, he uses his best endeavors to secure the faithful execution of the laws enacted. Compare *Kendall* v. *United States*, 12 Pet. 524, 613, 626.

"Checks and balances were established in order that this should be 'a government of laws and not of men.' As White said in the House, in 1789, an uncontrollable power of removal in the Chief Executive 'is a doctrine not to be learned in American governments.' Such power had been denied in Colonial Charters, and even under Proprietary Grants and Royal Commissions. It had been denied in the thirteen States before the framing of the Federal Constitution. The doctrine of the separation of powers was adopted by the Convention of 1787, not to promote efficiency but to preclude the exercise of arbitrary power. The purpose was, not to avoid friction, but, by means of the inevitable friction incident to the distribution of the governmental powers among three departments, to save the people from autocracy. In order to prevent arbitrary executive action, the Constitution provided in terms that presidential appointments be made with the consent of the Senate, unless Congress should otherwise provide; and this clause was construed by Alexander Hamilton in The Federalist, No. 77, as requiring like consent to removals. Limiting further executive prerogatives customary in monarchies, the Constitution empowered Congress to vest the appointment of inferior officers, 'as they think proper, in the President alone, in the Courts of Law, or in the Heads of Departments.' Nothing in support of the claim of uncontrollable power can be inferred from the silence of the Convention of 1787 on the subject of removal. For the outstanding fact remains that every specific proposal to confer such uncontrollable power upon the President was rejected. In America, as in England, the conviction prevailed then that the people must look to representative assemblies for the protection of their liberties. And protection of the individual, even if he be an official, from the arbitrary or capricious exercise of power was then believed to be an essential of free government." [Myers v. United States, 272 U. S. 52, 291-95 (1926) (dissent)].

ERIE RAILROAD CO. v. TOMPKINS
304 U. S. 64 (1938)

In this famous opinion, Mr. Justice Brandeis overruled the long-standing decision of *Swift* v. *Tyson.* Speaking for the majority of the Supreme Court, Brandeis held that there is no Federal common law and Congress has no power to declare substantive rules of common law applicable in a state. Except in matters governed by the Federal Constitution or by Acts of Congress, the law to be applied in any case by a Federal Court is the law of the state in which the cause of action arose.

From the formation of our government to the present time, there have been two opposing views as to the scope of the federal power granted by the applicable provisions of the Constitution. The narrower, states' rights view, taken by Marshall, Field and Holmes, is in accord with the Court's early ruling that there is no Federal common law of crimes. Brandeis espoused the states' rights doctrine in this opinion. The broader, or national, view was earlier subscribed by Story and endorsed by the Court for 94 years prior to this holding.

The footnotes in the case, valuable for reference, are omitted.

MR. JUSTICE BRANDEIS delivered the opinion of the Court.

The question for decision is whether the oft-challenged doctrine of *Swift* v. *Tyson* shall now be disapproved.

Tompkins, a citizen of Pennsylvania, was injured on a dark night by a passing freight train of the Erie Railroad Company while walking along its right of way at Hughestown in that State. He claimed that the accident occurred through negligence in the operation, or maintenance, of the train; that he was rightfully on the premises as licensee because on a commonly used beaten footpath which ran for a short distance alongside the tracks; and that he was struck by something which looked like a door projecting from one of the moving cars. To enforce that claim he brought an action in the federal court for southern New York, which had jurisdiction because the company is a corporation of that State. It denied liability; and the case was tried by a jury.

The Erie insisted that its duty to Tompkins was no greater than that owed to a trespasser. It contended, among other things, that its duty to Tompkins, and hence its liability, should be determnied in accordance with the Pennsylvania law; that under the law of Pennsylvania, as declared by its highest court, persons who use pathways along the railroad right of way – that is a longitudinal pathway as distinguished from a crossing – are to be deemed trespassers; and that the railroad is not liable for injuries to undiscovered trespassers resulting from its negligence, unless it be wanton or wilful. Tompkins denied that any such rule had been established by the decisions of the Pennsylvania courts; and contended that, since there was no statute of the State on the subject, the railroad's duty and liability is to be determined in federal courts as a matter of general law.

The trial judge refused to rule that the applicable law precluded recovery. The jury brought in a verdict of $30,000; and the judgment entered thereon was affirmed by the Circuit Court of Appeals, which held, 90 F. 2d 603, 604, that it was unnecessary to consider whether the law of Pennsylvania was as contended, because the question was one not of local, but of general, law and that "upon questions of general law the federal courts are free, in the absence of a local statute, to exercise their independent judgment as to what the law is; and it is well settled that the question of the responsibility of a railroad for injuries caused by its servants is one of general law. . . . Where the public has made open and notorious use of a railroad right of way for a long period of time and without objection, the company owes to persons on such permissive pathway a duty of care in the operation of its trains. . . . It is likewise generally recognized law that a jury may find that negligence exists toward a pedestrian using a permissive path on the railroad right of way if he is hit by some object projecting from the side of the train."

The Erie had contended that application of the Pennsylvania rule was required, among other things, by § 34 of the Federal Judiciary Act of September 24, 1789, c. 20, 28 U. S. C. § 725, which provides:

"The laws of the several States, except where the Constitution, treaties, or statutes of the United States otherwise require or provide, shall be regarded as rules of decision in trials at common law, in the courts of the United States, in cases where they apply."

Because of the importance of the question whether the federal court was free to disregard the alleged rule of the Pennsylvania common law, we granted certiorari.

First. Swift v. *Tyson,* 16 Pet. 1, 18, held that federal courts exercising jurisdiction on the ground of diversity of citizenship need not, in matters of general jurisprudence, apply the unwritten law of the State as declared by its highest court; that they are free to exercise an independent judgment as to what the common law of the State is – or should be; and that, as there stated by Mr. Justice Story:

"The true interpretation of the thirty-fourth section limited its application to state laws strictly local, that is to say, to the positive statutes of the state, and the construction thereof adopted by the local tribunals, and to rights and titles to things having a permanent locality, such as the rights and titles to real estate, and other matters immovable and intraterritorial in their nature and character. It never has been supposed by us, that the section did apply, or was intended to apply, to questions of a more general nature, not at all dependent upon local statutes or local usages of a fixed and permanent operation, as, for example, to the construction of ordinary contracts or other written instruments, and especially to questions of general commercial law, where the state tribunals are called upon to perform the like functions as ourselves, that is, to ascertain upon general reasoning and legal analogies, what is the true exposition of the contract or instrument, or what is the just rule furnished by the principles of commercial law to govern the case."

The Court in applying the rule of § 34 to equity cases, in *Mason* v. *United States,* 260 U. S. 545, 559, said: "The statute, however, is merely declarative of the rule which would exist in the absence of the statute." The federal courts assumed, in the broad field of "general law," the power to declare rules of decision which Congress was confessedly without power to enact as statutes. Doubt was repeatedly expressed as to the correctness of the construction given § 34, and as to the soundness of the rule which it introduced. But it was the more recent research of a competent scholar, who examined the original document, which established that the construction given to it by the Court was erroneous; and that the purpose of the section was merely to make certain that, in all matters except those in which some federal law is controlling, the federal courts exercising jurisdiction in diversity of citizenship cases would apply as their rules of decision the law of the State, unwritten as well as written.

Criticism of the doctrine became widespread after the decision of *Black & White Taxicab Co.* v. *Brown & Yellow Taxicab Co.*, 276 U. S. 518. There, Brown and Yellow, a Kentucky corporation owned by Kentuckians, and the Louisville and Nashville Railroad, also a Kentucky corporation, wished that the former should have the exclusive privilege of soliciting passenger and baggage transportation at the Bowling Green, Kentucky, railroad station; and that the Black and White, a competing Kentucky corporation, should be prevented from interfering with that privilege. Knowing that such a contract would be void under the common law of Kentucky, it was arranged that the Brown and Yellow reincorporate under the law of Tennessee, and that the contract with the railroad should be executed there. The suit was then brought by the Tennessee corporation in the federal court for western Kentucky to enjoin competition by the Black and White; an injunction issued by the District Court was sustained by the Court of Appeals; and this Court, citing many decisions in which the doctrine of *Swift v. Tyson* had been applied, affirmed the decree.

Second. Experience in applying the doctrine of *Swift* v. *Tyson,* had revealed its defects, political and social; and the benefits expected to flow from the rule did not accrue. Persistence of state courts in their own opinions on questions of common law prevented uniformity; and the impossibility of discovering a satisfactory line of demarcation between the province of general law and that of local law developed a new well of uncertainties.

On the other hand, the mischievous results of the doctrine had become apparent. Diversity of citizenship jurisdiction was conferred in order to prevent apprehended discrimination in state courts against those not citizens of the State. *Swift* v. *Tyson* introduced grave discrimination by non-citizens against citizens. It made rights enjoyed under the unwritten "general law" vary according to whether enforcement was sought in the state or in the federal court; and the privilege of selecting the court in which the right should be determined was conferred upon the non-citizen. Thus, the doctrine rendered impossible equal protection of the law. In attempting to promote uniformity of law throughout the United States, the doctrine had prevented uniformity in the administration of the law of the State.

The discrimination resulting became in practice far-reaching. This resulted in part from the broad province accorded to the so-called "general law" as to which federal courts exercised an independent judgment. In addition to questions of purely commercial law, "general law" was held to include the obligations under contracts entered into and to be performed within the State, the extent to which a carrier operating within a State may stipulate for exemption from liability for his own negligence or that of his employee; the liability for torts committed within the State upon persons resident or properly located there, even where the question of liability depended upon the scope of a property right conferred by the State; and the right to exemplary or punitive damages. Furthermore, state decisions construing local deeds, mineral conveyances, and even devises of real estate were disregarded.

In part the discrimination resulted from the wide range of persons held entitled to avail themselves of the federal rule by resort to the diversity of citizenship jurisdiction. Through this jurisdiction individual citizens willing to remove from their own State and become citizens of another might avail themselves of the federal rule. And, without even change of residence, a corporate citizen of the State could avail itself of the federal rule by re-incorporating under the laws of another State, as was done in the *Taxicab* case.

The injustice and confusion incident to the doctrine of *Swift* v. *Tyson* have been repeatedly urged as reasons for abolishing or limiting diversity of citizizenship jurisdiction. Other legislative relief has been proposed. If only a question of statutory construction were involved, we should not be prepared to abandon a doctrine so widely applied throughout nearly a century. But the unconstitutionality of the course pursued has now been made clear and compels us to do so.

Third. Except in matters governed by the Federal Constitution or by Acts of Congress, the law to be applied in any case is the law of the State. And whether the law of the State shall be declared by its Legislature in a statute or by its highest court in a decision is not a matter of federal concern. There is no federal general common law. Congress has no power to declare substantive rules of common law applicable in a State whether they be local in their nature or "general," be they commercial law or a part of the law of torts. And no clause in the Constitution purports to confer such a power upon the federal courts. As stated by Mr. Justice Field when protesting in *Baltimore* & *Ohio R. Co.* v. *Baugh,* 149 U. S. 368, 401, against ignoring the Ohio common law of fellow servant liability:

"I am aware that what has been termed the general law of the country – which is often little less than what the judge advancing the doctrine thinks at the time should be the general law on a particular subject has been often advanced in judicial opinions of this court to control a conflicting law of a State. I admit that learned judges have fallen into the habit of repeating this doctrine as a convenient mode of brushing aside the law of a State in conflict with their views. And I confess that, moved and governed by the authority of the great names of those judges, I have, myself, in many instances, unhesitatingly and confidently, but I think now erroneously, repeated the same doctrine. But, notwithstanding the great names which may be cited in favor of the doctrine, and notwithstanding the frequency with which the doctrine has been reiterated, there stands, as a perpetual protest against its repetition, the Constitution of the United States, which recognizes and preserves the autonomy and independence of the State – independence in their legislative and independence in their judicial departments. Supervision over either the legislative or the judicial action of the States is in no case permissible except as to matters by the Constitution specifically authorized or delegated to the United States. Any interference with either, except as thus permitted, is an invasion of the authority of the State and, to that extent, a denial of its independence."

The fallacy underlying the rule declared in *Swift* v. *Tyson* is made clear by Mr. Justice Holmes. The doctrine rests upon the assumption that there is "a transcendental body of law outside of any particular State but obligatory within it unless and until changed by statute," that federal courts have the power to use their judgment as to what the rules of common law are; and that in the federal courts "the parties are entitled to an independent judgment on matters of general law": "but law in the sense in which courts speak of it today does not exist without some definite authority behind it. The common law so far as it is enforced in a State, whether called common law or not, is not the common law generally but the law of that State existing by the authority of that State without regard to what it may have been in England or anywhere else. . . .

"The authority and only authority is the State, and if that be so, the voice adopted by the State as its own [whether it be of its Legislature or of its Supreme Court] should utter the last word." Thus the doctrine of *Swift* v. *Tyson* is, as Mr. Justice Holmes said, "an unconstitutional assumption of powers by courts of the United States which no lapse of time or respectable array of opinion should make us hesitate to correct." In disapproving that doctrine we do not hold unconstitutional § 34 of the Federal Judiciary Act of 1789 or any other Act of Congress. We merely declare that in applying the doctrine this Court and the lower courts have invaded rights which in our opinion are reserved by the Constitution to the several States.

Fourth. The defendant contended that by the common law of Pennsylvania as declared by its highest court in *Falchetti* v. *Pennsylvania R. Co.*, 307 Pa. 203; 160 A. 859, the only duty owed to the plaintiff was to refrain from wilful or wanton injury. The plaintiff denied that such is the Pennsylvania law. In support of their respective contentions the parties discussed and cited many decisions of the Supreme Court of the State. The Circuit Court of Appeals ruled that the question of liability is one of general law; and on that ground declined to decide the issue of state law. As we hold this was error, the judgment is reversed and the case remanded to it for further proceedings in conformity with our opinion.

Reversed.

Part IV

THE ECONOMIC VIEWS OF MR. JUSTICE BRANDEIS

A. *Business Relations*

NEW STATE ICE CO. v. LIEBMANN
285 U. S. 262, 280-311 (1932)

An Oklahoma statute declared that the manufacture, sale and distribution of ice is a public business and forbade anyone to engage in it without first having obtained a license from a state commission. A license was to issue only when existing facilities in the area were insufficient to meet the public needs. The majority of the Supreme Court held that the statute was violative of due process. The Court held that a state law infringing the liberty guaranteed to individuals by the Constitution cannot be imposed in the interest of legislative experimentation.

In his dissent, Mr. Justice Brandeis stated that due process is never violated when a state or government regulates any business under its police power if the business has become a matter of public concern. ". . . the State's power extends to every regulation of any business reasonably required and appropriate for the public protection." Where "there is reasonable ground for the legislative conclusion that in order to secure a necessary service at reasonable rates, it may be necessary to curtail the right to enter the calling, it is . . . consistent with the due process clause to do so, whatever the nature of the business."

He analyzed the situation in Oklahoma in great detail and concluded that the statute was not arbitrary, unreasonable, or capricious. In view of the presumption of validity, the function of the Court is merely to decide whether the legislature could reasonably conclude that such action was necessary.

Brandeis believed that "there must be power in the States and the Nation to remould, through experimentation, our economic practices and institutions to meet changing social and economic needs." He declared, "I cannot believe that the framers of the Fourteenth Amendment . . . intended to deprive us of the power to correct the evils of technological unemployment and excess productive capacity. . . ."

He also expressed the view that when excessive competition runs some people out of business, thus wasting their investment and needlessly raises prices or makes goods and services sporadically available, a state is justified in causing a monopoly which could correct these shortcomings.

This Oklahoma experiment was initiated during an economic depression, and the case presents a dichotomy of viewpoint, represented by Mr. Justice Sutherland, for the majority of the Court, and Mr. Justice Brandeis. Sutherland stated that nothing was "*more clearly settled*" than the proposition (quoting from *Burns Baking Co.* v. *Bryan,* 264 U. S. 504, 513 (1924)) that it is beyond the power of the state "under the guise of protecting the public, arbitrarily [to] interfere with private business or prohibit lawful occupations or impose unreasonable and unnecessary restrictions upon them." From Mr. Justice Brandeis' dissent one may conclude that perhaps the principle is not so *clearly settled* as Mr. Justice Sutherland believed. Brandeis cautioned the Supreme Court that while it had the power to strike down the experimental statute the Court should constantly be on its guard lest it crystallize its prejudices into legal principles. Thus, he stated, "Denial of the right to experiment may be fraught with serious consequences to the Nation. It is one of the happy incidents of the federal system that a single courageous State may, if its citizens choose, serve as a laboratory, and try novel social and economic experiments without risk to the rest of the country." Should we again be confronted with serious economic problems, it is not *clearly settled* what the Court would do if faced with further state "experimentation."

The identification of a specific brand of economic theory as being a part of the Constitution was criticised as far back as 1905 by Mr. Justice Holmes. In his dissent in *Lochner* v. *New York,* 198 U. S. 45, 75, he asserted that ". . . a constitution is not intended to embody a particular economic theory, whether of paternalism and the organic relation of the citizen to the State or of *laissez-faire.* It is made for people of fundamentally differing views, and the accident of our finding certain opinions natural and familiar or novel and even shocking ought not to conclude our judgment upon the question whether statutes embodying them conflict with the Constitution of the United States."

The footnotes in the case, valuable for reference, are omitted.

MR. JUSTICE BRANDEIS, dissenting.

Chapter 147 of the Session Laws of Oklahoma, 1925, declares that the manufacture of ice for sale and distribution is "a public business"; confers upon the Corporation Commission in respect to it the powers of regulation customarily exercised over public utilities; and provides specifically for securing adequate service. The statute makes it a misdemeanor to engage in the business without a license from the Commission; directs that the license shall not issue except pursuant to a prescribed written application, after a formal hearing upon adequate notice both to the community to be served and to the general public, and a showing upon competent evidence, of the necessity "at the place desired"; and it provides that the application may be denied, among other grounds, if "the facts proved at said hearing disclose that the facilities for the manufacture, sale and distribution of ice by some person, firm or corporation already licensed by said Commission at said point, community or place are sufficient to meet the public needs therein."

Under a license, so granted, the New State Ice Company is, and for some years has been, engaged in the manufacture, sale and distribution of ice at Oklahoma City, and has invested in that business $500,000. While is was so engaged, Liebmann, without having obtained or applied for a license, purchased a parcel of land in that city and commenced the construction thereon of an ice plant for the purpose of entering the business in competition with the plaintiff. To enjoin him from doing so this suit was brought by the Ice Company. Compare *Frost* v. *Corporation Commission*, 278 U. S. 515. Liebmann contends that the manufacture of ice for sale and distribution is not a public business; that it is a private business and, indeed, a common calling; that the right to engage in a common calling is one of the fundamental liberties guaranteed by the due process clause; and that to make his right to engage in that calling dependent upon a finding of public necessity deprives him of liberty and property in violation of the Fourteenth Amendment. Upon full hearing the District Court sustained that contention and dismissed the bill. 42 F. (2d) 913. Its decree was affirmed by the Circuit Court of Appeals. 52 F. (2d) 349. The case is here on appeal. In my opinion, the judgment should be reversed.

First. The Oklahoma statute makes entry into the business of manufacturing ice for sale and distribution dependent, in effect, upon a certificate of public convenience and necessity. Such a certificate was unknown to the common law. It is a creature of the machine age, in which plants have displaced tools and businesses are substituted for trades. The purpose of requiring it is to promote the public interest by preventing waste. Particularly in those businesses in which interest and depreciation charges on plants constitute a large element in the cost of production, experience has taught that the financial burdens incident to unnecessary duplication of facilities are likely to bring high rates and poor service. There, cost is usually dependent, among other things, upon volume; and division of possible patronage among competing concerns may so raise the unit cost of operation as to make it impossible to provide adequate service at reasonable rates. The introduction in the United States of the certificate of public convenience and necessity marked the growing conviction that under certain circumstances free competition might be harmful to the community and that, when it was so, absolute freedom to enter the business of one's choice should be denied.

Long before the enactment of the Oklahoma statute here challenged a like requirement had become common in the United States in some lines of business. The certificate was required first for railroads; then for street railways; then for other public utilities whose operation is dependent upon the grant of some special privilege. Latterly, the requirement had been widely extended to common carriers by motor vehicles which use the highways, but which, unlike street railways and electric light companies, are not dependent upon the grant of any special privilege. In Oklahoma the certificate was required, as early as 1915, for cotton gins – a business then declared a public one, and, like the business of manufacturing ice, conducted wholly upon private property. Sess. Laws, 1915, c. 176, § 3. See *Frost* v. *Corporation Commission*, 278 U. S. 515, 517. As applied to public utilities, the validity under the Fourteenth Amendment of the requirement of the certificate has never been successfully questioned.

Second. Oklahoma declared the business of manufacturing ice for sale and distribution a "public business"; that is, a public utility. So far as appears, it was the first State to do so. Of course, a legislature cannot by mere legislative fiat convert a business into a public utility. *Producers Transportation Co.* v. *Railroad Commission*, 251 U. S. 228, 230. But the conception of a public utility is not static. The welfare of the community may require that the business of supplying ice be made a public utility, as well as the business of supplying water or any other necessary commodity or service. If the business is, or can be made, a public utility, it must be possible to make the issue of a certificate a prerequisite to engaging in it.

Whether the local conditions are such as to justify converting a private business into a public one is a matter primarily for the determination of the state legislature. Its determination is subject to judicial review; but the usual presumption of validity attends the enactment. The action of the State must be held valid unless clearly arbitrary, capricious or unreasonable. "The legislature being familiar with local conditions is, primarily, the judge of the necessity of such enactments. The mere fact that a court may differ with the legislature in its views of public policy, or that judges may hold views inconsistent with the propriety of the legislation in question, affords no ground for judicial interference, . . ." *McLean* v. *Arkansas*, 211 U. S. 539, 547. Whether the grievances are real or fancied, whether the remedies are wise or foolish, are not matters about which the Court may concern itself. "Our present duty is to pass upon the statute before us, and if it has been enacted upon a belief of evils that is not arbitrary we cannot measure their extent against the estimate of the legislature." *Tanner* v. *Little,* 240 U. S. 369, 385. A decision that the legislature's belief of evils was arbitrary, capricious and unreasonable may not be made without enquiry into the facts with reference to which it acted.

Third. Liebmann challenges the statute – not an order of the Corporation Commission. If he had applied for a license and been denied one, we should have been obliged to enquire whether the evidence introduced before the Commission justified it in refusing permission to establish an additional ice plant in Oklahoma City. As he did not apply but challenges the statute itself, our enquiry is of an entirely different nature. Liebmann rests his defense upon the broad claim that the Federal Constitution gives him the right to enter the business of manufacturing ice for sale even if his doing so be found by the properly constituted authority to be inconsistent with the public welfare. He claims that, whatever the local conditions may demand, to confer upon the Commission power to deny that right is an unreasonable, arbitrary and capricious restraint upon his liberty.

The function of the Court is primarily to determine whether the conditions in Oklahoma are such that the legislature could not reasonably conclude (1) that the public welfare required treating the manufacture of ice for sale and distribution as a "public business"; and (2) that in order to ensure to the inhabitants of some communities an adequate supply of ice at reasonable rates it was necessary to give the Commission power to exclude the establishment of an additional ice plant in places where the community was already well served. Unless the Court can say that the Federal Constitution confers an absolute right to engage anywhere in the business of manufacturing ice for sale, it cannot properly decide that the legislators acted unreasonably without first ascertaining what was the experience of Oklahoma in respect to the ice business. The relevant facts appear, in part, of record. Others are matters of common knowledge to those familiar with the ice business. Compare *Muller* v. *Oregon,* 208 U. S. 412, 419, 420. They show the actual conditions, or the beliefs, on which the legislators acted. In considering these matters we do not, in a strict sense, take judicial notice of them as embodying statements of uncontrovertible facts. Our function is only to determine the reasonableness of the legislature's belief in the existence of evils and in the effectiveness of the remedy provided. In performing this function we have no occasion to consider whether all the statements of fact which may be the basis of the prevailing belief are well-founded; and we have, of course, no right to weigh conflicting evidence.

(A) In Oklahoma a regular supply of ice may reasonably be considered a necessary of life, comparable to that of water, gas and electricity. The climate, which heightens the need of ice for comfortable and wholesome living, precludes resort to the natural product. There, as elsewhere, the development of the manufactured ice industry in recent years has been attended by deep-seated alterations in the economic structure and by radical changes in habits of popular thought and living. Ice has come to be regarded as a household necessity, indispensable to the preservation of food and so to economical household management and the maintenance of health. Its commercial uses are extensive. In urban communities, they absorb a large proportion of the total amount of ice manufactured for sale. The transportation, storage and distribution of a great part of the nation's food supply is dependent upon a continuous, and dependable supply of ice. It appears from the record that in certain parts of Oklahoma a large trade in dairy and other products has been built up as a result of rulings of the Corporation Commission under the Act of 1925, compelling licensed manufacturers to serve agricultural communities; and that this trade would be destroyed if the supply of ice were withdrawn. We cannot say that the legislature of Oklahoma acted arbitrarily in declaring that ice is an article of primary necessity, in industry and agriculture as well as in the household, partaking of the fundamental character of electricity, gas, water, transportation and communication.

Nor can the Court properly take judicial notice that, in Oklahoma, the means of manufacturing ice for private use are within the reach of all persons who are dependent upon it. Certainly it has not been so. In 1925 domestic mechanical refrigeration had scarcely emerged from the experimental stage. Since that time, the production and consumption of ice manufactured for sale, far from diminishing, has steadily increased. In Oklahoma the mechanical household refrigerator is still an article of relative luxury. Legislation essential to the protection of individuals of limited or no means is not invalidated by the circumstance that other individuals are financially able to protect themselves. The businesses of power companies and of common carriers by street railway, steam railroad or motor vehicle fall within the field of public control, although it is possible, for a relatively modest outlay, to install individual power plants, or to purchase motor vehicles for private carriage of passengers or goods. The question whether in Oklahoma the means of securing refrigeration otherwise than by ice manufactured for sale and distribution has become so general as to destroy popular dependence upon ice plants is one peculiarly appropriate for the determination by this Court, which cannot have knowledge of all the relevant facts.

The business of supplying ice is not only a necessity, like that of supplying food or clothing or shelter, but the legislature could also consider that it is one which lends itself peculiarly to monopoly. Characteristically the business is conducted in local plants with a market narrowly limited in area, and this for the reason that ice manufactured at a distance cannot effectively compete with a plant on the ground. In small towns and rural communities the duplication of plants and in larger communities the duplication of delivery service, is wasteful and ultimately burdensome to consumers. At the same time the relative ease and cheapness with which an ice plant may be constructed exposes the industry to destructive and frequently ruinous competition. Competition in the industry tends to be destructive because ice plants have a determinate capacity, and inflexible fixed charges and operating costs, and because in a market of limited area the volume of sales is not readily expanded. Thus, the erection of a new plant in a locality already adequately served often causes managers to go to extremes in cutting prices in order to secure business. Trade journals and reports of association meetings of ice manufacturers bears ample witness to the hostility of the industry to such competition, and to its unremitting efforts, through trade associations, informal agreements, combination of delivery systems, and in particular through the consolidation of plants, to protect markets and prices against competition of any character.

That these forces were operative in Oklahoma prior to the passage of the Act under review, is apparent from the record. Thus, it was testified that in only six or seven localities in the States containing, in the aggregate, not more than 235,000 of the total population of approximately 2,000,000, was there "a semblance of competition"; and that even in those localities the prices of ice were ordinarily uniform. The balance of the population was, and still is, served by companies enjoying complete monopoly. Compare *Munn* v. *Illinois,* 94 U. S. 113, 131, 132; *Sinking Fund Cases,* 99 U. S. 700, 747; *Wabash, St. L. & P. Ry. Co.* v. *Illinois,* 118 U. S. 557, 569; *Spring Valley Water Works* v. *Schottler,* 110 U. S. 347, 354; *Budd* v. *New York,* 143 U. S. 517, 545; *Wolff Co.* v. *Industrial Court,* 262 U. S. 522, 528. Where there was competition, it often resulted to the disadvantage rather than the advantage of the public, both in respect to prices and to service. Some communities were without ice altogether, and the State was without means of assuring their supply. There is abundant evidence of widespread dissatisfaction with ice service prior to the Act of 1925, and of material improvement in the situation subsequently. It is stipulated in the record that the ice industry as a whole in Oklahoma has acquiesced in and accepted the Act and the status which it creates.

(B) The statute under review rests not only upon the facts just detailed but upon a long period of experience in more limited regulation dating back to the first year of Oklahoma's statehood. For 17 years prior to the passage of the Act of 1925, the Corporation Commission under § 13 of the Act of June 10, 1908, had exercised jurisdiction over the rates, practices and service of ice plants, its action in each case, however, being predicated upon a finding that the company complained of enjoyed a "virtual monopoly" of the ice business in the community which it served. The jurisdiction thus exercised was upheld by the Supreme Court of the State in *Oklahoma Light & Power Co.* v. *Corporation Commission*, 96 Okla. 19; 220 Pac. 54. The court said, at p. 24: "The manufacture, sale, and distribution of ice in many respects closely resemble the sale and distribution of gas as fuel, or electric current, and in many communities the same company that manufactures, sells and distributes electric current is the only concern that manufactures, sells, and distributes ice, and by reason of the nature and extent of the ice business it is impracticable in that community to interest any other concern in such business. In this situation, the distributor of such a necessity as ice should not be permitted by reason of the impracticability of any one else engaging in the business to charge unreasonable prices, and if such an abuse is persisted in, the regulatory power of the State should be invoked to protect the public." See also *Consumers Light & Power Co.* v. *Phipps*, 120 Okla. 223; 251 Pac. 63.

By formal orders, the Commission repeatedly fixed or approved prices to be charged in particular communities, required ice to be sold without discrimination and to be distributed as equitably as possible to the extent of the capacity of the plant; forbade short weights and ordered scales to be carried on delivery wagons and ice to be weighed upon the customer's request; and undertook to compel sanitary practices in the manufacture of ice and courteous service of patrons. Many of these regulations, other than those fixing prices, were embodied in a general order to all ice companies, issued July 15, 1921, and are still in effect. Informally, the Commission adjusted a much greater volume of complaints of a similar nature. It appears from the record that for some years prior to the Act of 1925 one day of each week was reserved by the Commission to hear complaints relative to the ice business.

As early as 1911, the Commission in its annual report to the Governor, had recommended legislation more clearly delineating its powers in this field:

"There should be a law passed putting the regulation of ice plants under the jurisdiction of the Commission. The Commission is now assuming this jurisdiction under an Act passed by the Legislature known as the anti-trust law. A specific law upon this subject would obviate any question of jurisdiction."

This recommendation was several times repeated, in terms revealing the extent and character of public complaint against the practices of ice companies.

The enactment of the so-called Ice Act in 1925 enlarged the existing jurisdiction of the Corporation Commission by removing the requirement of a finding of virtual monopoly in each particular case, compare *Budd* v. *New York,* 143 U. S. 517, 545, with *Brass* v. *Stoeser,* 153 U. S. 391, 402, 403; by conferring the same authority to compel adequate service as in the case of other public utilities; and by committing to the Commission the function of issuing licenses equivalent to a certificate of public convenience and necessity. With the exception of the granting and denying of such licenses and the exertion of wider control over service, the regulatory activity of the Commission in respect to ice plants has not changed in character since 1925. It appears to have diminished somewhat in volume.

In 1916, the Commission urged, in its report to the Governor, that all public utilities under its jurisdiction be required to secure from the Commission "what is known as a 'certificate of public convenience and necessity' before the duplication of facilities."

"This would prevent ruinous competition resulting in the driving out of business of small though competent public service utilities by more powerful corporations, and often consequent demoralization of service, or the requiring of the public to patronize two utilities in a community where one would be adequate."

Up to that time a certificate of public convenience and necessity to engage in the business had been applied only to cotton gins. Okla. Sess. Laws, 1915, c. 176, § 3. In 1917 a certificate from the Commission was declared prerequisite to the construction of new telephone or telegraph lines. In 1923 it was required for the operation of motor carriers. In 1925, the year in which the Ice Act was passed, the requirement was extended also to power, heat, light, gas, electric or water companies proposing to do business in any locality already possessing one such utility.

Fourth. Can it be said in the light of these facts that it was not an appropriate exercise of legislative discretion to authorize the Commission to deny a license to enter the business in localities where necessity for another plant did not exist? The need of some remedy for the evil of destructive competition, where competition existed, had been and was widely felt. Where competition did not exist, the propriety of public regulation had been proven. Many communities were not supplied with ice at all. The particular remedy adopted was not enacted hastily. The statute was based upon a long-established state policy recognizing the public importance of the ice business, and upon 17 years' legislative and administrative experience in the regulation of it. The advisability of treating the ice business as a public utility and of applying to it the certificate of convenience and necessity had been under consideration for many years. Similar legislation had been enacted in Oklahoma under similar circumstances with respect to other public services. The measure bore a substantial relation to the evils found to exist. Under these circumstances, to hold the Act void as being unreasonable, would, in my opinion involve the exercise not of the function of judicial review, but the function of a super-legislature. If the Act is to be stricken down, it must be on the ground that the Federal Constitution guarantees to the individual the absolute right to enter the ice business, however detrimental the exercise of that right may be to the public welfare. Such, indeed, appears to be the contention made.

Fifth. The claim is that manufacturing ice for sale and distribution is a business inherently private, and, in effect, that no state of facts can justify denial of the right to engage in it. To supply one's self with water, electricity, gas, ice or any other article, is inherently a matter of private concern. So also may be the business supplying the same articles to others for compensation. But the business of supplying to others, for compensation, any article or service whatsoever may become a matter of public concern. Whether it is, or is not, depends upon the conditions existing in the community affected. If it is a matter of public concern, it may be regulated, whatever the business. The public's concern may be limited to a single feature of the business, so that the needed protection can be secured by a relatively slight degree of regulation. Such is the concern over possible incompetence, which dictates the licensing of dentists, *Dent* v. *West Virginia,* 129 U. S. 114, 122; *Douglas* v. *Noble,* 261 U. S. 165, 170; or the concern over possible dishonesty, which led to the licensing of auctioneers or hawkers, *Baccus* v. *Louisiana,* 232 U. S. 334, 338. On the other hand, the public's concern about a particular business may be so pervasive and varied as to require constant detailed supervision and a very high degree of regulation. Where this is true, it is common to speak of the business as being a "public" one, although it is privately owned. It is to such businesses that the designation "public utility" is commonly applied; or they are spoken of as "affected with a public interest." *German Alliance Ins. Co.* v. *Lewis,* 233 U. S. 389, 408.

A regulation valid for one kind of business may, of

course, be invalid for another; since the reasonableness of every regulation is dependent upon the relevant facts. But so far as concerns the power to regulate, there is no difference in essence, between a business called private and one called a public utility or said to be "affected with a public interest." Whatever the nature of the business, whatever the scope or character of the regulation applied, the source of the power invoked is the same. And likewise the constitutional limitation upon that power. The source is the police power. The limitation is that set by the due process clause, which, as construed, requires that the regulation shall not be unreasonable, arbitrary or capricious; and that the means of regulation selected shall have a real or substantial relation to the object sought to be obtained. The motion of a distinct category of business "affected with a public interest," employing property "devoted to a public use," rests upon historical error. The consequences which it is sought to draw from those phrases are belied by the meaning in which they were first used centuries ago, and by the decision of this Court, in *Munn* v. *Illinois*, 94 U. S. 113, which first introduced them into the law of the Constitution. In my opinion, the true principle is that the State's power extends to every regulation of any business reasonably required and appropriate for the public protection. I find in the due process clause no other limitation upon the character or the scope of regulation permissible.

Sixth. It is urged specifically that manufacturing ice for sale and distribution is a common calling; and that the right to engage in a common calling is one of the fundamental liberties guaranteed by the due process clause. To think of the ice-manufacturing business as a common calling is difficult; so recent is it in origin and so peculiar in character. Moreover, the Constitution does not require that every calling which has been common shall ever remain so. The liberty to engage in a common calling, like other liberties, may be limited in the exercise of the police power. The slaughtering of cattle had been a common calling in New Orleans before the monopoly sustained in *Slaughter-House Cases,* 16 Wall. 36, was created by the legislature. Prior to the Eighteenth Amendment selling liquor was a common calling, but this Court held it to be consistent with the due process clause for a State to abolish the calling, *Bartemeyer* v. *Iowa,* 18 Wall. 129; *Mugler* v. *Kansas,* 123 U. S. 623, or to establish a system limiting the number of licenses, *Crowley* v. *Christensen,* 137 U. S. 86. Every citizen has the right to navigate a river or lake, and may even carry others thereon for hire. But the ferry privilege may be made exclusive in order that the patronage may be sufficient to justify maintaining the ferry service, *Conway* v. *Taylor's Executor,* 1 Black 603, 633, 634.

It is settled that the police power commonly invoked in aid of health, safety and morals, extends equally to the promotion of the public welfare. The cases just cited show that, while, ordinarily, free competition in the common callings has been encouraged, the public welfare may at other times demand that monopolies be created. Upon this principle is based our whole modern practice of public utility regulation. It is no objection to the validity of the statute here assailed that it fosters monopoly. That, indeed, is its design. The certificate of public convenience and invention is a device – a recent social-economic invention – through which the monopoly is kept under effective control by vesting in a commission the power to terminate it whenever that course is required in the public interest. To grant any monopoly to any person as a favor is forbidden even if terminable. But where, as here, there is reasonable ground for the legislative conclusion that in order to secure a necessary service at reasonable rates, it may be necessary to curtail the right to enter the calling, it is, in my opinion, consistent with the due process clause to do so, whatever the nature of the business. The existence of such power in the legislature seems indispensable in our ever-changing society.

It is settled by unanimous decisions of this Court,

that the due process clause does not prevent a State or city from engaging in the business of supplying its inhabitants with articles in general use, when it is believed that they cannot be secured at reasonable prices from the private dealers. Thus, a city may, if the local law permits, buy and sell at retail coal and wood, *Jones* v. *Portland,* 245 U. S. 217; or gasoline, *Standard Oil Co.* v. *Lincoln,* 275 U. S. 504. And a State may, if permitted by its own Constitution, build and operate warehouses, elevators, packing houses, flour mills or other factories, *Green* v. *Frazier,* 253 U. S. 233. As States may engage in a business, because it is a public purpose to assure to their inhabitants an adequate supply of necessary articles, may they not achieve this public purpose, as Oklahoma has done, by exercising the lesser power of preventing single individuals from wantonly engaging in the business and thereby making impossible a dependable private source of supply? As a State so entering upon a business may exert the taxing power all individual dealers may be driven from the calling by the unequal competition. If States are denied the power to prevent the harmful entry of a few individuals into a business, they may thus, in effect, close it altogether to private enterprise.

Seventh. The economic emergencies of the past were incidents of scarcity. In those days it was preeminently the common callings that were the subjects of regulation. The danger then threatening was excessive prices. To prevent what was deemed extortion, the English Parliament fixed the prices of commodities and of services from time to time during the four centuries preceding the Declaration of Independence. Like legislation was enacted in the Colonies; and in the States, after the Revolution. When the first due process clause was written into the Federal Constitution, the price of bread was being fixed by statute in at least two of the States, and this practice continued long thereafter. Dwelling houses when occupied by the owner are preeminently private property. From the foundation of our Government those who wished to lease residential property had been free of charge to tenants such rentals as they pleased. But for years after the World War had ended, the scarcity of dwellings in the City of New York was such that the State's legislative power was invoked to ensure reasonable rentals. The constitutionality of the statute was sustained by this Court. *Marcus Brown Holding Co.* v. *Feldman,* 256 U. S. 170. Similar legislation of Congress for the City of Washington was also upheld. *Block* v. *Hirsh,* 256 U. S. 135.

Eighth. The people of the United States are now confronted with an emergency more serious than war. Misery is wide-spread, in a time, not of scarcity, but of over-abundance. The long-continued depression has brought unprecedented unemployment, a catastrophic fall in commodity prices and a volume of economic losses which threatens our financial institutions. Some people believe that the existing conditions threaten even the stability of the capitalistic system. Economists are searching for the causes of this disorder and are reexamining the bases of our industrial structure. Business men are seeking possible remedies. Most of them realize that failure to distribute widely the profits of industry has been a prime cause of our present plight. But rightly or wrongly, many persons think that one of the major contributing causes has been unbridled competition. Increasingly, doubt is expressed whether it is economically wise, or morally right, that men should be permitted to add to the producing facilities of an industry which is already suffering from over-capacity. In justification of that doubt, men point to the excess-capacity of our productive facilities resulting from their vast expansion without corresponding increase in the consumptive capacity of the people. They assert that through improved methods of manufacture, made possible by advances in science and invention and vast accumulation of capital, our industries had become capable of producing from thirty to one hundred per cent. more than was consumed even in days of vaunted prosperity; and that the present capacity will, for a long time, exceed the needs of business. All agree that irregularity in employment—

the greatest of our evils—cannot be overcome unless production and consumption are more nearly balanced. Many insist there must be some form of economic control. There are plans for proration. There are many proposals for stabilization. And some thoughtful men of wide business experience insist that all projects for stabilization and proration must prove futile unless, in some way, the equivalent of the certificate of public convenience and necessity is made a prerequisite to embarking new capital in an industry in which the capacity already exceeds the production schedules.

Whether that view is sound nobody knows. The objections to the proposal are obvious and grave. The remedy might bring evils worse than the present disease. The obstacles to success seem insuperable. The economic and social sciences are largely uncharted seas. We have been none too successful in the modest essays in economic control already entered upon. The new proposal involves a vast extension of the area of control. Merely to acquire the knowledge essential as a basis for the exercise of this multitude of judgments would be a formidable task; and each of the thousands of these judgments would call for some measure of prophecy. Even more serious are the obstacles to success inherent in the demands which execution of the project would make upon human intelligence and upon the character of men. Man is weak and his judgment is at best fallible.

Yet the advances in the exact sciences and the achievements in invention remind us that the seemingly impossible sometimes happens. There are many men now living who were in the habit of using the age-old expression: "It is as impossible as flying." The discoveries in physical science, the triumphs in invention, attest the value of the process of trial and error. In large measure, these advances have been due to experimentation. In those fields experimentation has, for two centuries, been not only free but encouraged. Some people assert that our present plight is due, in part, to the limitations set by courts upon experimentation in the fields of social and economic science; and to the discouragement to which proposals for betterment there have been subjected otherwise. There must be power in the States and the Nation to remould, through experimentation, our economic practices and institutions to meet changing social and economic needs. I cannot believe that the framers of the Fourteenth Amendment, or the States which ratified it, intended to deprive us of the power to correct the evils of technological unemployment and excess productive capacity which have attended progress in the useful arts.

To stay experimentation in things social and economic is a grave responsibility. Denial of the right to experiment may be fraught with serious consequences to the Nation. It is one of the happy incidents of the federal system that a single courageous State may, if its citizens choose, serve as a laboratory; and try novel social and economic experiments without risk to the rest of the country. This Court has the power to prevent an experiment. We may strike down the statute which embodies it on the ground, that in our opinion, the measure is arbitrary, capricious or unreasonable. We have the power to do this, because the due process clause has been held by the Court applicable to matters of substantive law as well as to matters of procedure. But in the exercise of this high power, we must be ever on our guard, lest we erect our projudices into legal principles. If we would guide by the light of reason, we must let our minds be bold.

LOUISVILLE JOINT STOCK LAND BANK v. RADFORD

295 U. S. 555 (1935)

Speaking for a unanimous Court, Mr. Justice Brandeis in this opinion declared the original Frazier-Lemke Act unconstitutional because it deprived the mortgagee of five distinct property rights recognized under the law of Kentucky, without due process of law. The following rights were taken away from the mortgagee: (1) the right to retain the lien until the indebtedness thereby secured was paid, (2) the right to realize on the security by a judicial public sale, (3) the right to determine, subject to the discretion of the court, the time of such sale, (4) the right to bid for the property at the sale, and thus to assure having the mortgaged property devoted primarily to the satisfaction of the debt, and (5) the right to control the property during the period of default, subject only to the discretion of the court, and to have rents and profits collected by a receiver toward the satisfaction of the debt. Brandeis also stated that the Act could not be upheld under the bankruptcy power of Congress, for that power also is subject to the Fifth Amendment. The Fifth Amendment ordains that, "however great the Nation's need, private property shall not be thus taken even for a public use without just compensation. If the public interest requires, and permits, the taking of property of individual mortgagees in order to relieve the necessities of individual mortgagors," the proceedings by eminent domain must be invoked. In that manner, the burden of the relief granted in the public interest may, through taxation, be borne by the public. Thus, Brandeis indicates the relationship between the police power and the power of eminent domain, accepting the limitation of the power of the government to take away property.

An amended Act which preserved three of the five enumerated rights of mortgagees, although allegedly destructive of the other two, was later sustained in *Wright* v. *Vinton Branch of Mountain Trust Bank*, 300 U. S. 440 (1937).

This case is included here, in juxtaposition to the *New State Ice Co.* opinion to show that Mr. Justice Brandeis imposed limits on the extinction of property rights. It illustrates a restriction which he placed on the government's power to take away property. He conceived of property rights as a fundamental instrumentality of democracy, and the case confirms this viewpoint.

The footnotes in the case, valuable for reference, are omitted.

Mr. Justice Brandeis delivered the opinion of the Court.

This case presents for decision the question whether subsection (s) added to § 75 of the Bankruptcy Act by the Frazier-Lemke Act, June 28, 1934, c. 869, 48 Stat. 1289, is consistent with the Federal Constitution.

The federal court for western Kentucky, 8 F. Supp. 489, and the Circuit Court of Appeals for the Sixth Circuit, 74 F. (2d) 576, held it valid in this case; and it has been sustained elsewhere. In view of the novelty and importance of the question, we granted certiorari.

In 1922 (and in 1924) Radford mortgaged to the Louisville Joint Stock Land Bank a farm in Christian County, Kentucky, comprising 170 acres, then presumably of the appraised value of at least $18,000. The mortgages were given to secure loans aggregating $9,000, to be repaid in instalments over the period of 34 years with interest at the rate of 6 per cent. Radford's wife joined in the mortgages and the notes. In 1931 and subsequent years, the Radfords made default in their covenant to pay the taxes. In 1932 and 1933, they made default in their promise to pay the instalments of interest and principal. In 1933, they made default, also, in their covenant to keep the buildings insured. The Bank urged the Radfords to endeavor to refinance the indebtedness pursuant to the provisions of the Emergency Farm Mortgage Act, May 12, 1933, c. 25, 48 Stat. 41. After they had declined to do so, the Bank, having declared the entire indebtedness immediately payable, commenced, in June, 1933, a suit in the Circuit Court for Christian County against the Radfords and their tenant to foreclose the mortgages; and, invoking a covenant in the mortgage expressly providing therefor, sought the appointment of a receiver to take possession and control of the premises and to collect the rents and profits.

The application for the appointment of a receiver was denied, and all proceedings in the suit were stayed, upon request of the Conciliation Commissioner for Christian County appointed under § 75 of the Bankruptcy Act, as he stated that Radford desired to avail himself of the provisions of that section. Proceeding under it, Radford filed, in the federal court for western Kentucky, a petition praying that he be afforded an opportunity to effect a composition of his debts. The petition was promptly approved and a meeting of the creditors was held. But Radford failed to obtain the acceptance of the requisite majority in number and amount to the composition proposed. Then, the Bank offered to accept a deed of the mortgaged property in full satisfaction of the indebtedness to it and to assume the unpaid taxes. Radford refused to execute the deed; and on June 30, 1934, the state court entered judgment ordering a foreclosure sale.

Meanwhile, the Frazier-Lemke Act had been passed on June 28, 1934; and on August 6, 1934, and again on November 10, 1934, Radford filed amended petitions for relief thereunder. The second amended petition prayed that Radford be adjudged a bankrupt; that his property, whether free or encumbered, be appraised; and that he have the relief provided for in Paragraphs 3 and 7 of sub-section (s) of the Frazier-Lemke Amendment. That Act provides, among other things, that a farmer who has failed to obtain the consents requisite to a composition under § 75 of the Bankruptcy Act, may, upon being adjudged a bankrupt, acquire alternative options in respect to mortgaged property:

1. By Paragraph 3, the bankrupt may, if the mortgagee assents, purchase the property at its then appraised value, acquiring title thereto as well as immediate possession, by agreeing to make deferred payments as follows: 2½ per cent. within two years; 2½ per cent. within three years; 5 per cent. within 4 years; 5 per cent. within 5 years; the balance within six years. All deferred payments to bear interest at the rate of 1 per cent. per annum.

2. By Paragraph 7, the bankrupt may, if the mortgagee refuses his assent to the immediate purchase on the above basis, require the bankruptcy court to "stay all proceedings for a period of five years, during which five years the debtor shall retain possession of all or any part of his property, under the control of the court, provided he pays a reasonable rental annually for that part of the property of which he retains possession; the first payment of such rental to be made within six months of the date of the

order staying proceedings, such rental to be distributed among the secured and unsecured creditors; as their interests may appear, under the provisions of this Act. At the end of five years, or prior thereto, the debtor may pay into court the appraised price of the property of which he retains possession: *Provided,* That upon request of any lien holder on real estate the court shall cause a reappraisal of such real estate and the debtor may then pay the reappraised price, if acceptable to the lien holder, into the court, otherwise the original appraisal price shall be paid into court and thereupon the court shall, by an order, turn over full possession and title of said property to the debtor and he may apply for his discharge as provided for by this Act: *Provided, however,* That the provisions of this Act shall apply only to debts existing at the time this Act becomes effective."

Answering the amended petition, the Bank duly claimed that the Frazier-Lemke Act is, and the relief sought would be, unconstitutional. It prayed that Radford's amended petition be dismissed; that the Bank be permitted to pursue its remedies in the state court; and that it be allowed to proceed with the foreclosure sale in accordance with the judgment of that court. It refused to accept the composition and extension proposal offered by Radford; declined to consent to the proposed sale of that property to Radford at the appraised value or any value on the terms set forth in Paragraph 3; and also objected to his retaining possession thereof with the privilege of purchasing the same provided by Paragraph 7. The federal court overruled the Bank's objections; denied its prayers; adjudged Radford a bankrupt within the meaning of the Frazier-Lemke Act; and appointed a referee to take proceedings thereunder. There was no claim that the farm was exempt as a homestead or otherwise.

The referee ordered an appraisal of all of Radford's property, encumbered and unencumbered. The appraisers found that "the fair and reasonable value of the property of the debtor on which Louisville Joint

Stock Bank has a mortgage" and also the "market value of said land" was then $4,445. The referee approved the appraisal, although the Bank offered in open court to pay $9,205.09 in cash for the mortgaged property; and counsel for the bankrupt admitted that the Bank had a valid lien upon it for the amount so offered to be paid, and that, under the law, if the Bank's offer to purchase the property were accepted, all the money paid in in cash would be immediately returned to it in satisfaction of the mortgage indebtedness.

The Bank refused to consent to a sale of the mortgaged property to Radford at the appraised value and filed written objections to such sale and to the manner of payments prescribed by Paragraph 3 of subsection (s). Thereupon, the referee ordered that, for the period of five years, all proceedings for the enforcement of the mortgages be stayed; and that the possession of the mortgaged property, subject to liens, remain in Radford, under the control of the court, as provided in Paragraph 7 of subsection (s). The referee fixed the rental for the first year at $325; and ordered that for each subsequent year the rental be fixed by the court. It was stipulated, that the annual taxes and insurance premium amount to $105; and admitted that administration charges said to amount to $22.75 must be paid from the rental. All the orders of the referee were, upon a petition for a review, duly approved by the District Court; and its decree was affirmed by the Circuit Court of Appeals on February 11, 1935.

* * *

Fifth. The controlling purpose of the Act is to preserve to the mortgagor the ownership and enjoyment of the farm property. It does not seek primarily a discharge of all personal obligations — a function with which alone bankruptcy acts have heretofore dealt. Nor does it make provision of that nature by prohibiting, limiting or postponing deficiency judgments, as do some State laws. Its avowed object is to take from the mortgagee rights in the specific property held as security; and to that end "to scale down the indebtedness" to the present value of the property. As here applied it has taken from the Bank the following property rights recognized by the Law of Kentucky:

1. The right to retain the lien until the indebtedness thereby secured is paid.
2. The right to realize upon the security by a judicial public sale.
3. The right to determine when such sale shall be held, subject only to the discretion of the court.
4. The right to protect its interest in the property by bidding at such sale whenever held, and thus to assure having the mortgaged property devoted primarily to the satisfaction of the debt, either through receipt of the proceeds of a fair competitive sale or by taking the property itself.
5. The right to control meanwhile the property during the period of default, subject only to the discretion of the court, and to have the rents and profits collected by a receiver for the satisfaction of the debt.

Strong evidence that the taking of these rights from the mortgagee effects a substantial impairment of the security is furnished by the occurrences in the Senate which led to the adoption there of the amendment to the bill declaring that the Act "shall apply only to debts existing at the time this Act becomes effective." The bill as passed by the House applied to both preexisting and future mortgages. It was amended in the Senate so as to limit it to existing mortgages; and as so amended was adopted by both Houses pursuant to the report of the Conference Committee. This was done because, in the Senate, it was pointed out that the bill, if made applicable to future mortgages, would destroy the farmer's future mortgage credit.

Sixth. Radford contends that these changes in the position of the Bank wrought pursuant to the Act, do not impair substantive rights, because the Bank retains every right in the property to which it is entitled. The contention rests upon the unfounded assertion that its only substantive right under the mortgage is to have the value of the security applied to the satisfaction of the debt. It would be more accurate to say that the only right under the mortgage left to the Bank is the right to retain its lien until the mortgagor, sometime within the five-year period, chooses to release it by paying the appraised value of the property. A mortgage lien so limited in character and incident is of course legally conceivable. It might be created by contract under existing law. If a part of the mortgaged property were taken by eminent domain a mortgagee would receive payment on a similar basis. But the Frazier-Lemke Act does not purport to exercise the right of eminent domain; and neither the law of Kentucky nor Radford's mortgages contain any provision conferring upon the mortgagor an option to compel, at any time within five years, a release of the farm upon payment of its appraised value and a right to retain meanwhile possession, upon paying a rental to be fixed by the bankruptcy courts.

Equally unfounded is the contention that the mortgagee is not injured by the denial of possession for the five years, since it receives the rental value of the property. It is argued that experience has proved that five years is not unreasonably long, since a longer period is commonly required to complete a voluntary contract for the sale and purchase of a farm; or to close a bankruptcy estate; or to close a railroad receivership. And it is asserted that Radford is, in effect, acting as receiver for the bankruptcy court. Radford's argument ignores the fact that in ordinary bankruptcy proceedings and in equity receiverships, the court may in its discretion, order an immediate sale and closing of the estate; and it ignores, also, the fundamental difference in purpose between the delay permitted in those proceedings and that prescribed by Congress. When a court of equity allows a receivership to continue, it does so to prevent a sacrifice of the creditor's interest. Under the Act, the purpose of the delay in making a sale and of the prolonged possession accorded the mortgagor is to promote his interests at the expense of the mortgagee.

Home Building & Loan Assn. v. *Blaisdell,* 290 U. S. 398, upon which Radford relies, lends no support to his contention. There the statute left the period of the extension of the right of redemption to be determined by the court within the maximum limit of two years. Even after the period had been decided upon, it could, as was pointed out, "be reduced by order of the court under the statute, in case of a change in circumstances, . . ." (p. 447); and at the close of the period, the mortgagee was free to apply the mortgaged property to the satisfaction of the mortgage debt. Here, the option and the possession would continue although the emergency which is relied upon as justifying the Act ended before November 30, 1939.

Seventh. Radford contends further that the changes in the mortgagee's rights in the property, even if substantial, are not arbitrary and unreasonable, because they were made for a permissible public purpose. That claim appears to rest primarily upon the following propositions: (1) The welfare of the Nation demands that our farms be individually owned by those who operate them. (2) To permit widespread foreclosure of farm mortgages would result in transferring ownership, in large measure, to great corporations; would transform farmer-owners into tenants or farm laborers; and would tend to create a peasant class. (3) There was grave danger at the time of the passage of the Act, that foreclosure of farms would become widespread. The persistent decline in the prices of agricultural products, as compared with the prices of articles which farmers are obliged to purchase, had been accentuated by the long continued depression and had made it impossible for farmers to pay the charges accruing under existing mortgages. (4) Thus had arisen an emergency requiring congressional action. To avert the threatened calamity the Act presented an appropriate remedy. Extensive economic data, of which in large part we may take judicial notice, were submitted in support of these propositions.

The Bank calls attention, among other things, to the fact that the Act is not limited to mortgages of farms operated by the owners; that the finding of the lower courts that Radford is a farmer within the meaning the Act does not necessarily imply that he operates his farm; and that at least part of it must have been rented to another, since a tenant is joined as defendant in the foreclosure suit. Section 75 of the Bankruptcy Act (to which this Act is an amendment), provides in sub-section (r) that "the term 'farmer' means any individual who is personally bona fide engaged primarily in farming operations or the principal part of whose income is derived from farming operations." Thus, the Act affords relief not only to those owners who operate their farms, but also to all individual landlords the "principal part of whose income is derived" from the "farming operations" of share croppers or other tenants; and, among these landlords, to persons who are merely capitalist absentees.

It has been suggested that the number of farms operated by tenants was very large before the present depression; that the increase of tenancy had been progressive for more than half a century; that the increase has not been attributable, in the main, to foreclosures; and that, in some regions, the increase in tenancy has been marked during the period when farm incomes were large and farm values, farm taxes and farm mortgages were rising rapidly.

We have no occasion to consider either the causes or the extent of farm tenancy; or whether its progressive increase would be arrested by the provisions of the Act. Nor need we consider the occupations of the beneficiaries of the legislation. These are matters for the consideration of Congress; and the extensive provision for the refinancing of farm mortgages which Congress has already made, shows that the gravity of the situation has been appreciated. The province of the Court is limited to deciding whether the Frazier-Lemke Act as applied has taken from the bank without compensation, and given to

Radford, rights in specific property which are of substantial value. Compare *Ochoa* v. *Hernandez,* 230 U. S. 139, 161; *Loan Association* v. *Topeka,* 20 Wall. 655, 662, 664; *In re Dillard,* Fed. Cas. No. 3,912, p. 706. As we conclude that the Act as applied has done so, we must hold it void. For the Fifth Amendment commands that, however great the Nation's need, private property shall not be thus taken even for a wholly public use without just compensation. If the public interest requires, and permits, the taking of property of individual mortgagees in order to relieve the necessities of individual mortgagors, resort must be had to proceedings by eminent domain; so that, through taxation, the burden of the relief afforded in the public interest may be borne by the public.

Reversed.

COMPETITION

Louis D. Brandeis

This article first appeared in the *American Legal News,* v. 44, pp. 5-14, January 1913, and was reprinted in *The Curse of Bigness,* edited by Osmond K. Fraenkel and published in 1935 by Viking Press.

Practically all Americans agree there is a trust problem; but upon every matter relating to the problem there is the greatest diversity of opinion. In this wide divergence of view, two lines of cleavage may be drawn according as men take one or the other side of the two following important questions:

First, shall the industrial policy of American be that of competition, or that of monopoly?

Second, have we adequate governmental machinery to enforce whatever industrial policy America concludes to adopt, whether that policy be competition or monopoly?

Now, these two questions are frequently confused, but they are entirely distinct. The first is a question of economic policy, the second, the question of governmental machinery.

Some men who believe in competition think we have adequate governmental machinery now to secure competition, and all that is necessary is to enforce the Sherman law as it stands. Other men who believe in competition think we lack governmental machinery necessary to secure and maintain it, and that appropriate machinery should be devised and adopted for regulating competition. Likewise, some men who believe that private monopoly should be permissible think that the public will be best served if we simply repeal the Sherman law and let business take care of itself. Other men who believe in private monopoly think that we should devise and introduce new governmental machinery by which monopoly would be regulated.

Furthermore, there is a division among those who believe in the necessity of additional governmental machinery to enforce the policy either of competition or of monopoly; for they differ widely as to the nature of the machinery to be installed. This difference is not merely a difference in numerous and important details. They differ quite fundamentally as to the nature of the machinery to be employed—some persons maintaining that the new machinery shall be wholly judicial, that is, shall be such as will be enforced only through courts of law; other persons insisting that however much the judicial machinery is improved, there must also be introduced administrative machinery; that is, such as would be applied through some kind of a commission. Such a commission was proposed in the bill introduced by a Democrat, Senator Newlands, on August 21, 1911, under the title of Interstate Trade Commission, and another and more elaborate one was later introduced by a Progressive Republican, Senator La Follette, under the name of the Federal Trade Commission, and legislation of this character is strongly urged by the New Party.

For the purpose of this discussion most of the differences of view indicated can be eliminated. The question, "Shall we regulate competition or regulate monopoly?" assumes that there will be some regulation, and it is clear that in order to regulate either, the legal machinery must be greatly improved, and an administrative board of some kind, and with fairly broad powers, must be created to supplement the powers of the courts in dealing with this subject.

The only fundamental difference as between the New Party's program and that of its opponent relates to the economic policy to be enforced. All other differences are differences in degree or of emphasis.

In saying that the New Party stands for monopoly I do not mean that it wants to introduce monopoly generally in private industry, but merely that it accepts private monopoly as permissible, and the trusts as in themselves unobjectionable, requiring only that they be "good." It is prepared to protect existing trusts from dismemberment, if only they will be "good" hereafter, thus leaving them in the possession of the huge profits obtained through violations of law. But once we treat monopoly as permissible, we have given away the whole case of competition, for monopoly is the path of least effort in business, and is sure to be pursued, if opened.

On the other hand those who stand for competition do not advocate what has been frequently described as "unrestricted" or "destructive" competition. They demand a regulated competition or, if one may adopt the phrase, competition which is "good."

Regulation is essential to the preservation of competition and to its best development just as regulation is necessary to the preservation and development of civil or political liberty. To preserve civil and political liberty to the many we have found it necessary to restrict the liberty of the few. Unlicensed liberty leads necessarily to despotism or oligarchy. Those who are stronger must to some extent be curbed. We curb the physically strong in order to protect those physically weaker. The liberty of the merchant and manufacturer to lie in trade, formerly permissible, and expressed in the fine phrase *caveat emptor,* has yielded largely to the better business ethics supplemented by pure-food laws and postal-fraud prosecution. Formerly the interests of business and of the community were supposed to be best served by letting buyer and seller trade without restriction on native or acquired shrewdness. Those laws present examples of protecting those who, by reason of position or training are, in respect to particular business transactions, the weaker or unable to take care of themselves. Recognizing differences in position of employer and employee, we have similarly restricted theoretically freedom of contract by factory laws which prescribe conditions under which work may be performed and, to some extent, the hours of labor. Experience had shown that under the changed conditions in industry, it was necessary, in order that life and liberty of the worker be preserved, to put a restraint upon the theoretical freedom of the individual worker and the employer – the employer and the employee – to do as he chose in that respect.

The right of competition must be similarly limited; for excesses of competition lead to monopoly just as excesses of liberty have led to despotism. It is another case where the extremes meet.

What are those excesses of competition which should be prevented because they lead to monopoly? The answer to that question should be sought—not in theorizing, but in the abundant experiences of the last twenty-five years, during which the trusts have been developed. We have but to study the facts and ascertain:

"How did monopoly, wherever it obtained foothold, acquire its position?"

And we can, in the first place, give the comprehensive answer, which should relieve the doubts and fears of many: no monopoly in private industry in America has yet been attained by efficiency alone. No business has been so superior to its competitors in the processes of manufacture or of distribution as to enable it to control the market solely by reason of its superiority. There is nothing in our industrial history to indicate that there is any need whatever to limit the natural growth of a business in order to preserve competition. We may emphatically declare: "Give fair play to efficiency."

One has heard of late the phrases: "You can't make people compete by law." "Artificial competition is undesirable." These are truisms, but their implication is false. Believers in competition make no suggestion that traders be compelled to compete. They ask merely that no trader should be allowed to kill competition. Competition consists in trying to do things better than someone else; that is, making or selling a better article, or the same article as at lesser cost, or otherwise giving better service. It is not competition to resort to methods of the prize ring, and simply "knock the other man out." That is killing a competitor.

Clearly misleading is the phrase, "Natural monopoly should not be interfered with." There are no natural monopolies in the industrial world. The Oil Trust and the Steel Trust have sometimes been called "natural monopolies," but they are both most unnatural monopolies. The Oil Trust acquired its control of the market by ruthless conduct which was not only a sin against society, but in large part involved flagrant violations of law. Without the aid of criminal rebating the Standard Oil would not have acquired the vast wealth and power which enabled it to destroy its smaller competitors by price-cutting and similar processes. The course of the Tobacco Trust was similar in character.

The Steel Trust, while apparently free from the coarser forms of suppressing competition, acquired control of the market not through greater efficiency, but by buying up existing plants and particularly ore supplies at fabulous prices, and by controlling strategic transportation systems. A monopoly like the Steel Trust can hardly be called natural, when it resulted in the main by the purchase of a single huge concern – the Carnegie Company – for, at least, $250,000,000 more than its value, thus bribing Mr. Carnegie to retire from the field in which he was master; and by the purchase of its vast ore resources at many times their value.

It will be found that wherever competition has been suppressed it has been due either to resort to ruthless processes, or by improper use of inordinate wealth and power. The attempt to dismember existing illegal trusts is not, therefore, an attempt to interfere in any way with the natural law of business. It is an endeavor to restore health by removing a cancer from the body industrial. It is not an attempt to create competition artificially, but it is the removing of the obstacle to competition. The policy of regulated competition is distinctly a constructive policy. It is the policy of development as distinguished from the destructive policy of private monopoly. It has always in the past and must always in the future paralyze individual effort and initiative and deaden enterprise. Business progress demands that the industrial advance be unobstructed and private monopoly's highways of industrial and commercial development kept open.

Earnest argument is constantly made in support of monopoly by pointing to the wastefulness of competition. Undoubtedly competition involves some waste. What human activity does not? The wastes of democracy are among the greatest obvious wastes, but we have compensations in democracy which far outweigh that waste and make it more efficient than absolutism. So it is with competition. Incentive and development which are incident to the former system of business result in so much achievement that the accompanying waste is relatively insignificant. The margin between that which men naturally do and which they can do is so great that a system which urges men on to action, enterprise, and initiative is preferable in spite of the wastes that necessarily attend that process. I say, "necessarily" because there have been and are today wastes incidental to competition that are unnecessary. Those are the wastes which attend that competition which do not develop, but kill. Those wastes the law can and should eliminate. It may do so by regulating competition.

It is, of course, true that the unit in business may be too small to be efficient. The larger unit has been a common incident of monopoly. But a unit too small for efficiency is by no means a necessary incident of competition. It is also true that the unit in business may be too large to be efficient, and this is no uncommon incident of monopoly. In every business concern there must be a size-limit of greatest efficiency. What that limit is will differ in different businesses and under varying conditions in the same business. But whatever the business or organization there is a point where it would become too large for efficient and economic management, just as there is a point where it would be too small to be an efficient instrument. The limit of efficient size is exceeded when the disadvantages attendant upon size outweigh the advantages, when the centrifugal force exceeds the centripetal. Man's work often outruns the capacity of the individual man; and, no matter what the organization, the capacity of an individual man usually determines the success or failure of a particular enterprise, not only financially to the owners, but in service to the community. Organization can do much to make concerns more efficient. Organization can do much to make larger units possible and profitable. But the efficiency even of organization has its bounds; and organization can never supply the combined judgment, initiative, enterprise, and authority which must come for the chief executive officers. Nature sets a limit to their possible accomplishment. As the Germans say, "Care is taken that the trees do not scrape the skies."

That mere size does not bring success is illustrated by the record of our industrial system during the past ten years. This record, if examined, will show that:

(1) Most of the trusts which did not secure monopolistic positions have failed to show marked success as compared with the independent concerns.

This is true of many existing trusts, for instance, of the Newspaper Trust, the Writing Paper Trust, the Upper Leather Trust, the Sole Leather Trust, the Woolen Trust, the Paper Bag Trust, the International Mercantile Marine, and those which have failed, like the Cordage Trust, the Mucilage Trust, the Flour Trust, should not be forgotten.

(2) Most of those trusts which have shown marked success secured monopolistic positions either by controlling the whole business themselves, or by doing so in combination with others. And their success has been due mainly to their ability to fix prices.

This is true, for instance, of the Standard Oil Trust, the Shoe Machinery Trust, the Tobacco Trust, the Steel Trust, the Pullman Car Company.

(3) Most of the trusts which did not secure for themselves monopoly in the particular branch of trade, but controlled the situation only through price agreements with competitors, have been unable to hold their own share of the market as against the independents.

This is true, for instance, of the Sugar Trust, the Steel Trust, the Rubber Trust.

(4) Most of the efficiently managed trusts have found it necessary to limit the size of their own units for production and for distribution.

This is true, for instance, of the Tobacco Trust, the Standard Oil Trust, the Steel Trust.

These general rules are, of course, subject to exceptions due to instances of conspicuous ability on the part of managers or unusual trade conditions.

Lack of efficiency is ordinarily manifested either (1) in rising cost of product, (2) in defective quality of goods produced, or (3) in failure to make positive advances in processes and methods.

The third of these manifestations is the most serious of all. In this respect monopoly works like poison which infects the system for a long time before it is discovered, and yet a poison so potent that the best of management can devise no antidote.

Take the case of the Steel Trust. It inherited through the Carnegie Company the best organization and the most efficient steel makers in the world. It has had since its organization exceptionally able management. It has almost inexhaustible resources. It produces on so large a scale that practically no experimental expense would be unprofitable if it brought the slightest advance in the art. And yet in only ten years after its organization, high American authority — the *Engineering News,* declares:

"We are today something like five years behind Germany in iron and steel metallurgy, and such innovations as are being introduced by our iron and steel manufacturers are most of them merely following the lead set by foreigners years ago.

"We do not believe this is because American engineers are any less ingenious or original than those of Europe, though they may indeed be deficient in training and scientific education compared with those of Germany. We believe the main cause is the wholesale consolidation which has taken place in American industry. A huge organization is too clumsy to take up the development of an original idea. With the market closely controlled and certain of profits by following standard methods, those who control our trusts do not want the bother of developing anything new.

"We instance metallurgy only by way of illustration. There are plenty of other fields of industry where exactly the same condition exists. We are building the same machines and using the same methods as a dozen years ago, and the real advances in the art are being made by European inventors and manufacturers."

This judgment is confirmed by the "Menace of the Broken Rail."

The Steel Trust was organized in 1901. It has dominated the steel trade of America. Its power has been particularly great in respect to rails, partly because of the system of inter-locking directorates. Steel Trust directors are also directors in railroad companies, owning more than one half of the railroad mileage in the United States. Ten years after the organization of the Steel Trust, the country was aroused by one or two shocking railroad accidents. The accidents appeared to result from broken rails. The Interstate Commerce Commission was led to make an investigation into the general subject and found that whereas in 1902 there were 72 derailments due to broken rails, there were in 1911, 249 derailments due to the same cause. In the past decade—the era of the Steel Trust – there have been 2,059 derailments due to broken rails, resulting in 106 killed and injured. Of course, all of these rails were not made by the Steel Trust, and the strain put upon rails has increased with the increase in the weight of equipment more than ever before; but the fact that articles produced by the Steel Trust have failed to keep pace with the requirements of transportation to such an extent as to require an investigation by the Government certainly indicates a marked limitation upon the efficiency of the greatest of all industrial units. Another instance of this character of inefficiency was disclosed recently in the ably managed Shoe Machinery Trust.

The Shoe Machinery Trust, the result of combining directly and indirectly more than a hundred different concerns, acquired substantially a monopoly of all the essential machinery used in bottoming boots and shoes. Its energetic managers were conscious of the constant need of improving and developing inventions and spent large sums in efforts to do so. Nevertheless, in the year 1910 they were confronted with a competitor so formidable that the Company felt itself obliged to buy him off, though in violation of the law and at a cost of about $5,000,000. That competitor, Thomas G. Plant, a shoe manufacturer who had resented the domination of the trust, developed an extensive system of shoe machinery, which is believed to be superior to the Trust's own system, which represents the continuous development of that Company and its predecessors for nearly half a century.

H. B. Endicott, one of the leading shoe manufacturers of the country, and now a director in the Shoe Machinery Trust, publicly declared, after examining the Plant system: "In my judgment, and that of my experts, what you (Plant) have shown us was by far the most perfect set of working machinery that we had ever seen, or expected to see."

But the efficiency of monopolies, even if established, would not justify their existence unless the community should reap benefit from the efficiency; experience teaches us that whenever trusts have developed efficiency, their fruits have been absorbed almost wholly by the trusts themselves. From such efficiency as they have developed the community has gained substantially nothing. For instance:

The Standard Oil Trust, an efficiently managed monopoly, increased the prices of its principal products (refined oil, naphtha, and paraffin wax) between 1895 and 1898, and 1903 to 1906 by 46 per cent. The profits per gallon on crude oil used increased from 1882 to 1906 from $1.78 per gallon to $3.05 per gallon. The profits of the marketing companies of the Trust increased from 88 cents per gallon of illuminating oil in 1898 to $1.50 per gallon in 1906. The profits on naphtha per gallon nearly doubled between 1898 and 1906.

The Tobacco Trust [*is*] an efficiently managed monopoly. Between 1899 and 1907 the selling price (less taxes) on smoking tobacco rose from 21.1 cents per pound to 30.1 cents; the profit per pound from 2.8 cents per pound to 9.8 cents. The selling price of plug tobacco rose from 24.9 cents per pound to 30.4 cents; the profit per pound from 1.9 cents to 8.7 cents.

In the snuff business the Tobacco Trust controlled 96 per cent of the market. The extortion was even greater. The selling price of snuff (less taxes) rose from 29.2 cents per pound in 1900 to 37.1 cents in 1907; whereas the cost decreased from 22.6 cents per pound to 20.8 cents. Thus the profit per pound exacted by the Trust rose from 6.6 cents per pound to 16.3 cents per pound. In other words, in 1907 on every pound of snuff sold by the Trust there was exacted from the public a profit of about 81 per cent on its cost.

The following statement of the Commissioner of Corporations illustrated the power and disposition of the Trust to absorb whatever profits existed:

"The results of the Spanish War tax upon tobacco products especially illustrate the monopolistic power of the combination. When that tax was imposed in

1898, prices were generally raised. In 1901 and 1902 the tax was reduced to its former basis, but the combination was powerful enough to keep its prices at the higher level. It thus absorbed practically all the benefit of the reduction, adding millions yearly to its income. The episode shows the unforeseen results of fiscal legislation affecting monopolistic conditions not fully recognized. The tax reduction, of course, was intended to benefit the consumers. As a matter of fact, it benefited almost solely the controlling interest in the industry."

The Steel Trust [is] a corporation of reputed efficiency. The high prices maintained by it in the industry are matters of common knowledge. In less than ten years it accumulated for its shareholders or paid out as dividends on stock representing merely water, over $650,000,000.

Compare with this record of increased or stationary prices and of growing profits, the record of strictly competitive manufacturing businesses where the selling prices have shown a marked tendency to decrease and the ratio of profits has been almost uniformly lessened. For instance:

The Book Paper business furnishes a conspicuous example of this. In important mills the average selling-price of book paper declined from 7.08 cents per pound in 1889 to 4.24 cents in 1899, and to 3.99 in 1910; the ratio of profit per pound declined from 19 per cent on cost in 1889 to 13 per cent in 1899 and 7 per cent in 1910. This reduction is the more noteworthy because the principal raw material used—wood—(like wages) has steadily risen in price during the period.

The proposed Government commission to fix prices would not greatly relieve the evils attendant upon monopoly. It might be effective in preventing private monopoly from taking excessive profits, but Government price-regulation would be powerless to secure to the public the low prices commonly attendant upon competition. In other words, price-fixing might reduce the trust's profits, but it would fail materially to reduce the trust's prices; because the limitation of the monopoly's profits would, by lessening this incentive, surely reduce the monopoly's efficiency.

Capital and property will yield, according to the degree of the judgment and efficiency applied in management, vastly different returns. To secure the successful management of any private business reward must be proportionate to success. The establishment of any rule fixing a maximum return on capital would, by placing a limit upon the fruits of achievement, tend to lessen efficiency. For efficiency is naturally reflected in large net earnings; and as no ready means exists for determining whether greater net earnings are due to greater efficiency in management or to excessive profits, large net earnings would be followed by compulsory reduction of prices, and such reduction by a lessening of effort. To take from a private business the natural fruits of efficiency would create a sense of injustice suffered, which would paralyze effort and individual enterprise, and produce slipshod management. The attempt to secure low prices through price-fixing would prove as impotent as the statutes which have sought to protect the public in respect to railroad rates by limiting the dividends of railroads. The permissible dividends generally exhausted the profits. No selling price for monopoly products could be set constitutionally at a point lower than that which would allow a reasonable return on capital. And in the absence of comparative data from any competing businesses producing the same article at less cost, it would be practically impossible to determine that the cost should be lower.

The success of the Interstate Commerce Commission has been invoked as an argument in favor of licensing monopoly, and regulating it by a similar commission.

If the experience of the Interstate Commerce Commission is carefully inquired into, it will be found to present argument against, rather than in favor of, the proposition that the evils naturally attendant upon industrial private monopolies can be avoided through establishing such an industrial commission.

In the first place, the success of the Interstate Commerce Commission has been effective principally in preventing rate increases and in stopping discrimination. The great reductions in railroad rates which have been made in the last 24 years (during the life of the Commission) have been due, in not rare instances, to action of the Interstate Commerce Commission. In those instances where the Commission has reduced rates (as distinguished from preventing increases) the Commission rested its decision largely on the ground that existing rates amounted to discrimination against particular places or articles, or the lower rates were justified by a comparison with other rates of the same or other companies. Price fixing of that nature applied to industrial trusts would afford little protection to the public.

In the second place, there is a radical difference between attempts to fix rates for transportation and similar public services and fixing prices in industrial businesses. The striking characteristic of the railroad problems of the whole country is their uniformity. Problems of transportation, while varying infinitely in detail, are largely the same throughout the whole country, and they are largely the same yesterday, today, and tomorrow. For this reason the Commission reaches its decision as to the reasonableness of a rate most frequently by a comparison of what is charged upon the same or other railroad for a similar service. In spite, therefore, of the numerous problems as to the reasonableness of rates with which the Interstate Commerce Commission is confronted, their task would be a relatively simple one as compared with that which would necessarily arise if prices were to be fixed in the field of industry. In industry we have, instead of uniformity, infinite variety; instead of stability, constant change.

In the third place, the problems of the Interstate Commerce Commission, relatively simple as they are by reason of the character of the service to be regulated, already far exceed the capacity of that or any single board. A single question of rates, like that involved in the Spokane and intermountain rate cases has been before the Commission awaiting final adjudication nearly twenty years. Think of the infinite questions which would come before an industrial commission seeking to fix rates, and the suffering of the community from the inability of that body to dispose of them promptly and efficiently. It would require not only one but hundreds of commissioners to protect the American people from the extortions of monopolies, even if protection were possible at all.

Everyone admits that the reasonableness of the railroads' rates is in some degree at least dependent upon the cost of the service. The Commission has been in existence twenty-four years and no data exist today for determining with reasonable accuracy the cost of any service upon the railroads, and indeed none can exist until a valuation of the railroads is made.

Since private monopoly is not beneficial to the community, there can remain but two questions:

First, can we preserve competition where it exists?

Second, can we restore competition where it has been suppressed?

To both the answer is, Yes.

Diagnosis shows monopoly to be an artificial, not a natural, product. Competition, therefore, may be preserved by preventing that course of conduct by which in the past monopolies have been established. If we had in the past undertaken by appropriate legal and administrative machinery to prevent our financiers and others from carrying out agreements to form monopolies; if we had seriously attempted to prevent those methods of destructive or unfair competition, as are manifest in "cut-throat competition" – discrimination against customers who will not deal exclusively with the combination; if we had made any persistent, intelligent effort to stop advantages gained by railroad discrimination espionage, or the practice of establishing "fake independents," or to stop those who have secured control of essential raw material from denying business rivals access to it – few of the trusts, of which we now complain, would have come into existence, or would, at all events, have acquired power to control the market. We made no serious attempt to stop monopoly — certainly no intelligent attempt; partly because we lacked knowledge, partly because we lacked desire; for we had a sneaking feeling that perhaps, after all, a private monopoly might be a good thing, and we had no adequate governmental machinery to employ for this purpose. But in the past twenty-two years we have acquired much experience with trusts. We know their ways. We have learned what the defects in the existing machinery are; and if we will but remedy those defects by appropriate legal and administrative machinery — somewhat on the lines proposed in the La Follette-Stanley and Newlands bills — and supplement the prohibition of monopoly by the regulation of competition, we shall be able, not only to preserve the competition we now enjoy, but gradually regain the free soil upon which private monopoly has encroached, and we may be assured that, despite all industrial changes, the day of industrial liberty has not yet passed.

THE MENACE OF THE TRUSTS

Louis D. Brandeis

This statement was made by Brandeis before a Senate Committee Hearing on Trust Legislation, December 14, 1911. It is reprinted from Lief, *The Social and Economic Views of Mr. Justice Brandeis* (New York, The Vanguard Press, 1930) pp. 372-375.

To a greater or less extent in small business the owners are beginning to recognize that there is but one principle by which lasting success can be attained, and it is this: Those who do the work shall get in some fair proportion what they produce. The share to which capital as such is entitled is small. All the rest should go to those, high and low, who do the work.

This is the idea which our New England people are working out in their modest business concerns and they are thus finding a way to perpetuate their business and get out of it not only satisfaction and contentment on the part of the working people but contentment and success for themselves.***

If we are to work out a satisfactory system of profit sharing as a means of reconciling capital and labor, it can only be done by reducing the return of capital and the purveyors of capital and letting the people who do the work, be they managers, the skilled handicraftmen, or day laborers, take all that is earned above a reasonable return on the capital invested.

The management of the steel corporation has not only failed to work out a proper solution of this vexed problem, but its conduct has tended in the opposite direction. The wages in the steel industry through this period of the trust, so far as made public, compared unfavorably with the period before 1892. In many respects they are absolutely lower than 1892. In other respects they are relatively lower, if the cost of living be taken into consideration. The increase in wages of the day laborers from 1892 to 1907 amounted to about eighteen percent, but the cost of living increased in that period four or five percent more. The wages of skilled laborers during the same period were reduced from five to forty percent.

Nor is this all, or to my mind the most important consideration in the trust's treatment of labor, important as it is. The most serious ground for criticizing the Steel Trust is that the hours of labor have been shockingly increased since 1892.***

You cannot have true American citizenship, you cannot preserve political liberty, you cannot secure American standards of living unless some degree of industrial liberty accompanies it. And the United States Steel Corporation and these other trusts have stabbed industrial liberty in the back. They have crushed it out among large groups of our people so completely that it will require years to restore our industries to a condition of health. This social unrest is what is really the matter with business. Well-founded unrest; reasoned unrest; but the manifestations of which are often unintelligent and sometimes criminal.***

Until we had these great trusts, or the great corporations which preceded them, workers could secure justice through their unions. Abuses of the trade unions have been innumerable. Individuals of slight education, of slight training, are elevated many times by shallow popularity to positions which can be filled adequately only by men possessing great minds and great characters. No wonder, then, that these leaders made mistakes; make grievous errors. The extraordinary thing is that they have not made more mistakes. It is one of the most promising symptoms in American democracy that with all the difficulties attending such positions the labor leaders on the whole have done so little that is wrong. And you, gentlemen, Members of the Senate and Members of the House who are called upon to consider questions affecting "big business," must weigh well these by-products. For by their by-products shall you know the trusts.***

If you do anything which tends to accelerate this pace toward the conversion of American capital into stock exchange securities, by just so much will you increase the difficulty of solving the problem of the Money Trust, which already baffles the best minds of the country.

And there are still other baneful by-products of the industrial trusts. Mr. [George W.] Perkins has asserted that these great corporations are not private businesses but public businesses. He has asserted that the numerous stockholders are partners in the enterprise with J. P. Morgan & Co. and others, as if that were "a consummation devoutly to be wished."

To my mind this is a condition to be regretted rather than to be welcomed and presents features of a highly serious character. Such numerous small stockholding creates in the corporation a condition of irresponsible absentee landlordism; that is, the numerous small stockholders in the steel corporation, in the tobacco company, and in the other trusts occupy a position which is dangerous to society. They have a certain degree of wealth without responsibility. Their only desire is dividends. Their demand upon the managers is at most to maintain or increase their dividends. They have no power or responsibility; they have no relations to the employees; they are remote; often thousands of miles from the people who are toiling for them. Thus we have reproduced in industry the precise conditions which brought all the misery upon Ireland and upon other countries where absentee landlordism has prevailed. Large dividends are the bribes which the managers tender the small investor for the power to use other peoples' money.***

The trust problem can never be settled right for the American people by looking at it through the spectacles of bonds and stocks. You must study it through the spectacles of people's rights and people's interests; must consider the effect upon the development of the American democracy. When you do that you will realize the perils to our institutions which attend the trusts; you will realize the danger of letting the people learn that our sacred Constitution protects not only vested rights but vested wrongs. The situation is a very serious one; unless wise legislation is enacted we shall have as a result of that social unrest a condition which will be more serious than that produced by the fall of a few points in stock-exchange quotations.

LIGGETT CO. v. LEE
288 U. S. 517, 541 (1932)

In the majority opinion, the Supreme Court held invalid that portion of the Florida Anti-Chain Store Law which levied heavier license taxes on stores located in more than one county than on stores in the same county. The Court stated that the county line furnishes no reasonable basis for such a classification. In this dissent, Mr. Justice Brandeis held that the validity of the statute should be sustained in the absence of proof that local conditions did not warrant it. Brandeis discussed the use of a license fee to discourage chain store operations within a state and the matter of state restraints on corporate size and activity as being constitutionally unobjectionable.

The following are excerpts from the dissent, omitting case citations and footnotes.

MR. JUSTICE BRANDEIS, dissenting in part.

In my opinion, the judgment of the Supreme Court of Florida should be affirmed.

Florida Laws, 1931, Chapter 15,624 is legislation of the type popularly called Anti-Chain Store Laws. The statute provides for the licensing of retail stores by the State, the counties and the municipalities—a system under which large revenues may be raised. But the raising of revenue is obviously not the main purpose of the legislation. Its chief aim is to protect the individual, independently-owned, retail stores from the competition of chain stores. The statute seeks to do this, by subjecting the latter to financial handicaps which may conceivably compel their withdrawal from the State. An injunction against its enforcement is sought on the ground that the law violates rights guaranteed by the Federal Constitution.

The Florida law is general in its terms. It prohibits the operation, after September 30, 1931, of any retail store without securing annually a license; and provides, among other things, for annual fees which are in part graduated. If the owner operates only one store the state fee is $5; if more than one, the fee for the additional stores rises by step increases, dependent upon both the number operated and whether all operated are located in a single county. The highest fee is for a store in excess of 75. If all of the stores are located in a single county, the fee for each store in excess of 75 is $40; if all are not located in the same county the fee is $50. Under this law, the owner of 100 stores not located in a single county pays for each store operated, on the average, $33.65; and if they were located in a single county the owner would pay for each store, on the average, $25.20. If the 100 stores were independently owned (although operated cooperatively as a so-called "voluntary chain") the annual fee for each would be only $5. The statute provides that the licenses shall issue to expire on September 30th of each calendar year. This suit was begun September 30th, 1931. The first license year had expired before the case was heard in Court.

In its main features, this statute resembles the Indiana law discussed in *Tax Commissioners* v. *Jackson*, 283 U. S. 527. For the reasons there stated, the Court sustains like provisions in the Florida statute. But it declares arbitrary, and hence invalid, the novel provision imposing heavier license fees where the multiple stores of a single owner are located in more than one county, because it is "unable to discover any reasonable basis for this classification." There is nothing in the record to show affirmatively that the provision may not be a reasonable one in view of conditions prevailing in Florida. Since the presumption of constitutionality must prevail in the absence of some factual foundation of record for overthrowing the statute, its validity should, in my opinion, be sustained. . . .

• • •

Whether the citizens of Florida are wise in seeking to discourage the operation of chain stores is, obviously, a matter with which this Court has no concern. Nor need it, in my opinion, consider whether the differences in license fees employed to effect such discouragement are inherently reasonable, since the plaintiffs are at liberty to refuse to pay the compensation demanded for the corporate privilege and withdraw from the State, if they consider the price more than the privilege is worth. But a review of the legislation of the several States by which all restraints on corporate size and activity were removed, and a consideration of the economic and social effects of such removal, will help to an understanding of the Anti-Chain Store Laws; and will show that the discriminatory license fees prescribed by Florida, even if treated merely as a form of taxation, were laid for a purpose which may be appropriately served by taxation, and that the specific means employed to favor the individual retailer are not constitutionally objectionable.

Second. The prevalence of the corporation in America has led men of this generation to act, at times, as if the privilege of doing business in corporate form were inherent in the citizen; and has led them to accept the evils attendant upon the free and unrestricted use of the corporate mechanism as if these evils were the irescapable price of civilized life and, hence, to be borne with resignation. Throughout the greater part of our history a different view prevailed. Although the value of this instrumentality in commerce and industry was fully recognized, incorporation for business was commonly denied long after it had been freely granted for religious, educational and charitable purposes. It was denied because of fear. Fear of encroachment upon the liberties and opportunities of the individual. Fear of the subjection of labor to capital. Fear of monopoly. Fear that the absorption of capital by corporations, and their perpetual life, might bring evils similar to those which attended mortmain. There was a sense of some insidious menace inherent in large aggregations of capital, particularly when held by corporations. So, at first, the corporate privilege was granted sparingly; and only when the grant seemed necessary in order to procure for the community some specific benefit otherwise unattainable. The later enactment of general incorporation laws does not signify that the apprehension of corporate domination had been overcome. The desire for business expansion created an irresistible demand for more charters; and it was believed that under general laws embodying safeguards of universal application the scandals and favoritism incident to special incorporation could be avoided. The general laws, which long embodied severe restrictions upon size and upon the scope of corporate activity, were, in part, an expression of the desire for equality of opportunity.

* * *

Third. Able, discerning scholars having pictured for us the economic and social results of thus removing all limitations upon the size and activities of business corporations and of vesting in their managers vast powers once exercised by stockholders—results not designed by the States and long unsuspected. They show that size alone gives to giant corporations a social significance not attached ordinarily to smaller units of private enterprise. Through size, corporations, once merely an efficient tool employed by individuals in the conduct of private business, have become an institution—an institution which has brought such concentration of economic power that so-called private corporations are sometimes able to dominate the State. The typical business corporation of the last century, owned by a small group of individuals, managed by their owners, and limited in size by their personal wealth, is being supplanted by huge concerns in which the lives of tens or hundreds of thousands of employees and the property of tens or hundreds of thousands of investors are subjected, through the corporate mechanism, to the control of a few men. Ownership has been separated from control; and this separation has removed many of the checks which formerly operated to curb the misuse of wealth and power. And as ownership of the shares is becoming continually more dispersed, the power which formerly accompanied ownership is becoming increasingly concentrated in the hands of a few. The changes thereby wrought in the lives of the workers, of the owners and of the general public, are so fundamental and far-reaching as to lead these scholars to compare the evolving "corporate system" with the feudal system; and to lead other men of insight and experience to assert that this "master institution of civilised life" is committing it to the rule of a plutocracy.

The data submitted in support of these conclusions indicate that in the United States the process of absorption has already advanced so far that perhaps two-thirds of our industrial wealth has passed from individual possession to the ownership of large corporations whose shares are dealt in on the stock exchange; that 200 non-banking corporations, each with assets in excess of $90,000,000, control directly about one-fourth of all our national wealth, and that their influence extends far beyond the assets under their direct control; that these 200 corporations, while nominally controlled by about 2,000 directors, are actually dominated by a few hundred persons—the negation of industrial democracy. Other writers have shown that, coincident with the growth of these giant corporations, there has occurred a marked concentration of individual wealth; and that the resulting disparity in incomes is a major cause of the existing depression. Such is the Frankenstein monster which States have created by their corporation laws.

Fourth. Among these 200 corporations, each with assets in excess of $90,000,000 are five of the plaintiffs. These five have in the aggregate $820,000,000 of assets; and they operate, in the several States, an aggregate of 19,718 stores. A single one of these giants operates nearly 16,000. Against these plaintiffs, and other owners of multiple stores, the individual retailers of Florida are engaged in a struggle to preserve their independence—perhaps a struggle for existence. The citizens of the State, considering themselves vitally interested in this seemingly unequal struggle, have undertaken to aid the individual retailers by subjecting the owners of multiple stores to the handicap of higher license fees. They may have done so merely in order to preserve competition. But their purpose may have been a broader and deeper one. They may have believed that the chain store, by furthering the concentration of wealth and of power and by promoting absentee ownership, is thwarting American ideals; that it is making impossible equality of opportunity; that it is converting independent tradesmen into clerks; and that it is sapping the resources, the vigor and the hope of the smaller cities and towns.

The plaintiffs insist that no taxable difference exists between the owner of multiple stores and the owner of an individual store. A short answer to the contention has already been given, so far as required for the decision of this case. It is that the license fee is not merely taxation. The fee is the compensation exacted for the privilege of carrying on intrastate business in corporate form. As this privilege is one which a State may withhold or grant, it may charge such compensation as it pleases. Nothing in the Federal Constitution requires that the compensation demanded for the privilege should be reasonable. Moreover, since the authority to operate many stores, or to operate in two or more counties, is certainly a broader privilege than to operate only one store, or in only one county, there is in this record no basis for a finding that it is unreasonable to make the charge higher for the greater privilege.

A more comprehensive answer should, however, be given. The purpose of the Florida statute is not, like ordinary taxation, merely to raise revenue. Its main purpose is social and economic. The chain store is treated as a thing menacing the public welfare. The aim of the statute, at the lowest, is to preserve the competition of the independent stores with the chain stores; at the highest, its aim is to eliminate altogether corporate chain stores from retail distribution. The legislation reminds of that by which Florida and other States, in order to eliminate the "premium system" in merchandising, exacted high license fees of merchants who offered trading stamps with their goods. . . .

The plaintiffs discuss the broad question whether the power to tax may be used for the purpose of curbing, or of exterminating, the chain stores by whomsoever owned. It is settled that a State "may carry out a policy" by "adjusting its revenue laws and taxing system in such a way as to favor certain industries or forms of industry." . . . And since the Fourteenth Amendment "was not intended to compel the State to adopt an iron rule of equal taxation," . . . it may exempt from taxation kinds of business which it wishes to promote; . . . and may burden more heavily kinds of business which it wishes to discourage. . . . To do that has been the practice also of the Federal Government. It protects, by customs duties, our manufacturers and producers from the competition of foreigners. . . . It protects, by the oleomargarine laws, our farmers and dairymen from the competition of other Americans. . . . It eliminated, by a prohibitive tax, the issue of state bank notes in competition with those of national banks. . . . Such is the constitutional power of Congress and of the state legislatures. The wisdom of its exercise is not the concern of this Court.

* * *

Since business must yield to the paramount interests of the community in times of peace as well as in times of war, a State may prohibit a business found to be noxious and, likewise, may prohibit incidents or excrescences of a business otherwise beneficient. . . . Businesses may become as harmful to the community by excessive size, as by monopoly or the commonly recognized restraints of trade. If the State should conclude that bigness in retail merchandising as manifested in corporate chain stores menaces the public welfare, it might prohibit the excessive size or extent of that business as it prohibits excessive size or weight in motor trucks or excessive height in the buildings of a city. . . . It was said in *United States* v. *U. S. Steel Corp.*, 251 U. S. 417, 451, that the Sherman Anti-Trust Act did not forbid large aggregations; but the power of Congress to prohibit corporations of a size deemed excessive from engaging in interstate commerce was not questioned.

The elimination of chain stores, deemed harmful or menacing because of their bigness, may be achieved by levelling the prohibition against the corporate mechanism—the instrument by means of which excessive size is commonly made possible. Or, instead of absolutely prohibiting the corporate chain store, the State might conclude that it should first try the more temperate remedy of curbing the chain by imposing the handicap of discriminatory license fees. . . . And the State's power to make social and economic experiments is a broad one.

* * *

There is a widespread belief that the existing unemployment is the result, in large part, of the gross inequality in the distribution of wealth and income which giant corporations have fostered; that by the control which the few have exerted through giant corporations, individual initiative and effort are being paralyzed, creative power impaired and human happiness lessened; that the true prosperity of our past came not from big business, but through the courage, the energy and the resourcefulness of small men; that only by releasing from corporate control the faculties of the unknown many, only by reopening to them the opportunities for leadership, can confidence in our future be restored and the existing misery be overcome; and that only through participation by the many in the responsibilities and determinations of business, can Americans secure the moral and intellectual development which is essential to the maintenance of liberty. If the citizens of Florida share that belief, I know of nothing in the Federal Constitution which precludes the State from endeavoring to give it effect and prevent domination in intrastate commerce by subjecting corporate chains to discriminatory license fees. To that extent, the citizens of each State are still masters of their destiny.

INTERNATIONAL NEWS SERVICE v. ASSOCIATED PRESS

248 U. S. 215, 248-267 (1918)

The Supreme Court affirmed an injunction forbidding the International News Service from taking and gainfully using uncopyrighted news released by Associated Press, until its commercial value to Associated Press had passed, on the ground that it was unfair competition. The Court recognized a quasi-property right of AP in news accounts it released publicly after expenditure of time and money to gather the news. The unfair competition was created by the misappropriation of the news.

Brandeis' dissent apparently was founded upon two basic issues: (1) concern that the majority opinion would foster new and perpetual monopolies in unpatented and uncopyrighted material and (2) the thought that the scope of protection furnished by the doctrine of unfair competition required an adjustment of conflicting social and economic interests. In his opinion, the majority decision "would effect an important extension of property rights" which would conflict with the "free use of knowledge and ideas."

Mr. Justice Brandeis felt that the problem should

be left to the legislature. Recognizing the common law's capacity for growth, "But with the increasing complexity of society, the public interest tends to become omnipresent; and the problems presented by new demands for justice cease to be simple. Then the creation or recognition by courts of a new private right may work serious injury to the general public, unless the boundaries of the right are definitely established and wisely guarded." Thus, resort to legislation has increased as the social and economic matrix of society has become more complex. He identified the difficulties of the problem here involved, concluding, "Courts are ill-equipped to make the investigations . . . Courts would be powerless to prescribe the detailed regulations essential to full enjoyment of the rights conferred or to introduce the machinery required for enforcement of such regulations. Considerations such as these should lead us to decline to establish a new rule of law in the effort to redress a newly-disclosed wrong, although the propriety of some remedy appears to be clear."

Notwithstanding Brandeis' concern, the INS case has been restricted narrowly to the misappropriation of news, stock market quotations and the like. Perhaps, the reluctance of the courts to extend the doctrine, in no small measure, may be due to the forcefulness of his dissent. In fact, Judge Wyzanski in *Triangle Publications, Inc.* v. *New England Newspaper Publishing Co.*, 46 F. Supp. 198, 204 (1942) remarked, "I could hardly be unmindful of the probability that a majority of the present justices of the Supreme Court of the United States would follow the dissenting opinion of Mr. Justice Brandeis in the INS case . . . because they share his view that monopolies should not be readily extended, and his faith that legislative remedies are to be preferred to judicial innovations for problems where adjustment of many competing interests is necessary."

The footnotes in the case, valuable for reference, are omitted.

MR. JUSTICE BRANDEIS, dissenting.

There are published in the United States about 2,500 daily papers. More than 800 of them are supplied with domestic and foreign news of general interest by the Associated Press—a corporation without capital stock which does not sell news or earn or seek to earn profits, but serves merely as an instrumentality by means of which these papers supply themselves at joint expense with such news. Papers not members of the Associated Press depend for their news of general interest largely upon agencies organized for profit. Among these agencies is the International News Service which supplied news to about 400 subscribing papers. It has, like the Associated Press, bureaus and correspondents in this and foreign countries; and its annual expenditure in gathering and distributing news is about $2,000,000. Ever since its organization in 1909, it has included among the sources from which it gathers news, copies (purchased in the open market) of early editions of some papers published by members of the Associated Press and the bulletins publicly posted by them. These items, which constitute but a small part of the news transmitted to its subscribers, are generally verified by the International News Service before transmission; but frequently items are transmitted without verification; and occasionally even without being re-written. In no case is the fact disclosed that such item was suggested by or taken from a paper or bulletin published by an Associated Press member.

No question of statutory copyright is involved. The sole question for our consideration is this: Was the International News Service properly enjoined from using, or causing to be used gainfully, news of which it acquired knowledge by lawful means (namely, by reading publicly posted bulletins or papers purchased by it in the open market) merely because the news had been originally gathered by the Associated Press and continued to be of value to some of its members, or because it did not reveal the source from which it was acquired?

The "ticker" cases, the cases concerning literary and artistic compositions, and cases of unfair competition were relied upon in support of the injunction. But it is admitted that none of those cases affords a complete analogy with that before us. The question presented for decision is new; and it is important.

News is a report of recent occurrences. The business of the news agency is to gather systematically knowledge of such occurrences of interest and to distribute reports thereof. The Associated Press contended that knowledge so acquired is property, because it costs money and labor to produce and because it has value for which those who have it not are ready to pay; that it remains property and is entitled to protection as long as it has commercial value as news; and that to protect it effectively the defendant must be enjoined from making, or causing to be made, any gainful use of it while it retains such value. An essential element of individual property is the legal right to exclude others from enjoying it. If the property is private, the right of exclusion may be absolute; if the property is affected with a public interest, the right of exclusion is qualified. But the fact that a product of the mind has cost its producer money and labor, and has a value for which others are willing to pay, is not sufficient to ensure to it this legal attribute of property. The general rule of law is, that the noblest of human productions—knowledge, truths ascertained, conceptions, and ideas—become, after voluntary communication to others, free as the air to common use. Upon these incorporeal productions the attribute of property is continued after such communication only in certain classes of cases where public policy has seemed to demand it. These exceptions are confined to productions which, in some degree, involve creation, invention, or discovery. But by no means all such are endowed with this attribute of property. The creations which are recognized as property by the common law are literary, dramatic, musical, and other artistic creations; and these have also protection under the copyright statutes. The inventions and discoveries upon which this attribute of property is conferred only by statute, are the few comprised within the patent law. There are also many other cases in which courts interfere to prevent curtailment of plaintiff's enjoyment of incorporeal productions; and in which the right to relief is often called a property right, but is such only in a special sense. In those cases, the plaintiff has no absolute right to the protection of his production; he has merely the qualified right to be protected as against the defendant's acts, because of the special relation in which the latter stands or the wrongful method or means employed in acquiring the knowledge or the manner in which it is used. Protection of this character is afforded where the suit is based upon breach of contract or of trust or upon unfair competition.

The knowledge for which protection is sought in the case at bar is not of a kind upon which the law has heretofore conferred the attributes of property; nor is the manner of its acquisition or use nor the purpose to which it is applied, such as has heretofore been recognized as entitling a plaintiff to relief.

First. Plaintiff's principal reliance was upon the "ticker" cases; but they do not support its contention. The leading cases on this subject rest the grant of relief, not upon the existence of a general property right in news, but upon the breach of a contract or trust concerning the use of news communicated; and that element is lacking here. In *Board of Trade* v. *Christie Grain & Stock Co.,* 198 U. S. 236, 250, the court said the Board "does not lose its right by communicating the result [the quotations] to persons, even if many, in confidential relations to itself, under a contract not to make it public, and strangers to the trust will be restrained from getting at the knowledge by inducing a breach of trust and using knowledge obtained by such a breach." And it is also stated there (page 251): "Time is of the essence in matters like this, and it fairly may be said that, if the contracts with the plaintiff are kept, the information will not become public property until the plaintiff has gained its reward." The only other case in this court which relates to this subject is *Hunt* v. *N. Y. Cotton Exchange,* 205 U. S. 322. While the opinion there refers the protection to a general property right in the quotations, the facts are substantially the same as those in the *Christie Case,* which is the chief authority on which the decision is based. Of the cases in the lower federal courts and in the state courts it may be said, that most of them too can, on their facts, be reconciled with this principle, though much of the language of the courts cannot be. In spite of anything that may appear in these cases to the contrary it seems that the true principle is stated in the *Christie Case,* that the collection of quotations "stands like a trade secret." And in *Dr. Miles Medical Co.* v. *Park* & *Sons Co.,* 220 U. S. 373, 402, this court says of a trade secret: "Any one may use it who fairly, by analysis and experiment, discovers it. But the complainant is entitled to be protected against invasion of its right in the process by fraud or by breach of trust or contract." See *John D. Park* & *Sons Co.* v. *Hartman,* 153 Fed. Rep. 24, 29.

The leading English case, *Exchange Telegraph Co.* v. *Gregory* & *Co.* [1896], 1 Q. B. 147, is also rested clearly upon a breach of contract or trust, although there is some reference to a general property right. The later English cases seem to have rightly understood the basis of the decision, and they have not sought to extend it further than was intended. Indeed, we find the positive suggestion in some cases that the only ground for relief is the manner in which knowledge of the report of the news was acquired.

If the news involved in the case at bar had been posted in violation of any agreement between the Associated Press and its members, questions similar to those in the "ticker" cases might have arisen. But the plaintiff does not contend that the posting was wrongful or that any papers were wrongfully issued by its subscribers. On the contrary it is conceded that both the bulletins and the papers were issued in accordance with the regulations of the plaintiff. Under such circumstances, for a reader of the papers purchased in the open market, or a reader of the bulletins publicly posted, to procure and use gainfully, information therein contained, does not involve inducing anyone to commit a breach either of contract or of trust, or committing or in any way abetting a breach of confidence.

Second. Plaintiff also relied upon the cases which hold that the common-law right of the producer to prohibit copying is not lost by the private circulation of a literary composition, the delivery of a lecture, the exhibition of a painting or the performance of a dramatic or musical composition. These cases rest upon the ground that the common law recognizes such productions as property which, despite restricted communication, continues until there is a dedication to the public under the copyright statutes or otherwise. But they are inapplicable for two reasons. (1) At common law, as under the copyright acts, intellectual productions are entitled to such protection only if there is underneath something evincing the mind of a creator or originator, however modest the requirement. The mere record of isolated happenings, whether in words or by photographs not involving artistic skill, are denied such protection. (2) At common law, as under the copyright acts, the element in intellectual productions which secures such protection is not the knowledge, truths, ideas, or emotions which the composition expresses, but the form or sequence in which they are expressed; that is, "some new collocation of visible or audible points,—of lines, colors, sounds, or words." See *White-Smith Music Co.* v. *Apollo Co.*, 209 U. S. 1, 19; *Kalem Co.* v. *Harper Brothers*, 222 U. S. 55, 63. An author's theories, suggestions, and speculations, or the systems, plans, methods, and arrangements of an originator, derive no such protection from the statutory copyright of the book in which they are set forth; and they are likewise denied such protection at common law.

That news is not property in the strict sense is illustrated by the case of *Sports and General Press Agency, Ltd.* v. *"Our Dogs" Publishing Co., Ltd.* [1916], 2 K. B. 880, where the plaintiff, the assignee of the right to photograph the exhibits at a dog show, was refused an injunction against defendant who had also taken pictures of the show and was publishing them. The court said that, except in so far as the possession of the land occupied by the show enabled the proprietors to exclude people or permit them on condition that they agree not to take photographs (which condition was not imposed in that case), the proprietors had no exclusive right to photograph the show and could therefore grant no such right. And, it was further stated that, at any rate, no matter what conditions might be imposed upon those entering the grounds, if the defendant had been on top of a house or in some position where he could photograph the show without interfering with the physical property of the plaintiff, the plaintiff would have no right to stop him. If, when the plaintiff creates the event recorded, he is not entitled to the exclusive first publication of the news (in that case a photograph) of the event, no reason can be shown why he should be accorded such protection as to events which he simply records and transmits to other parts of the world, though with great expenditure of time and money.

Third. If news be treated as possessing the characteristics not of a trade secret, but of literary property, then the earliest issue of a paper of general circulation or the earliest public posting of a bulletin which embodies such news would, under the established rules governing literary property, operate as a publication, and all property in the news would then cease. Resisting this conclusion, plaintiff relied upon the cases which hold that uncopyrighted intellectual and artistic property survives private circulation or a restricted publication; and it contended that in each issue of each paper, a restriction is to be implied that the news shall not be used gainfully in competition with the Associated Press or any of its members. There is no basis for such an implication. But it is also well settled that where the publication is in fact a general one, even express words of restriction upon use are inoperative. In other words, a general publication is effective to dedicate literary property to the public, regardless of the actual intent of its owner. In the cases dealing with lectures, dramatic and musical performances, and art exhibitions, upon which plaintiff relied, there was no general publication in print comparable to the issue of daily newspapers or the unrestricted public posting of bulletins. The principles governing those cases differ more or less in application, if not in theory, from the principles governing the issue of printed copies; and in so far as they do differ, they have no application to the case at bar.

Fourth. Plaintiff further contended that defendant's practice constitutes unfair competition, because there is "appropriation without cost to itself of values created by" the plaintiff; and it is upon this ground that the decision of this court appears to be based. To appropriate and use for profit, knowledge and ideas produced by other men, without making compensation or even acknowledgment, may be inconsistent with a finer sense of propriety; but, with the exceptions indicated above, the law has heretofore sanctioned the practice. Thus it was held that one may ordinarily make and sell anything in any form, may copy with exactness that which another has produced, or may otherwise use his ideas without his consent and without the payment of compensation, and yet not inflict a legal injury; and that ordinarily one is at perfect liberty to find out, if he can by lawful means, trade secrets of another, however valuable, and then use the knowledge so acquired gainfully, although it cost the original owner much in effort and in money to collect or produce.

Such taking and gainful use of a product of another which, for reasons of public policy, the law has refused to endow with the attributes of property, does not become unlawful because the product happens to have been taken from a rival and is used in competition with him. The unfairness in competition which hitherto has been recognized by the law as a basis for relief, lay in the manner or means of conducting the business; and the manner or means held legally unfair, involves either fraud or force for the doing of acts otherwise prohibited by law. In the "passing off" cases (the typical and most common case of unfair competition), the wrong consists in fraudulently representing by word or act that defendant's goods are those of plaintiff. See *Hanover Milling Co.* v. *Metcalf*, 240 U. S. 403, 412-413. In the other cases, the diversion of trade was effected through physical or moral coercion, or by inducing breaches of contract or of trust by enticing away employees. In some others, called cases of simulated competition, relief was granted because defendant's purpose was unlawful; namely, not competition but deliberate and wanton destruction of plaintiff's business.

That competition is not unfair in a legal sense, merely because the profits gained are unearned, even if made at the expense of a rival, is shown by many cases besides those referred to above. He who follows the pioneer into a new market, or who engages in the manufacture of an article newly introduced by another, seeks profits due largely to the labor and expense of the first adventurer; but the law sanctions, indeed encourages, the pursuit. He who makes a city known through his product, must submit to sharing the resultant trade with others who, perhaps for that reason, locate there later. *Canal Co.* v. *Clark,* 13 Wall. 311; *Elgin National Watch Co.* v. *Illinois Watch Co.,* 179 U. S. 665, 673. He who has made his name a guaranty of quality, protests in vain when another with the same name engages, perhaps for that reason, in the same lines of business, provided, precaution is taken to prevent the public from being deceived into the belief that what he is selling was made by his competitor. One bearing a name made famous by another is permitted to enjoy the unearned benefit which necessarily flows from such use, even though the use proves harmful to him who gave the name value. *Brown Chemical Co.* v. *Meyer,* 139 U. S. 540, 544; *Howe Scale Co.* v. *Wyckoff, Seamans* & *Benedict,* 198 U. S. 118; *Donnell* v. *Herring-Hall-Marvin Safe Co.,* 208 U. S. 267; *Waterman Co.* v. *Modern Pen Co.,* 235 U. S. 88. See *Saxlehner* v. *Wagner,* 216 U. S. 375.

The means by which the International News Service obtains news gathered by the Associated Press is also clearly unobjectionable. It is taken from papers bought in the open market or from bulletins publicly posted. No breach of contract such as the court considered to exist in *Hitchman Coal* & *Coke Co.* v. *Mitchell,* 245 U. S. 229, 254; or of trust such as was present in *Morison* v. *Moat,* 9 Hare, 241; and neither fraud nor force is involved. The manner of use is likewise unobjectionable. No reference is made by word or by act to the Associated Press, either in transmitting the news to subscribers or by them in publishing it in their papers. Neither the International News Service nor its subscribers is gaining or seeking to gain in its business a benefit from the reputation of the Associated Press. They are merely using its product without making compensation. See *Bamforth* v. *Douglass Post Card* & *Machine Co.,* 158 Fed. Rep. 355; *Tribune Co. of Chicago* v. *Associated Press,* 116 Fed. Rep. 126. That, they have a legal right to do; because the product is not property, and they do not stand in any relation to the Associated Press, either of contract or of trust, which otherwise precludes such use. The argument is not advanced by characterizing such taking and use a misappropriation.

It is also suggested, that the fact that defendant does not refer to the Associated Press as the source of the news may furnish a basis for the relief. But the defendant and its subscribers, unlike members of the Associated Press, were under no contractual obligation to disclose the source of the news; and there is no rule of law requiring acknowledgment to be made where uncopyrighted matter is reproduced. The International News Service is said to mislead its subscribers into believing that the news transmitted was originally gathered by it and that they in turn mislead their readers. There is, in fact, no representation by either of any kind. Sources of information are sometimes given because required by contract; sometimes because naming the source gives authority to an otherwise incredible statement; and sometimes the source is named because the agency does not wish to take the responsibility itself of giving currency to the news. But no representation can properly be implied from omission to mention the source of information except that the International News Service is transmitting news which it believes to be credible.

Nor is the use made by the International News Service of the information taken from papers or bulletins of Associated Press members legally objectionable by reason of the purpose for which it was employed. The acts here complained of were not done for the purpose of injuring the business of the Associated Press. Their purpose was not even to divert its trade, or to put it at a disadvantage by lessening defendant's necessary expenses. The purpose was merely to supply subscribers of the International News Service promptly with all available news. The suit is, as this court declares, in substance one brought for the benefit of the members of the Associated Press, who would be proper, and except for their number perhaps necessary, parties; and the plaintiff conducts the suit as representing their interest. It thus appears that the protection given by the injunction is not actually to the business of the complainant news agency; for this agency does not sell news nor seek to earn profits; but is a mere instrumentality by which 800 or more newspapers collect and distribute news. It is these papers severally which are protected; and the protection afforded is not from competition of the defendant, but from possible competition of one or more of the 400 other papers which receive the defendant's service. Furthermore, the protection to these Associated Press members consists merely in denying to other papers the right to use, as news, information which, by authority of all concerned, had theretofore been given to the public by some of those who joined in gathering it; and to which the law denies the attributes of property. There is in defendant's purpose nothing on which to base a claim for relief.

It is further said that, while that for which the Associated Press spends its money is too fugitive to be recognized as property in the common-law courts, the defendant cannot be heard to say so in a court of equity, where the question is one of unfair competition. The case presents no elements of equitable title or of breach of trust. The only possible reason for resort to a court of equity in a case like this is that the remedy which the law gives is inadequate. If the plaintiff has no legal cause of action, the suit necessarily fails. *Levy* v. *Walker,* L. R. 10 Ch. D. 436, 449. There is nothing in the situation of the parties which can estop the defendant from saying so.

Fifth: The great development of agencies now furnishing country-wide distribution of news, the vastness of our territory, and improvements in the means of transmitting intelligence, have made it possible for a news agency or newspapers to obtain, without paying compensation, the fruit of another's efforts and to use news so obtained gainfully in competition with the original collector. The injustice of such action is obvious. But to give relief against it would involve more than the application of existing rules of law to new facts. It would require the making of a new rule in analogy to existing ones. The unwritten law possesses capacity for growth; and has often satisfied new demands for justice by invoking analogies or by expanding a rule or principle. This process has been in the main wisely applied and should not be discontinued. Where the problem is relatively simple, as it is apt to be when private interests only are involved, it generally proves adequate. But with the increasing complexity of society, the public interest tends to become omnipresent; and the problems presented by new demands for justice cease to be simple. Then the creation or recognition by courts of a new private right may work serious injury to the general public, unless the boundaries of the right are definitely established and wisely guarded. In order to reconcile the new private right with the public interest, it may be necessary to prescribe limitations and rules for its enjoyment; and also to provide administrative machinery for enforcing the rules. It is largely for this reason, that, in the effort to meet the many new demands for justice incident to a rapidly changing civilization, resort to legislation has latterly been had with increasing frequency.

The rule for which the plaintiff contends would effect an important extension of property rights and a corresponding curtailment of the free use of knowledge and of ideas; and the facts of this case admonish us of the danger involved in recognizing such a property right in news, without imposing upon news-gatherers corresponding obligations. A large majority of the newspapers and perhaps half the newspaper readers of the United States are dependent for their news of general interest upon agencies other than the Associated Press. The channel through which about 400 of these papers received, as the plaintiff alleges, "a large amount of news relating to the European war of the greatest importance and of intense interest to the newspaper reading public" was suddenly closed. The closing to the International News Service of these channels for foreign news (if they were closed) was due not to unwillingness on its part to pay the cost of collecting the news, but to the prohibitions imposed by foreign governments upon its securing news from their respective countries and from using cable or telegraph lines running therefrom. For aught that appears, this prohibition may have been wholly undeserved; and at all events the 400 papers and their readers may be assumed to have been innocent. For aught that appears, the International News Service may have sought then to secure temporarily by arrangement with the Associated Press the latter's foreign news service. For aught that appears, all of the 400 subscribers of the International News Service would gladly have then become members of the Associated Press, if they could have secured election thereto. It is possible, also, that a large part of the readers of these papers were so situated that they could not secure prompt access to papers served by the Associated Press. The prohibition of the foreign governments might as well have been extended to the channels through which news was supplied to the more than a thousand other daily papers in the United States not served by the Associated Press; and a large part of their readers may also be so located that they can not procure prompt access to papers served by the Associated Press.

A legislature, urged to enact a law by which one news agency or newspaper may prevent appropriation of the fruits of its labors by another, would consider such facts and possibilities and others which appropriate enquiry might disclose. Legislators might conclude that it was impossible to put an end to the obvious injustice involved in such appropriation of news, without opening the door to other evils, greater than that sought to be remedied. Such appears to have been the opinion of our Senate which reported unfavorably a bill to give news a few hours' protection; and which ratified, on February 15, 1911, the convention adopted at the Fourth International American Conference; and such was evidently the view also of the signatories to the International Copyright Union of November 13, 1908; as both these conventions expressly exclude news from copyright protection.

Or legislators dealing with the subject might conclude, that the right to news values should be protected to the extent of permitting recovery of damages for any unauthorized use, but that protection by injunction should be denied, just as the courts of equity ordinarily refuse (perhaps in the interest of free speech) to restrain actionable libels, and for other reasons decline to protect by injunction mere political rights; and as Congress has prohibited courts from enjoining the illegal assessment or collection of federal taxes. If a legislature concluded to recognize property in published news to the extent of permitting recovery at law, it might, with a view to making the remedy more certain and adequate, provide a fixed measure of damages, as in the case of copyright infringement.

Or again, a legislature might conclude that it was unwise to recognize even so limited a property right in published news as that above indicated; but that a news agency should, on some conditions, be given full protection of its business; and to that end a remedy by injunction as well as one for damages should be granted, where news collected by it is gainfully used without permission. If a legislature concluded (as at least one court has held, *New York & Chicago Grain & Stock Exchange* v. *Board of Trade,* 127 Illinois, 153) that under certain circumstances news-gathering is a business affected with a public interest, it might declare that, in such cases, news should be protected against appropriation, only if the gatherer assumed the obligation of supplying it, at reasonable rates and without discrimination, to all papers which applied therefor. If legislators reached that conclusion, they would probably go further, and prescribe the conditions under which and the extent to which the protection should be afforded; and they might also provide the administrative machinery necessary for ensuring to the public, the press, and the news agencies, full enjoyment of the rights so conferred.

Courts are ill-equipped to make the investigations which should precede a determination of the limitations which should be set upon any property right in news or of the circumstances under which news gathered by a private agency should be deemed affected with a public interest. Courts would be powerless to prescribe the detailed regulations essential to full enjoyment of the rights conferred or to introduce the machinery required for enforcement of such regulations. Considerations such as these should lead us to decline to establish a new rule of law in the effort to redress a newly-disclosed wrong, although the propriety of some remedy appears to be clear.

B. *Labor Relations*

LABOR RELATIONS

LOUIS D. BRANDEIS

The following statements are excerpts from the testimony of Brandeis before the United States Commission on Industrial Relations, published in Senate Document, 64th Congress, 1st Session, vol. 26 (Serial Vol. 6936), pp. 7657-81. Extracts of the testimony have been published in *The Curse of Bigness* (ed. Osmond K. Fraenkel), New York, The Viking Press, 1935, pp. 70-95.

COMMISSIONER WEINSTOCK: * * * For the information of the commission, will you be good enough to point out, Mr. Brandeis, what you have observed to be the mistakes of employers in dealing with labor. Will you brief them?

MR. BRANDEIS: I think the main mistake that the employers have made has been a failure to acquire understanding of the conditions and facts concerning labor. There has been ignorance in this respect on the part of employers—ignorance due in large part to lack of imagination. Employers have not been able to think themselves into the labor position. They do not understand labor and many successful business men have never recognized that labor presents the most important problem in the business. One of the ablest business men I ever came in contact with, and who later made some very important advances in dealing with labor problems, said to me when I first had occasion to discuss a pressing labor problem with him: "I want to take up the labor question when I get around to it." He had been proceeding for years with a reorganization of his business in all other respects—in respect to distribution, in respect to financing and factory organization—but he postponed taking up the labor question until he should be through with all the other problems. Now, he was a man who looked upon business as applied science—as something to be thought out. His was a master mind; he was also a man of splendid heart and character in every way. But he had held the traditions generally prevailing that labor was something you could leave to the superintendents of your factories. He held an attitude similar to that which the chairman called attention to as being the attitude of directors who had testified here. Instead of recognizing that in most businesses the labor problem is the most important one, even from the business standpoint; that if you solve that satisfactorily all other problems are comparatively simple—it had seemed to him one that could be left to a subordinate. The fact that this man, whose record as a business man is very high, both in character and ability, was putting off the labor question until he got through with all the others, shows why labor has been so often misunderstood by employers.

The other cause of employers' difficulties is a failure to think clearly. The employers' refusal to deal with a union is ordinarily due to erroneous reasoning or false sentiment. The man who refuses to deal with the union acts ordinarily from a good motive. He is impressed with "union dictation." He is apt to think "this is my business and the American has the right of liberty of contract." He honestly believes that he is standing up for a high principle and is willing often to run the risk of having his business ruined rather than abandon that principle. They have not thought out clearly enough that liberty means exercising one's rights consistently with a like exercise of rights by other people; that liberty is distinguished from license in that it is subject to certain restrictions, and that no one can expect to secure liberty in the sense in which we recognize it in America without having his rights curtailed in those respects in which it is necessary to limit them in the general public interest. The failure of many employers to recognize these simple truths is a potent reason why employers have not been willing to deal with unions. I think our employers, as a rule, are kind-hearted; they mean to do right; they mean to be just; and there is no difference between the men who have fought the hardest against labor unions and those who have yielded to and dealt with labor unions in that respect, except that the former have not had that education which comes from actual active co-operation with unions in the solution of these problems.

I had my first practical experience in dealing with labor problems while acting for manufacturers in the effort to settle or prevent strikes. I found if I wanted to bring about a settlement it was absolutely necessary that the head of the business be brought into the conference. If the employer was a large corporation, nothing less than the president would do, and on the other hand we required the president of the international union to deal with the man in real authority. My effort was to bring these two men together and make each understand the problems of the other. And when I could bring that about, when I could make the union understand the employers' problem and the employer the union's problem, a settlement was almost certain. The next step was to make the individual employee feel that whatever the system of dealing, either through superintendents or otherwise, that there was no individual in that employ who was so insignificant but that if he believed a wrong was done him, he could, in the last analysis, appeal to the highest official of the corporation. When once that principle was established, the danger of a rupture between employer and employee was usually passed. The labor men felt faith; they felt that they could deal with the employer in full confidence; and under those circumstances I found that the laboring man would accept the definite statement of the corporation as to what they could afford to pay and what they could not afford to pay. I offered the union representative the opportunity of going through the employer's books; offered them every facility to learn the actual facts and requested their suggestions. They withdrew manfully from the opposition, for they were convinced they were being dealt with fairly, and that the rights of each individual laboring man were recognized as important as those of the biggest official. The corporation operated many factories, but the president was not burdened with numerous appeals. The fact that he recognized that there was nothing more important than the rights of the individual laboring man to human treatment was all the assurance needed.

* * *

COMMISSIONER WEINSTOCK: On the other hand, Mr. Brandeis, what are the mistakes of organized labor, as you see them?

MR. BRANDEIS: Well, in many ways they are similar—they are the correlative of the mistakes of the employers.

I think in the first place the commonest mistake is a belief that the employer is earning a tremendous amount of money at the expense of labor. Taking all things into consideration, the employer rarely earns "a tremendous amount of money." He earns in a great many cases far less than is proper for the industry. The margins of earnings in most business is less than it should be—less than is required for safety. The workingmen are mostly unfamiliar with large figures and are misled by them. They do not readily understand percentages, and they do not consider the risk that is involved. Very few workmen appreciate how necessary it is that there should sometimes be large profits in order to set off the losses. Few people care to advertise their losses, but the profits are advertised freely, and very often are exaggerated.

Now, what the employer needs most is to have proper representatives of labor understand the problems of his business; how serious they are, how great is the chance of losing money, how relatively small is the chance of making large profits, and how great is the percentage of failure. Put a competent representative of labor on your board of directors; make him grapple with the problems of whether to do or not to do a specific thing, and undertake to balance the advantages and disadvantages presented, and he will get a realizing sense of how difficult it is to operate a business successfully and what the dangers are of the destruction of the capital in the business. A few years ago, when union leaders were demanding from my client an increase in wages, and I asked them: "How much do you think the employer ought to earn before he increases your wages?" they named a figure which was far above his actual earnings, and I said to them: "Gentlemen, the books are open. If you can find either that more is being earned, or can show any way in which the employer can earn more than he is earning, the balance shall go to you." That put the responsibilities upon the labor leaders; they came to realize the difficulties under which the employer was laboring and acquiesced in the situation. The second cause of discord is the natural distrust felt by labor due largely to their lack of knowledge and of opportunities for knowledge.

The third cause is the sense of being subject to the power of the employer. That feeling of subjection cannot be removed without changing the conditions under which industry is being carried on. Perhaps the greatest of labor's mistakes is the practice, in many trades or communities, of restricting production. That is a very serious difficulty. Nothing would do so much to win the employer to collective bargaining as action on the part of the labor leaders favoring increased production. If employers could be satisfied that unionism meant increased production and better discipline and that the unions were striving for that result, a large part of the apprehension of employers would be removed and collective bargaining would be wisely extended.

Both labor and employers should bear constantly in mind that each is his brother's keeper; that every employer is injured by any single employer who does labor a wrong; and that every laboring man and every union is injured by every individual unionist who does an employer a wrong. The influence of a single wrongful act by one who can be classified, is tremendous. It affects every other member of the class. When an employer acts improperly toward his employees, it is the business of other employers to see that such conduct is prevented, for his wrong will injure them. And in the same way any lack of fairness and any act of lawlessness on the part of labor is certain to injure other workers and the unions as a whole, and the individual members of labor unions with employers.

* * *

COMMISSIONER COMMONS: I had thought of asking Mr. Brandeis questions on the boycott, on the open shop, and on the preferential union shop, from a legal standpoint, but if you are going to close at this hour, I suppose we cannot talk longer at this time, but I can ask him those questions at a later time.

CHAIRMAN WALSH: I understand that it will be impossible for Mr. Brandeis to appear again today.

MR. BRANDEIS: I could, perhaps, answer the question as to the preferential shop.

COMMISSIONER COMMONS: I wanted to ask with regard to the legal aspects of it. I understand that the opinion of the courts is that the closed-shop demands of unions is an illegal demand. I think that is the statement of the anthracite-coal strike commission. On the other hand, the records of the anthracite-coal strike commission take the ground that there should be only an open shop. The question is, has the employer the right to maintain only a non-union shop if he desires—that is, has he the right to refuse to recognize a union or employ union men? Further, if it is legal to have the closed shop, why should it be legal to prescribe a preferential union shop?

MR. BRANDEIS: I think the preferential union shop—I have never heard any question raised, and I do not see how any question can be raised, as to the legality of the preferential union shop. The preferential union shop is this: It is a shop in which union standards and conditions prevail, and in which the employer agrees, other things being equal, that he will employ union men—that he will give the union man a preference over a non-union man. Now, that preferential union shop has seemed to me, certainly in many trades, to be a necessity if we are to have an effective union. I had, in early dealings with labor problems, found this situation to be very common where there was a perfectly honest open shop—that is, where the employer was willing to deal with the union fairly and squarely, making a contract with the union and agreeing with that union that he would not change conditions in his shop except upon negotiation with the union, but allow men in that shop to be either union or non-union men—the better that worked, the stronger was the tendency of the men to drop out of the union. They felt that they were getting all of the benefits of the union without having to submit to any of its burdens. So a relatively small part of the men had to bear the burden of the union, not only in money, but in the administrative work of the union and in submission to those restrictions which are put upon the members of the union for the common benefit. So in the perfect operation of the union shop, in those instances, conditions existed which undermined the union itself. The very perfection of the operation of the open-shop agreement worked to the detriment of the union. Furthermore, it was unfair and was demoralizing to the non-union men to get the benefits of the union without in any way contributing either by restriction or by money.

The question then came up as to how you can secure to the employer and others certain liberty of action and at the same time maintain the union. Justice and practical experience showed the necessity of creating some incentive to join the union, and, on the other hand, some disadvantage in not joining the union. On the whole the most advantageous incentive was to give preference in employment to him who joined the union; to say to the man who joins that union: "I will give you preference, but you must be up to the standard; you must be as good as the other man." And if the union cannot supply such men, then, that you may take some non-union man. Under this system the closed shop is avoided. In the preferential union shop certain men are given preference over other men; and that is the principle which underlies the protocol in the garment workers' trade.

COMMISSIONER COMMONS: Do you advise unions now giving up the closed-shop idea and asking for the preferential shop?

MR. BRANDEIS: I do; and I think such a course would remove to a large extent the opposition of employers to unionism, and their refusing to enter into agreements with unions.

COMMISSIONER COMMONS: Is your reason legal or given on legal grounds?

MR. BRANDEIS: It is partly legal, partly sentimental, and partly a recognition of economic rights and a sound social policy.

COMMISSIONER COMMONS: Employers that now stand for the open shop, what is your advice to them?

MR. BRANDEIS: I should say to those employers who stand for the open shop, that they ought to recognize that it is for their interests as well as that of the community that unions should be powerful and responsible; that it is to their interests to build up the unions, to aid as far as they can in making them stronger, and to create conditions under which the unions shall be led by the ablest and most experienced men. A large part of all union activity today, and in the past, has been devoted to the struggle for existence; and that fact accounts also for a large part of union excesses. As nearly as possible union existence should be assured so that the efforts of the leaders might be devoted to solving the fundamental and difficult problems of discipline and organization, and the working out of other problems of the trades.

C. *Appraisal of Mr. Justice Brandeis' Economic Views*

THE INDUSTRIAL LIBERALISM OF JUSTICE BRANDEIS

DONALD R. RICHBERG

Donald R. Richberg is a senior partner of the Washington, D. C. law firm, Davies, Richberg, Tydings, Beebe and Landa. His distinguished government service included the chairmanship of the National Recovery Act Board in 1935. He is the author of a number of books, among them are *Government and Business Tomorrow* (1943), *Old Faith and Fancies New* (1949), and *My Hero* (autobiography, 1954). This article is reprinted from 31 Columbia Law Review 1094-1103 (1931).

In his introduction to that brilliant volume of Jerome Frank on *Law and the Modern Mind*,[1] Judge Mack observes that "the last two decades have made it abundantly clear that the just decision of causes requires a careful weighing of social and economic considerations not to be found in the strict body of the law itself." And he commends Mr. Frank for demonstrating that not only must we consider "the social and economic facts upon which legal decisions should properly be predicated, but that the very thought processes of the judge and jurist himself must be tested and freed from persistently childish notions that have no place in an adult civilization."

It may be generally conceded that Justice Brandeis has so constantly and carefully tested his own thought processes as to free them to an exceptional degree from those "childish notions" which seem to persist to some extent in all adult thought—and which commonly become radio-active when the judicial conservative rebukes the legislative radical. It is, therefore, not only interesting but comforting to examine, behind the social and economic facts upon which the Brandeis opinions have been predicated, the thought processes from which they have arisen. One is free from any embarrassing fear that the investigation may expose a philosophy of life that never developed beyond the day dreams of childhood. But there is a question which must be fairly faced in reviewing his views of industry, with their disturbing consistency over a period of sweeping industrial change: Will Justice Brandeis be time-justified in his persistent protest against "bigness"; or is bigness the product of an irresistible force which if now misdirected should be harnessed and wisely directed in the service of mankind?

It may be well to restate the question in the clear language of Professor Beard:[2] "Is the America of tomorrow to be the society of 'the new freedom' so effectively portrayed by Mr. Brandeis and the President who appointed him? Or will the march of integration in finance and industry override the small enterprises which they sought to preserve against extinction?"

For more than twenty years, at least, whether discussing the problems of worker, manager or consumer, Mr. Brandeis has opposed monopoly and concentration and advocated competition and the preservation of small business units. He has pointed out the inefficiencies as well as the oppressions of big business operations. He has steadfastly sought to maintain the individual satisfactions and social advantages of a multiplicity of units of production and distribution, which should insure a competitive incentive for improvement and progress and a competitive check on excessive individual gain. The consequences of these thought processes are written deep into his judicial opinions. If these ideas are progressive our civilization must refuse submission to its conquering enemy. If these ideas are reactionary, our civilization must protect itself against the destructive experiments now being carried on by its well-meaning but ruthless friend.

It is probably fair to assume that the industrial liberalism of Justice Brandeis arises out of a deep rooted individualism, which is not only intensely concerned with his own freedom of thought and act, but is profoundly sympathetic with the desire of any other human being to stand erect, to tower above environment, to maintain an individual sovereignty subject to no political or economic Caesars.

"The makers of our Constitution undertook to secure conditions favorable to the pursuit of happiness. They recognized the significance of man's spiritual nature, of his feelings, of his intellect. They knew that only a part of the pain, pleasure, and satisfactions of life are to be found in material things. They sought to protect Americans in their beliefs, their thoughts, their emotions, and their sensations. They conferred, as against the Government, the right to be let alone—the most comprehensive of rights and the right most valued by civilized men." [3]

But political freedom is not enough. "Can any man be really free who is constantly in danger of becoming dependent upon somebody and something else than his own exertion and conduct?" [4] The answer is quite clear: "You cannot have true American citizenship, you cannot preserve political liberty, you cannot secure American standards of living unless some degree of industrial liberty accompanies it." [5]

For the wage earner this liberty can only be obtained through participation in the responsibilities of a business enterprise:

"The social justice for which we are striving is an incident of our democracy, not the main end. It is rather the result of democracy—perhaps its finest expression—but it rests upon democracy, which implies the rule by the people. And, therefore, the end for which we must strive is the attainment of rule by the people, and that involves industrial democracy as well as political democracy. That means that the problems of a trade should no longer be the problems of the employer alone. The problems of his business, and it is not the employer's business alone, are the problems of all in it. The union cannot shift upon the employer the responsibility for conditions nor can the employer insist upon determining, according to his will, the conditions which shall exist." [6]

For the business man this liberty can only be obtained through preserving his responsibility for the welfare of an industrial unit. The extinction of a multitude of small units and the transformation of their independent owners into dependent employees of "big business" extinguishes economic democracy upon which political democracy—and liberty—depend.

"Already the displacement of the small independent business man by the huge corporation with its myriad of employees, its absentee ownership, and its financier control presents a grave danger to our democracy. The social loss is great; and there is no economic gain. But the process of capitalizing free Americans is not an inevitable one. It is largely the result of unwise, man-made, privilege creating law, which has stimulated existing tendencies to inequality instead of discouraging them." [7]

Thus we find clearly stated a common interest of employer and employee, who would be free citizens of a democracy, in combating the tendency toward concentration and monopoly. Each loses not only his individual freedom but his capacity to cooperate with the other—a capacity dependent on the opportunity for personal relations.

"The grave objection to the large business is that, almost inevitably, the form of organization, the absentee stock holdings, and its remote directorship prevent participation, ordinarily, of employees in such management. The executive officials become stewards in charge of the details of the operation of the business, they alone coming into direct relation with labor. Thus we lose that necessary cooperation which naturally flows from contact between employers and employees—and which the American aspirations for democracy demand. It is in the resultant absolutism that you will find the fundamental cause of prevailing unrest; no matter what is done with the superstructure, no matter how it may be improved in one way or the other, unless we eradicate that fundamental difficulty, unrest will not only continue, but, in my opinion, will grow worse." [8]

This loss of liberty, this degradation of democracy is accompanied, according to Mr. Brandeis, by "no economic gain"—a conclusion which will incite heated opposition. But the inefficiency of large organizations, their drift into bureaucracy, red tape, inertia and decadence is a favorite theme of this champion of "smallness." When he argued against the railroad demand for an advance in freight rates, in 1911, he massed his statistics to prove that scientific management, instead of seeking higher rates, would produce lower costs and increased business. But, he argued, scientific management had been sacrificed to "bigness":

"I ask the Commission to consider whether there is not a causal connection between the fact of bigness, the fact of this extraordinary gross, and the fact of the reduced net; whether it is not a fact that the Pennsylvania system, the New York Central system, and indeed, to a less extent, the Baltimore & Ohio system have not exceeded what may be called the limit of greatest efficiency. Because, obviously, in all human institutions there must be a limit of greatest efficiency. These railroads are run by men; and, preeminently, they are determined by one or two men. Everybody in his experience knows his own limitations; knows how much less well he can do many things than a few things. There undoubtedly is a limit with a railroad, as in the case of other institutions, where they may be too small; but there is another limit where they may be too large—where the centrifugal force will be greater than the centripetal, and where, by reason of the multiplicity of problems and the distance to the circumference, looseness of administration arises that overcomes any advantage from size, overcomes it so far as to make it relatively a losing proposition. . . .

"I say, therefore, may not that be one of the causes of the trouble, which some of the railroads believe themselves to be in? And this question, this bigness, or, as I would be inclined to call it, this curse of bigness, has other incidents than the ones I have mentioned." [9]

These political-economic views of Justice Brandeis are of the utmost importance in a consideration of his contribution to the development of American law. No doctrine of *laissez faire* permits him to isolate industrial evolution from the making and enforcement of the law. The legislatures and the courts do not sit idly by while through concentration and utilization of economic power, strong willed industrialists make over our civilization. This transformation "is largely the result of unwise, man-made, privilege creating law." It is because of what our law-makers have *done,* as well as because of what they have failed to do, that monopolies have grown great.

"The small man needs the protection of the law; but the law becomes the instrument by which he is destroyed." [10]

The point of the lawyer's argument was emphasized in the dissenting opinion of the judge filed six years later: [11]

"The refusal to permit a multitude of small rivals to cooperate, as they have done here, in order to protect themselves and the public from the chaos and havoc wrought in their trade by ignorance, may result in suppressing competition in the hardwood industry. These keen business rivals, who sought through cooperative exchange of trade information to create conditions under which alone rational competition is possible, produce in the aggregate about one-third of the hardwood lumber of the country. This Court held in *United States* v. *U. S. Steel Corporation,* 251 U. S. 417, that it was not unlawful to vest in a single corporation control of fifty per cent of the steel industry of the country; and in *United States* v. *United Shoe Machinery Co.,* 247 U. S. 32, the Court held that it was not unlawful to vest in a single corporation control of practically the whole shoe machinery industry. May not these hardwood lumber concerns, frustrated in their efforts to rationalize competition, be led to enter the inviting field of consolidation? And, if they do, may not another huge trust, with highly centralized control over vast resources, natural, manufacturing, and financial, become so powerful as to dominate competitors, wholesalers, retailers, consumers, employees, and, in large measure, the community?"

Not even in the field of public utilities should there

be an acceptance of private monopoly, according to this philosophy.

"It has been suggested that we accept the proposed monopoly in transportation but provide safeguards.

"This would be like surrendering liberty and substituting despotism with safeguards. There is no way in which to safeguard people from despotism except to prevent despotism. There is no way to safeguard the people from the evils of a private transportation monopoly except to prevent the monopoly. The objections to despotism and to monopoly are fundamental in human nature. They rest upon the innate and ineradicable selfishness of man. They rest upon the fact that absolute power inevitably leads to abuse. They rest upon the fact that progress flows only from struggle." [12]

Some years ago Justice Brandeis made an effort to summarize certain of his views in a letter which can be quoted with propriety here as an aid in the interpretation of more public expressions: [13]

"Refuse to accept as inevitable any evil in business (*e.g.*, irregularity of employment). Refuse to tolerate any immoral practice (*e.g.*, espionage). But do not believe that you can find a universal remedy for evil conditions or immoral practices in effecting a fundamental change in society (as by State Socialism). And do not pin too much faith in legislation. Remedial institutions are apt to fall under the control of the enemy and to become instruments of oppression.

"Seek for betterment within the broad lines of existing institutions. Do so by attacking evil *in situ;* and proceed from the individual to the general. Remember that progress is necessarily slow; that remedies are necessarily tentative; that because of varying conditions there must be much and constant enquiry into facts . . . and much experimentation; and that always and everywhere the intellectual, moral and spiritual development of those concerned will remain an essential—and the main factor—in real betterment.

"This development of the individual is, thus, both a necessary means and the end sought. For our objective is the making of men and women who shall be free, self-respecting members of a democracy—and who shall be worthy of respect. Improvement in material conditions of the worker and ease are the incidents of better conditions—valuable mainly as they may ever increase opportunities for development.

"The great developer is responsibility. Hence no remedy can be hopeful which does not devolve upon the workers participation in the responsibility for the conduct of business; and their aim should be the eventual assumption of full responsibility—as in cooperative enterprises. This participation in and eventual control of industry is likewise an essential of obtaining justice in distributing the fruits of industry.

"But democracy in any sphere is a serious undertaking. It substitutes self-restraint for external restraint. It is more difficult to maintain than to achieve. It demands continuous sacrifice by the individual and more exigent obedience to the moral law than any other form of government. Success in any democratic undertaking must proceed from the individual. It is possible only where the process of perfecting the individual is pursued. His development is attained mainly in the processes of common living. Hence the industrial struggle is essentially an affair of the Church and is its imperative task."

It may be a dangerous, even a presumptuous, effort to attempt a distillation of the utterances of a keen and subtle thinker in order to isolate the essence of a philosophy. All intelligent reasoning, and particularly that of a lawyer or a judge, proceeds from a multitude of uncertain generalizations to a particular conclusion which may be described as an expedient certainty. In order to give this conclusion the sanction of apparent inevitableness the uncertainties of its origin cannot be too clearly revealed. In the classic language of Justice Holmes: "The decision will depend on a judgment or intuition more subtle than any articulate major premise." [14] For this very reason the "instinctive preferences and inarticulate syllogisms" of a jurist are of greater importance than the language of particular opinions—if they can be discovered.

Lawyers and laymen casually acquainted with the life and works of Justice Brandeis might assume that he was possessed by instinctive sympathy with the underdog, and that the onward and ruthless march of big business, the rapid growth in his generation of political and economic despotism with increasing submergence of the "little fellow," invoked this sympathy and drove him to pull the big man down in order to lift the little man up. Without questioning the existence of this sympathy, it may be suggested that a love of equity is at least secondary in the Brandeis philosophy to a passion for liberty and a faith in democracy as the political method of its production.

Is there not a flash from the inmost life in his plea for "the right to be let alone—the most comprehensive of rights and the right most valued by civilized men." [15] Here is the reckless superlative of passion and faith.

Why should workers have a voice in the control of industry? There is little materialistic reasoning in his answer: no mere economic advantage is stressed. He is not content with any program that runs the "great risk of improving their material condition and reducing their manhood . . . the United States is a democracy and . . . we must have above all things, men. It is the development of manhood to which any industrial and social system should be directed. . . . Men must have industrial liberty as well as good wages." [16]

Why should independent business be saved from absorption into monopolistic combinations? It is because "the United States Steel Corporation and these other trusts have stabbed industrial liberty in the back. . . . The trust problem can never be settled right for the American people by looking at it through the spectacles of bonds and stocks. You must study it through the spectacles of people's rights and people's interests; must consider the effect upon the development of the American democracy."[17] The writer of these lines understands that democracy is not a political program. It is a religion.

It is interesting to note how "individualistic" and non-"socialistic" are the justifications for social legislation which proceed from this exponent of liberty and democracy.

"The liberty of each individual must be limited in such a way that it leaves to others the possibility of individual liberty; the right to develop must be subject to that limitation which gives everybody else the right to develop; the restriction is merely an adjustment of the relations of one individual to another." [18]

There is no sublimation of society, as a composite being of greater worth than the individual human, in this argument. There is no artificial concept of the State as an entity whose health and happiness is more important than individual health and happiness. The primary obligation whose fulfillment must be compelled by law is not that of individuals to society, but of society to individuals. The distinction is fundamental and there is no confusion in the mind of a real individualist.

"Universal suffrage necessarily imposes upon the State the obligation of fitting its governors—the voters—for their task; and the freedom of the individual is as much an essential condition of successful democracy as his education." [19]

The function of our government as viewed by Justice Brandeis is not merely the preservation of an assumed "natural" liberty, but a positive duty through cooperative aid to set men free from the tyrannies that otherwise might be imposed by nature and other human beings. Here is the authority and the reason for both social legislation and anti-trust legislation; for permitting "industrial combatants to push their struggle to the limits of the justification of self-interest," or for setting "the limits of permissible contest." [20] In the opinion just quoted he wrote: "All rights are derived from the purposes of the society in which they exist; above all rights rises duty to the community." But this is no deification of society. It is merely a reference to the liberties of the many which may not be infringed by arbitrary exercises of individual liberty. The purposes of our society are vigorously asserted in another opinion: [21]

"Those who won our independence believed that

the final end of the State was to make men free to develop their faculties, and that in its government the deliberative forces should prevail over the arbitrary. They valued liberty both as an end and as a means. They believed liberty to be the secret of happiness and courage to be the secret of liberty."

If this be a faithful description of the original purpose of our society—and who will question it?—there can be little doubt of the value and steadfastness of the work of Justice Brandeis as an expounder and defender of the Constitution of the United States and the government which "we, the people," undertook to establish thereunder. And if the trend of the times is moving contrary to the current of his thought, must we not conclude that his is the historic American spirit and that the rulers of modern industrial empires are aliens to that spirit?

With his realistic approach to all problems, with his patient researches into actualities, Justice Brandeis cannot be unaware that the independent worker or business man, for whom he would preserve liberty, shows precious little of the courage that is the "secret of liberty." He must observe the hordes of "white collar men" who, lacking the vigor and self-reliance to organize themselves for self-improvement, give support to the claim that their services are not worth more than their miserable wages. He must observe the hundreds of "company unions" of wage earners who demonstrate their incapacity for any greater responsibility than that of taking orders. He must observe the decadent futility of many old and anciently militant national unions. He must observe the thousands of once independent merchants and manufacturers, who, after a few years of feeble protesting against "trusts" and "chain-stores," have resigned themselves to life-time dependence upon the favor of remote controllers.

After years of such observations how often may the liberty loving judge wonder for whom the American democracy is to be preserved? To one who could see but a little way ahead—and behind, the prospect—and retrospect, might be discouraging. But to the reader of history who, in its reflected light, seeks also to look beyond tomorrow and tomorrow, there may be a more cheerful view.

Every generation has known a receding and an oncoming enemy of freedom. The man on horseback has come and conquered and has been defeated, time and time again. The new tyrannies of economic power will likewise rise and fall. Happily there is already much evidence that banker control is a passing phase. The huge vertical and horizontal "trusts" of the present day must have great directors to survive. They require double Napoleons, who as yet have not been found. The dinosaur perished not from lack of power, but from lack of brain. Perhaps the already demonstrated incapacity of human beings to administer wisely their superhuman organizations may bring about decentralization and revive democracy. Or, without disintegration, a redistribution of the control of vast enterprises may be achieved as the product of industrial-social engineering. Man, who survived the monstrosities of the prehistoric era, may survive the monstrosities of his own creation in the era of megalomania.

The industrial ideals of Justice Brandeis may remain shining long after the lights of modern business have gone out, and may aid generations yet unborn to move forward on the world-old path toward liberty.

Footnotes to
INDUSTRIAL LIBERALISM OF JUSTICE BRANDEIS, BY DONALD RICHBERG

1. Brentano's, 1930.
2. Introduction to THE SOCIAL AND ECONOMIC VIEWS OF MR. JUSTICE BRANDEIS (Vanguard Press, 1930).
3. Dissenting opinion in Olmstead v. United States, 277 U. S. 438, 478, 48 Sup. Ct. 564, 572 (1928).
4. Address before National Congress on Charities and Correction, Boston, June 8, 1911.
5. Statement in a hearing before a committee of the United States Senate on anti-trust legislation, December 14, 1911.
6. Statements before United States Commission on Industrial Relations, made April 16, 1914 and January 23, 1915.
7. Cutthroat Prices (Nov. 15, 1913) 128 HARPER'S WEEKLY 10.

8. Statements before United States Commission on Industrial Relations, *supra*, note 6.
9. Brief and argument before Interstate Commerce Commission, January 3, 11, 1911.
10. Statement before House Committee on Interstate and Foreign Commerce, January 9, 1915.
11. Dissenting opinion in American Column & Lumber Co. v. United States, 257 U. S. 377, 418, 42 Sup. Ct. 114, 123 (1921).
12. Address to New England Dry Goods Association, Boston, February 11, 1908.
13. Letter to Robert W. Bruere, February 25, 1922.
14. Lochner v. New York, 198 U. S. 45, 76, 25 Sup. Ct. 539, 547 (1905).
15. Olmstead v. United States, *loc. cit.*, *supra*, note 3.
16. See note 6, *supra*.
17. See note 5, *supra*.
18. Statement in behalf of a minimum wage law before New York State Factory Investigating Commission, January 22, 1915.
19. See note 4, *supra*.
20. Dissenting opinion in Duplex Printing Press Co. v. Deering, 254 U. S. 443, 488, 41 Sup. Ct. 172, 184 (1921).
21. Concurring opinion in Whitney v. California, 274 U. S. 357, 375, 47 Sup. Ct. 641, 648 (1927).

Part V
MR. JUSTICE BRANDEIS EVALUATED
LAW AND THE UNIVERSITIES

PAUL A. FREUND

This is a portion of the Tyrrell Williams Memorial Lecture, delivered by Professor Paul A. Freund of the Harvard Law School at the School of Law of Washington University (St. Louis) on April 30, 1953. In it Professor Freund, using Brandeis as an example, illustrates how a lawyer can translate into institutions the ideals and purposes of a society. The statement is reprinted from 1953 Washington University Law Quarterly 367, 373-374.

Professor Freund was Law Secretary to Mr. Justice Brandeis in 1932-1933. He has been in government service at various times and has argued many important cases before the United States Supreme Court. He is the author of *Understanding the Supreme Court* (1949) and other publications.

* * *

I can think of no better example than the career at the bar of Mr. Justice Brandeis. The ideas of Brandeis were simple and "in the air." Indeed, they had been in the air from the beginning of Western thought down through the nineteenth-century populists and muckrakers and utopians. He believed that in order to conserve and develop our greatest natural resource, the talents of ordinary people, there must be diffusion of both political power (hence Federalism) and economic power, and a corresponding diffusion of responsibility. Preachers, publicists and politicians were spreading the gospel, but it was the lawyer's function to translate these aspirations into the structure of our institutions, and this was the distinctive contribution of a Brandeis. Called upon to settle a garment workers' strike, he seized the occasion to establish a plan of continuous collaboration between management and labor.[10] Confronted by findings of waste and injustices in the field of industrial life insurance, he devised a system of savings bank life insurance, giving to workers more assured protection at lower cost and, just as important, demonstrating that the business could be carried on successfully by men with modest emoluments and without the prestige and ramifying power of the conventional financier of the era.[11] Impressed by the need of regulating competition and preventing monopoly, for to regulate monopoly seemed to him a fruitless task, he formulated the scheme of what became the Federal Trade Commission (for whose later checkered career he was of course not responsible).[12] Faced with the problem of controlling a public utility, he drew up for the regulation of the gas company in Boston a sliding scale whereby as rates to consumers were reduced dividends to stockholders could be increased, thus relying, for bodies corporate as well as for individuals, on the encouragement of inner impulses rather than external compulsion.[13] This is not the place to appraise the merits or defects of each of these devices. It is only important to observe how a lawyer can make political and economic and even moral ideals of ancient lineage come alive in the institutions of twentieth century industrial civilization.

* * *

MEMORIAL TRIBUTES TO MR. JUSTICE BRANDEIS

The following selections are from the Proceedings of the Bar of the Supreme Court of the United States and Meeting of the Court in Memory of Associate Justice Louis D. Brandeis, December 21, 1942 (Washington, n.p., 1942).

REMARKS OF JUDGE LEARNED HAND

Judge Learned Hand is one of America's distinguished jurists. He has been on the federal bench since 1909 and retired as a judge of the U. S. Court of Appeals, 2d Circuit, in 1951. His papers and addresses were edited by Irving Dilliard in 1953 (2d ed.), *The Spirit of Liberty.*

A man's life, like a piece of tapestry, is made up of many strands which interwoven make a pattern; to separate a single one and look at it alone, not only destroys the whole, but gives the strand itself a false value. So it must be with what I say today; this is no occasion to appraise the life and work of the man whose memory we have met to honor. It would be impossible at this time to do justice to the content of so manifold a nature and so full a life; its memorial stands written at large, chiefly in the records of his court; perhaps best preserved in the minds of living men and women. Before passing to my theme, I can therefore do no more than allude to much that I can ill afford to leave out: for instance, to his almost mystic reverence for that court, whose tradition seemed to him not only to consecrate its own members, but to impress its sacred mission upon all who shared in any measure in its work, even menially. To his mind nothing must weaken its influence or tarnish its lustre; no matter how hot had been the dispute, how wide the final difference, how plain the speech, nothing ever appeared to ruffle or disturb his serenity, or to suggest that he harbored anything but regard and respect for the views of his colleagues, however far removed from his own. Nor can I more than mention the clear, ungarnished style which so well betrayed the will that lay behind; the undiverted purpose to clarify and convince. How it eschewed all that might distract attention from the thought to its expression. The telling phrase, the vivid metaphor, the far-fetched word that teases the reader and flatters him with the vanity of recognition—these must not obtrude upon that which alone mattered: that conviction should be carried home. So put it that your hearers shall not be aware of the medium; so put it that they shall not feel you, yet shall be possessed of what you say. If style be the measure of the man, here was evidence of that insistence upon fact and reason which was at once his weapon and his shield. Others too must speak of the fiery nature which showed itself when stirred, but, which for the most part lay buried beneath an iron control of that ascesis, which seemed so to increase that towards the end one wondered at times whether like some Eastern sage the body's grosser part had not been quite burnt away and mere spirit remained; of those quick flashes of indignation at injustice, pretence, or oppression. These and much more which would make the figure stand out more boldly against its background, I shall not try to portray:—I must leave them to others who can speak more intimately and with more right.

At the risk of which I spoke a moment ago, I mean to choose a single thread from all the rest, which I venture to believe leads to the heart and kernel of his thinking, and—at least at this present—to the best of his teaching. I mean what I shall describe as his hatred of the mechanization of life. This he carried far indeed; as to it he lived at odds with much of the movement of his time. In many modern contrivances which to most of us seem innocent acquisitions of mankind—the motor car for instance—he saw a significance hostile to life's deeper, truer values. If he compromised as to a very few, the exceptions only served to emphasize the consistency of his conviction that by far the greater part of what passes for improvement, and is greedily converted into necessity, is tawdry, vain and destructive of spiritual values. In addition he also thought that the supposed efficiency with which these wants were supplied was illusory, even technologically. He had studied large industrial aggregations as few have and was satisfied that long before consolidation reached its modern size, it began to go to pieces at the top. There was a much earlier limit to human ability; minds did not exist able to direct such manifold and intricate structures. But that was only an incident; the important matter was the inevitable effect of size upon the individual, even though it neither limited nor impaired efficiency. Allied with this was his attitude towards concentration of political power which appeared so often in what he said from the bench. Indeed, his determination to preserve the autonomy of the states—though it went along with an unflinching assertion of federal power in matters which he reckoned truly national—amounted almost to an obsession. Haphazard as they might be in origin, and even devoid of much present significance, the states were the only breakwater against the ever pounding surf which threatened to submerge the individual and destroy the only kind of society in which personality could survive.

As is the case with all our convictions, the foundation for all this lay in his vision of the Good Life. It is, I know, a little incongruous to quote from another's vision of the Good Life who was in most respects at the opposite pole of belief and feeling but nevertheless there comes to my mind a scrap from the inscription above the gate of the Abbey of Thelême.

"Here enter you, pure, honest, faithful, true,

* * *

"Come, settle here a charitable faith,
"Which neighborly affection nourisheth."

He believed that there could be no true community save that built upon the personal acquaintance of each with each; by that alone could character and ability be rightly gauged; without that "neighborly affection" which would result no "faith" could be nourished, "charitable" or other. Only so could the latent richness which lurks in all of us come to flower. As the social group grows too large for mutual contact and appraisal, life quickly begins to lose its flavor and its significance. Among multitudes relations must become standardized; to standardize is to generalize, and to generalize is to ignore all those authentic features which mark, and which indeed alone create, an individual. Not only is there no compensation for our losses, but most of our positive ills have directly resulted from great size. With it has indeed come the magic of modern communication and quick transport; but out of these has come the sinister apparatus of mass suggestion and mass production. Such devices, always tending more and more to reduce us to a common model, subject us—our hard-won immunity now gone—to epidemics of hallowed catchword and formula. The herd is regaining its ancient and evil primacy; civilization is being reversed, for it has consisted of exactly the opposite process of individualization—witness the history of law and morals. These many inventions are a step backward; they lull men into the belief that because they are severally less subject to violence, they are more safe; because they are more steadily fed and clothed, they are more secure from want; because their bodies are cleaner, their hearts are purer. It is an illusion; our security has actually diminished as our demands have become more exacting; our comforts we purchase at the cost of a softer fibre, a feebler will and an infantile suggestibility.

I am well aware of the reply to all this; it is on every tongue. "Do not talk to us," you say, "of the tiny city utopias of Plato or Aristotle; or of Jefferson with his dream of a society of hardy, self-sufficient freeholders, living in proud, honorable isolation, however circumscribed. Those days are gone forever, and they are well lost. The vast command over Nature which the last century gave to mankind and which is but a fragmentary earnest of the future, mankind will not forego. The conquest of disease, the elimination of drudgery, the freedom from famine, the enjoyment of comfort, yes even that most doubtful gift, the not too distant possession of a leisure we have not yet learned to use—on these, having once tasted them, mankind will continue to insist. And, at least so far as we have gone, they appear to be conditioned upon the cooperation and organization of great numbers. Perhaps we may be able to keep and to increase our gains without working on so vast a scale; we do not know; show us and we may try; but for the present we prefer to keep along the road which has led us so far, and we will not lend an auspicious ear to jeremiads that we should retrace the steps which have brought us in sight of so glorious a consummation."

It is hard to see any answer to all this; the day has clearly gone forever of societies small enough for their members to have personal acquaintance with each other, and to find their station through the appraisal of those who have any first-hand knowledge of them. Publicity is an evil substitute, and the art of publicity is a black art; but it has come to stay, every year adds to its potency and to the finality of its judgments. The hand that rules the press, the radio, the screen and the far spread magazine, rules the country; whether we like it or not, we must learn to accept it. And yet it is the power of reiterated suggestion and consecrated platitude that at this moment has brought our entire civilization to imminent peril of destruction. The individual is as helpless against it as the child is helpless against the formulas with which he is indoctrinated. Not only is it possible by these means to shape his tastes, his feelings, his desires and his hopes; but it is possible to convert him into a fanatical zealot, ready to torture and destroy and to suffer mutilation and death for an obscene faith, baseless in fact and morally monstrous. This, the vastest conflict with which mankind has ever been faced, whose outcome still remains undecided, in the end turns upon whether the individual can survive; upon whether the ultimate value shall be this wistful, cloudy, errant, You or I, or that Great Beast, Leviathan, that phantom conjured up as an *ignis fatuus* in our darkness and a scapegoat for our futility.

We Americans have at last chosen sides; we believe that if it may be idle to seek the Soul of Man outside Society, it is certainly idle to seek Society outside the Soul of Man. We believe this to be the transcendent stake; we will not turn back; in the heavens we have seen the sign in which we shall conquer or die. But our faith will need again and again to be refreshed; and from the life we commemorate today we may gain refreshment. A great people does not go to its leaders for incantations or liturgies by which to propitiate fate or to cajole victory; it goes to them to peer into the recesses of its own soul, to lay bare its deepest desires; it goes to them as it goes to its poets and its seers. And for that reason it means little in what form this man's message may have been; only the substance of it counts. If I have read it aright, this was that substance: "You may build your Towers of Babel to the clouds; you may contrive ingeniously to circumvent Nature by devices beyond even the understanding of all but a handful; you may provide endless distractions to escape the tedium of your barren lives; you may rummage the whole planet for your ease and comfort. It shall avail you nothing; the more you struggle, the more deeply you will be enmeshed. Not until you have the courage to meet yourselves face to face; to take true account of what you find; to respect the sum of that account for itself and not for what it may bring you; deeply to believe that each of you is a holy vessel unique and irreplaceable; only then will you have taken the first steps along the path of Wisdom. Be content with nothing less; let not the heathen beguile you to their temples, or the Sirens with their songs. Lay up your treasure in the Heaven of your hearts, where moth and rust do not corrupt and thieves cannot break through and steal."

REMARKS OF PROFESSOR PAUL A. FREUND

Paul A. Freund is Charles Stebbins Fairchild Professor of Law at Harvard Law School. He is author of *On Understanding the Supreme Court* (1949) and other works.

How shall one encompass in a few faltering words the life we have come to commemorate—a life so beautiful, so various, so fruitful? The achievements of Mr. Justice Brandeis were so many, his knowledge so profound, his resourcefulness so formidable, that it would be easy to mistake these for the measure of the man. These were, indeed, the marks of a dedicated life; but it was the dedication that gave it greatness. To realize the promise of America through law —that men might share to the limit of their capacity in the American adventure—was the end to which he devoted all his talents and his energies. In him the lawyer's genius was dedicated to the prophet's vision, and the fusion produced a magnificent weapon for righteousness. In his hand the sword was fringed with fire.

Thus dedicated, his life had the simplicity of greatness. All his labors were given coherence and direction and moral intensity by being made to serve two fundamental beliefs: That responsibility is the developer of men, and that excessive power is the great corrupter. "Care is taken," he liked to quote from the German, "that the trees do not scrape the skies." He believed with Lord Acton that all power corrupts and that great power corrupts greatly. He believed with the Stoic philosophers that no man is so like unto himself as each is like to all. For him the democratic faith was not, however, simply dogma. Partly it was parental inheritance from the Pilgrims of '48; but above all it was confirmed by the rich experience of life. Convinced as he was that ordinary men have great capacity for moral and intellectual growth, through the sharing of responsibility, and that the limits of capacity in even the best of men are soon reached, the democratic faith was for him grounded in urgent necessity no less than in moral duty.

This faith transformed his tireless mastery of detail into the pursuit of an ideal. At the bar he brought his great gifts of analysis, of painstaking study, and of constructive statesmanship to the service of his belief in the common man. In the field of labor relations, he devised a plan of industrial peace which called for continuous collaboration between employer and labor, a continuous sharing in the responsibilities of management. In the field of finance, he insisted on the limitations of mortal understanding in endeavoring from the vantage point of the exchanges to direct giant industrial enterprises. Perhaps his proudest achievement while at the bar was the establishment of the system of savings bank industrial life insurance in Massachusetts. This system, as he envisaged it, would not simply give added security and so additional freedom to the workers; more than that, it would be a demonstration of what could be accomplished in an undertaking of modest size by ordinary men working without the prestige of position that has come to those who manage large aggregations of other people's money.

All his views were grounded in the same distrust of bigness, the same sense of urgency that the energies of all men should be released and utilized. He was profoundly attached to the principle of Federalism. He lost no opportunity to advise young lawyers that the United States was not Wall Street or even Washington; that if one went there on a tour of duty one should not overstay his time; that talents and training should be taken back to the home community.

On the bench his sense of the fallibility of judgment did not leave him. It remained as a guiding canon in the decision of constitutional cases. He would not be seduced by the attractions of opportunism. His own integrity and his faith in the integrity of traditions were too strong. When the Court was prepared, as in the first Tennessee Valley Authority case, to announce constitutional doctrine which had his full approval, he none the less raised his voice in protest at what he regarded as an unwarranted anticipation of the constitutional question. No inconsiderable part of his labors on the Court went into the exacting art of staying the judicial hand lest it decide more than was required by the case at bar. In the one or two instances in which it may be suggested that he departed from his canon of judicial parsimony—instances where he took occasion to cast constitutional doubt on declaratory judgments and on a general Federal common law—it is worth observing that the departures were in the interest of confining the powers of the Federal courts. No one was more sensitive than he to the limitations on the function of the Court; and yet no one succeeded more notably that he in combining the role of judge and teacher. One remembers the preparation of the first opinion of a Term, which had finally passed what seemed to be the ultimate revision, and the Justice's disquieting observation: "The opinion is now convincing, but what can we do"—and he was always excessively generous in the use of the plural—"but what can we do to make it more instructive?"

His conception of the office to which he had been called is revealed by glimpses into what only seem to be the small incidents of his character, for in the perfect harmony of his life nothing that became a part of it could be trivial. He could never quite reconcile himself to the grandeur of the Court's new edifice, lest the power of the Court might in some measure come to rest on the majesty of office rather than on the inward strength of the appeal to reason. So dominant was his devotion to reason that his opinions attempted even to satisfy unsuccessful counsel. No relevant argument was to pass unnoticed, and if a petition for rehearing was filed, the Justice felt a sense of failure, though I never quite understood why the intransigence of the advocate should be a fault attributed to the judge. No one who ever heard the Justice deliver a major opinion from the bench could fail to understand the symbolism, and more than symbolism, of the occasion: the patient earnestness with which he explained to the small assemblage the facts of the case and the reasons for the decision, as if in acknowledgment that the Court is a lawgiver only as its decrees find rational acceptance, as if in the hope that none might go away unpersuaded.

Those who had an opportunity to observe his judicial labors would wish to speak, I am sure, of his method of work. Every case that fell to him for opinion gave fresh occasion for the application of his principle that knowledge should precede understanding, and understanding should precede judging. Unremitting toil was taken as a matter of course, some of it performed in those dim hours of which his secretaries—the fraility of youthful nature being what it is—could speak, I suspect, only circumstantially. It is no secret that his opinions went through dozens, even scores, of painstaking revisions. If they have a quality that is monumental and massive, it is only because they were granite-hewn and sculptured with infinite care. Those who shared in some small way in this undertaking were given an unforgettable experience of whole-souled devotion to a great calling,

> "All can grow the flower now,
> For all have got the seed."

Those who knew him would say these things, but

they would speak finally and above all of his moral intensity, his spiritual greatness. His was the quality that by a word could lift the heart, by a nod enkindle the spirit. His moral judgments were stern, and they probed deep. To him unemployment was "the most sinful waste." The persecution of helpless people brought him not only the common sense of grief, but even more strongly a sense of shame at the slowness with which the nations of the earth made protest. He was not a sentimentalist. He could not be swayed from a course he believed morally right by being told that it would involve unfortunate hardships. He realized that victories cannot be won without a struggle and that a price must be paid for every advance.

In a life fraught with more than one man's share of sharp encounters, his faith in the understanding and morality of the multitude gave him serenity. He never yielded to despair, and to gloom only when he found too many men complacent. Moral obtuseness and faintness of heart were the enemies to be dreaded. So it was that when he was asked in the dark days of 1933 whether he believed the worst was over, he could answer almost cheerfully that the worst had happened before 1929. He had his own formula for success: brains, rectitude, singleness of purpose, and time. To flagging spirits he would hold these up as a banner that could never be struck.

It is fitting that we pause at this moment in the world's history to contemplate his life and draw strength from his spirit. For was it not of such a spirit that the poet of another war has spoken: "The pride of the United States leaves the wealth and finesse of the cities and all returns of commerce and agriculture and all the magnitude of geography or shows of exterior victory to enjoy the breed of full-sized men or one full-sized man unconquerable and simple."

REMARKS OF ATTORNEY GENERAL FRANCIS BIDDLE

Francis Biddle was a judge of the U. S. Circuit Court of Appeals, 3d Circuit, 1939-1940. He served as Solicitor General of the U. S., 1940, and as Attorney General of the U. S., 1941-1945. He was U. S. member of the International Military Tribunal, 1945-1946. Judge Biddle is the author of *Mr. Justice Holmes* (1942), *The World's Best Hope* (1949), *The Fear of Freedom* (1951) and other books and articles. He now resides in Washington, D. C.

We are gathered today to honor the memory of a great American—Louis D. Brandeis. In paying our tribute to that memory we speak for the Bar and the Bench. Yet we speak too not only as lawyers, gathered to record his extraordinary contribution to the profession in which we have spent our lives, but as Americans, joined now for a moment that we may try to express what he did for our country. It is timely that at this moment we should think of Mr. Justice Brandeis in this broader sense, for those inherent values that he held dear are being desperately defended throughout the world. As we fight today we are redefining among ourselves and among those with whom we are allied the meaning and the reality of those values. If this war touches us more deeply than any war, it is to the extent that we feel the essentials of our freedom beyond the sounds of words that we and others have spoken. To ourselves we must, day by bitter day, rediscover and reaffirm what constitutes our old American faith.

Brandeis spent his life in such a continued reaffirmation. I suggest, Mr. Chief Justice, that here is a very rare and very moving thing to remember; to remember again in the years that will come after this war, terrible years, or years of hope and growth, according as we shape them. Today again men are dying for the faith they cherish; Brandeis lived for that same faith, quietly dedicated his life to the service of his country. To be sure he was too fundamentally simple to think of anything he did as a dedication. But as much as anyone I have ever known he was innately selfless. Nor was it the selflessness of a man who held off the world. Brandeis lived intensely in his world—a world where the economic struggle for power, the wretched inequalities between comfort and suffering, the failure of the accepted democratic processes to give scope to the needs of a new industrial era enlisted his heart as well as his mind.

His preparation for his twenty-three years on this Court thus transcended his wide and varied experience in practice which had brought him to the front of his profession. But in the practice the same qualities stood forth: there was the battle for cheap insurance which led to the adoption of the savings bank insurance legislation in Massachusetts; the successful campaign for lower gas rates in Boston; the Ballinger-Pinchot investigation which resulted in centering public attention on the vital need of immediate and effective conservation programs; his chairmanship of the board of arbitration in the needle trades; his representation of the interests of consumers and workmen in many fields.

Although he was frugal and ascetic, living a life of steady concentration and immense work on the problems before him, his singleness of purpose never limited the friendly sympathy of his nature, or the curiosity of his mind. He was without prejudices, as he was without cliches. The asceticism and his fundamentally moral outlook gave him in the eyes of many of his friends the quality of a saint. Mr. Justice Holmes felt this reverence for his younger associate. "Whenever he left my house," Holmes wrote of him in 1932, "I was likely to say to my wife, 'There goes a really good man * * *.' In the moments of discouragement that we all pass through, he always has had the happy word that lifts up one's heart. It came from knowledge, experience, courage, and the high way in which he always has taken life."

Yet Justice Brandeis had none of the mystic essence which we associate with sainthood. He was practical, realistic, patient, persistent. He brought the mind of a trained social scientist to the analysis of legal opinion and decision, a method which is beautifully illustrated in his brief in support of the Oregon law fixing a ten-hour day for women wage earners. Three pages argue the law; the other ninety-seven diagnose factory conditions and their effect on individual workers and the public health. This approach has had a profound influence on the method of presenting arguments in cases involving social legislation, and, I suggest, on the outlook of courts to social problems. That judges today are more realistic, less given to the assumption of accepted dogmas, more mature and more curious-minded, is largely due to the influences of Brandeis. "What we must do in America," he once said, a few years before he was made a judge, "is not to attack our judges but to educate them. All judges should be made to feel, as many judges already do, that the things needed to protect liberty are radically different from what they were fifty years back * * *. In the past the courts have reached their conclusions largely deductively from preconceived notions and precedents. The method I have tried to employ in arguing cases before them has been inductive, reasoning from the facts."

I hesitate to suggest that Brandeis had a philosophy of life for I do not think of him primarily as a philosopher. Do not philosophers deal with generalities that take shapes of the universal and glitter above and below the realm of the restless particular? Unlike Mr. Justice Holmes, who, distrustful though he was of the essences, yet felt that the nature of man was to indulge in their formulation, Brandeis, clear in his first principles, was truly empirical in his preoccupations. While Holmes' doubts were philosophic, Brandeis' were scientific. "I have no general philosophy," he said. "All my life I have thought only in connection with the facts that came before me * * * We need not so much reason as to see and understand facts and conditions." He believed profoundly that behind every argument is someone's ignorance, and that disputes generaly arise from misunderstanding. President Wilson knew this when, after the hearings on the Justice's appointment which had lasted for three months, he wrote Senator Culbertson, the chairman of the Judiciary Committee: "I cannot speak too highly of his impartial, impersonal, orderly, and constructive mind, his rare analytical powers, his deep human sympathy, his profound acquaintance with the historical roots of our institutions * * * his knowledge of economic conditions and the way they bear upon the masses of the people."

Mr. Justice Brandeis' fundamental thought running through the whole frame and direction of his efforts, was always of man—"Man (to quote Albert Lief) struggling with oppressive forces in society. Man's right to full development. The infinite possibilities in human creativeness. Man's limitations, too. But especially the breadth of national achievement which can come when energies are released." He voiced this approach many times, never more profoundly than in his testimony before the Commission on Industrial Relations in 1914, more remarkable for having been delivered extemporaneously. "We must," he told the Committee, "bear in mind all the time that however much we may desire material improvement and must desire it for the comfort of the individual, the United States is a democracy and that we must have, above all things, men. It is the development of manhood to which any industrial and social system should be directed."

That, I believe, was the chief reason why he was so deeply concerned with the growth of huge corporations as presenting a grave danger to Ameircan Democracy by what he called "capitalizing free Americans." In his dissenting opinion in *Liggett* v. *Lee* he spoke of the "widespread belief * * * that by the control which the few have exerted through giant corporations, individual initiative and effort are being paralyzed, creative power impaired, and human happiness lessened; that the true prosperity of our past came not from big business, but through the courage, the energy, and the resourcefulness of small men * * *."

His belief, therefore, in preserving our fundamental rights protected by the Constitution, was no matter of individual preference, however strongly felt; a free climate of thought is indispensable for the development of individual men. * * *

He believed in seeking "for betterment within the broad lines of existing institutions," as he once wrote Robert W. Bruere, for progress is necessarily slow, and remedies necessarily tentative. "The development of the individual is," he added, "both a necessary means and the end sought. For our objective is the making of men and women who shall be free, self-respecting members of a democracy—and who shall be worthy of respect * * *. The great developer is responsibility."

He believed, never doubting, in Democracy. But he knew it to be a serious undertaking which "substitutes self-restraint for external restraint." He knew also that Democracy "demands continuous sacrifice by the individual and more exigent obedience to the moral law than any other form of government." Its success may proceed from the individual and "his development is attained mainly in the process of common living."

And so Brandeis believed that every man in this country should have an actual opportunity, and not only what he termed "a paper opportunity." He was convinced that industrial unrest would not be removed until the worker was given, through some method, a share in the management and responsibility of the business. The social justice for which we are striving was for him not the end but a necessary incident of our democracy. The end is the development of the people by self-government in the fullest sense, which involves industrial as well as political democracy.

Thus holding that Democracy was based on the theory that men were entitled to the pursuit of life and of happiness, and that equal opportunity advances civilization, he saw the threat to this way of life from the opposing view that one race was superior to the other. Less than a year after the first World War had begun he expressed this fundamental difference of conception, speaking before the New Century Club in Boston, twenty-seven years ago: "America," he said, "dedicated to liberty and brotherhood of man, rejected heretofore the arrogant claim that one European race is superior to another. America has believed that each race had something of peculiar value which it could contribute to the attainment of those high ideals for which it is striving. America has believed that in differentiation, not in uniformity, lies the path of progress. Acting on this belief, it has advanced human happiness and it has prospered."

Today Brandeis takes his place in the moving stream of history as a great American whose life work brought nearer to fulfillment the essentially American belief in equality of opportunity and individual freedom—the dream that Jefferson, whom Brandeis once referred to as the "first civilized American," had cherished, and Lincoln, sprung from such different roots. Brandeis is in their tradition, the American tradition of those who affirm the integrity of men and women.

RESPONSE OF MR. CHIEF JUSTICE HARLAN F. STONE

Chief Justice Stone was a professor of law and dean of Columbia University School of Law, 1902-1924. He served as Attorney General of the U. S., 1924-1925, and was appointed associate justice of the U. S. Supreme Court on March 2, 1925. He became chief justice of the Supreme Court in 1941 and died while serving in that capacity in 1946. He wrote *Law and Its Administration* (1915), and his selected opinions have been compiled by Alfred Lief in *Public Control of Business* (1940).

Mr. Attorney General, you are right in speaking of Justice Brandeis as a great American. It is because he was a great American, devoted to the law, using the lawyer's learning with skill, resourcefulness and, above all, with wisdom, that he was a great lawyer and law giver. We think of him as a great American because of his abiding faith in the principles of liberty, justice, and equality of opportunity which were proclaimed by those characteristically American documents, the first Virginia Bill of Rights, the Declaration of Independence, and the Constitution. His Americanism contemplated a society in which our continued adherence to those principles of government should, in all the vicissitudes of our history, bring to every man the opportunity to live the good and efficient life.

For him those principles were not concerned alone with the tyrannies of eighteenth century government which gave them birth. They were equally to be taken as guaranties that the social and economic injustices which attend the development of a dynamic and increasingly complex society should not prevail. In his mind the phrase "law and order" meant more than the suppression of lawless violence by government. It signified a state of society to be achieved by a new and better understanding of social values, and by just laws which should check those social forces that in a changing order tend to withhold from men freedom and equality of opportunity. Only as we are aware of his passion for freedom and justice for all men, and of the means by which he translated it into action through a profound understanding of both the function of law in a changing world and the techniques by which law may be adapted to the needs of a free society, do we gain insight into the true sources of his power and influence as a judge.

Most progress in the law has been won by those who have had the vision to perceive the necessity for bringing under its protection or suitable control the forces which, for good or evil, affect the good order and freedom of society, and who, seeing, have possessed the craftsmanship with which to make the necessary adjustment of old laws to new needs. Progress in the law has never been easy or swift. Apart from the legitimate demand for continuity in a system of law founded on precedent, we have sometimes been slow to perceive those resemblances which call for the extension of old precedents to new facts and events, and those differences of the new from the old which make necessary the qualification of precedent or the development of new doctrine.

Some centuries passed before judges and legislators were persuaded that the law should take notice of fraud or deceit as well as robbery and larceny, and before they recognized that if the law compels men to perform contracts it should equally impose an obligation to repay money procured through fraud or mistake. When Lord Mansfield was engaged in his great work of adapting a feudal common law to the requirements of a commercial England, his studies of the practices of merchants as a basis for an enlightened expansion of the law were regarded as a daring judicial innovation. The innovation was, in truth, no more and no less than the application of all the resources of the creative mind to the perpetual problem of attuning the law to the world in which it is to function. It was such a mind that Justice Brandeis brought to the service of the country and of this Court, when he took his seat on the Bench in 1916. The twentieth century had already brought to the courts new problems which had been as little envisaged by the law as had been the customs and practices of merchants before Mansfield's day. The demands for the protection of the interests of workingmen and for the creation of new administrative agencies, the growing inequalities in bargaining power of different classes in the community, and the recognized need for repressing monopoly and for regulating public utilities and large aggregations of capital, all called for the adaptation of the principles of the common law and of constitutional interpretation to new subjects, which often bore but a superficial resemblance to those with which lawyers and judges had been traditionally concerned.

These were problems to tax the technical skill and training of lawyers and judges, but their solution demanded also sympathetic understanding of their nature and of the part which the legal traditions of yesterday can appropriately play in securing the ordered society of today. In the long history of the law few judges have been so richly endowed for such an undertaking as was Justice Brandeis. His career at the Bar had revealed his constant interest in finding ways by which the existing machinery of the law could continue to serve the good order of society notwithstanding the new stresses to which it was being subjected.

Despite the demands of a busy practice he had had the inclination and had found the time to give freely of his professional services for the protection of the public from the abuses of monopoly and the misuse of financial power, from the injury suffered where labor disputes are not adjusted by peaceable means, and from the wrongs inflicted by the misconduct of recreant public officials. In all this his aims were persistently constructive. Aware that permanent gain in social progress, because of its very nature, must be slow, he was content with small reforms, with few steps at a time and short ones, so long as they were forward. He was convinced that progress would not ultimately be attained by resort to methods which required any surrender of his ideal of freedom and justice for all; that our constitutional system, administered with wisdom and good will, had within it all the potentialities for realization of that ideal without altering the essential character of institutions. Social conscience and vision, infinite patience, an extraordinary capacity for sustained intellectual effort, and serene confidence that truth revealed will ultimately prevail, were the special gifts of character and personality which he devoted to his judicial service. These are gifts seldom united in any one person, but they would have been inadequate for the task without his insight into the true significance of a system of law which is the product of some 700 years of Anglo-American history.

Justice Brandeis knew that throughout the development of the common law the judge's decision of today, which is also the precedent for tomorrow, has drawn its inspiration—and the law itself has derived its vitality and capacity for growth—from the very facts which, in every case, frame the issue for decision. And so, as the first step to decision, he sought complete acquaintance with the facts as the generative source of the law. By exhaustive research to discover the social and economic need and consequences of regulation of wages and hours of labor, of ratemaking for public utilities, of the sources and evils of monopoly, and in many another field, he laid the firm foundation of those judicial decisions which for nearly a quarter of a century were to point the way for the development of law adapted to the industrial civilization of the twentieth century. For what availed it that judges and lawyers knew all the laws in the ancient books, if they were unaware of the significance of the new experience to which those laws were not to be applied. In the facts, quite as much as in the legal principles set down in the lawbooks, he found the materials for the synthesis of judicial decision. In that synthesis the law itself was but the means to a social end—the protection and control of those interests in society which are the special concern of government and hence the law.

This end was to be attained within the limits set by the command of Constitution and statutes, and the restraints of precedent and of doctrines by common consent regarded as binding, through the reasonable accommodation of the law to changing social and economic needs. In such a process the law itself was on trial. The need for its continuity was to be weighed against the pressing demands of new facts, and in the light of the teachings of experience, out of which our legal system has grown. These were the guideposts marking the way to decision for Justice Brandeis, as they had been for other judges. What gave his judicial career its high distinction was his clear recognition that these are boundaries within which the judge has scope for freedom of choice of the rule of law which he is to apply, and that his choice within those limits may rightly depend upon social and economic considerations whose weight may turn the scales of judgment in favor of one rule rather than another.

It is the fate of those who tread unfamiliar paths to be misunderstood. There were many, when Justice Brandeis came to this Court, who had forgotten or never knew, and some perhaps who were not interested in knowing, that this was the judicial process which, throughout the history of law, has in varying degree served to renew its vitality and to continue its capacity for growth. It was the method of the great judges of the past, who had consciously or unconsciously practiced the creative art by which familiar legal doctrines have been moulded to the needs of a later day. This is better understood today than it was twenty-five years ago. In the fullness of time we have seen the shafts of criticism which were directed at Brandeis the lawyer and Judge turned harmlessly aside by the general recognition of his integrity of mind and purpose and of his judicial wisdom.

He was emphatic in placing the principles of constitutional decision in a different category from those which are guides to decision in cases where the law may readily be altered by legislative action. He never lost sight of the fact that the Constitution is primarily a great charter of government, and often repeated Marshall's words: "It is *a constitution* we are expounding" * * * "intended to endure for ages to come, and, consequently, to be adapted to the various *crises* of human affairs." Hence, its provisions were to be read not with the narrow literalism of a municipal code or a penal statute, but so that its high purposes should illumine every sentence and phrase of the document and be given effect as a part of a harmonious framework of government. Notwithstanding the doctrine of *stare decisis,* judicial interpretations of the Constitution, since they were beyond legislative correction could not be taken as the final word.

They were open to reconsideration, in the light of new experience and greater knowledge and wisdom. Emphasis of the purposes of the Constitution as a charter of government, and the generality of its restraints under the Due Process Clause, precluded the notion that it had adopted any particular set of social and economic ideas, to the exclusion of others which fair-minded men might hold, however much he might disagree with them. He was the stalwart defender of civil liberty and the rights of minorities. In the specific constitutional guaranties of individual liberty and of freedom of speech and religion, and in the adherence by all who wield the power of government to the principles of the Constitution, he saw the great safeguards of a free and progressive society.

Justice Brandeis revered this Court as an institution which he held to be the indispensable implement for the maintenance of our federal system. He believed that the Court's continued strength and influence depend more than all else upon the thoroughness, integrity and disinterestedness with which its justices do its work. Because of that belief he withdrew from every other activity; the work of the Court was the absorbing interest of his life. Intelligent and disinterested study and the force of reason at the conference table he held to be the only dependable guaranties of the adequate performance of its great task. Although often in the minority, he never sought or desired any other assurance that the Court would meet its responsibilities.

Justice Brandeis' active judicial service covered a period of twenty-three years, from 1916 to 1939. His opinions, appearing in Volumes 242 to 305 of our reports, cover every phase of the wide range of questions which came before the Court in this transition period. They bear internal evidence of the prodigious labor and painstaking care with which they were prepared. In cases involving the validity of legislation or the application of statute or common law to new fact situations, his opinions, like his briefs at the Bar, give us the results of his extensive researches into the social and economic backgrounds of the questions presented, buttressed by expert opinion and accounts of the experience in other states and countries. His statements of fact and law were simple, direct, orderly, powerful, proceeding to their conclusion with convincing logic. In their discussions of the principles of constitutional government and of civil liberty they rise to heights of dignity and power which place them among the great examples of legal literature. He was never willing to sacrifice clarity to the turn of a phrase, for he wished above all to be understood. For laymen as well as lawyers his opinions are a compendium of the legal aspects of the social and economic phenomena of our times. Together they constitute one of the most important chapters of the history of this Court.

Apart from the work of the Court his life was centered in his home and in the intimate associations with family and friends. His substantial means were devoted largely to charity and by choice his home life was austere in its simplicity. He exercised a unique personal influence over the lives of men and women, young and old, who came to him from every walk of life to seek guidance and inspiration in his counsel. He revived their faith that—in a world troubled by declining standards—right, justice, and truth must remain the guiding principles of human conduct. Despite his great intellectual vigor and activity, his life was singularly placid, unruffled by the misunderstandings or criticism of others, however unmerited. This was the outer manifestation of an inner life, untroubled and serene, because given to great ends, with truth as the ultimate goal.

The time has not yet come to bring into its proper perspective a career so unusual and so far-reaching in its influence, but we can appraise now the great service which he rendered by his devotion and loyalty to the Court as an institution and by the scholarship, integrity, and independence with which he performed his judicial labors. We know that because he sat as a judge on this Court the course of constitutional interpretation has been altered and that courts, in the process of adjudication, must henceforth, far more than in the past, look for light beyond the law books to the experience of the world in which we live.

We see him now as one of the influential men of his time * * * taking his rightful place among that small group of great figures of the law who have given to it new strength, and to us renewed assurance of its adequacy and hence that it will endure.

Footnotes to

LAW AND THE UNIVERSITIES

BY PAUL A. FREUND

* * *

10. LIEF, BRANDEIS, THE PERSONAL HISTORY OF AN AMERICAN IDEAL 183-191 (1936); MASON, BRANDEIS: A FREE MAN'S LIFE 291-315 (1946). [A recent conversation with Mr. Meyer Perlstein, International Vice-president of the I.L.G.W.U., who participated in these proceedings in 1910, reveals that the plan was known as the "Protocol of Peace." It was Mr. Filene, President of the famous Boston department store bearing his name, who called in Justice Brandeis. Other members of the tripartite panel were Hamilton Holt and Morris Hillquit. Among the specific proposals which were adopted was the "preferential union shop" as a compromise between the then much disputed "open" versus "closed" union shop. Mr. Perlstein whole-heartedly agrees that the credit is due Justice Brandeis, Ed.]

11. LIEF, *op. cit., supra,* note 10, at 98-106; MASON, THE BRANDEIS WAY (1938).

12. LIEF, *op. cit., supra,* note 10, at 287-292; MASON, *op. cit., supra,* note 10, at 402-404.

13. LIEF, *op. cit., supra,* note 10, at 76-84; MASON, *op. cit., supra,* note 10, at 126-140.

EPILOGUE

REMARKS OF ASSISTANT SECRETARY OF STATE DEAN ACHESON

These remarks were made by Assistant Secretary of State, later Secretary of State, Dean Acheson on behalf of Justice Brandeis' Law Secretaries at the funeral service for the Justice on October 7, 1941.

In this moment of farewell to the Justice, I should like to speak very briefly of what he has meant in the lives of a score of men who have had the great joy and the great fortune of serving him so intimately as his secretaries. We are the fortunate ones, but what he has meant to us is not very different from what he has meant to hundreds of young men and women who have grown up under his influence.

We are scattered over the country, some are on the bench, some are teaching, some are in the practice of law, some are in the service of the Government. But today to all of us there comes a surge of memories. It is almost impossible from among the strands of memory to select those which are most significant, but there are two strands, I believe, which have been woven deeply into our lives.

I need not say how great an influence upon us it was to begin our work under the guiding hand of the Justice and to know the brilliance of his mind, but our relationship was far more than that between young men and one of the greatest and most revered figures of our time. What gave it life, what gave it endurance was the depth of affection which the warmth of his interest and solicitude for us inspired.

Throughout these years we have brought him all of our problems and all our troubles, and he had time for all of us. In talk with him the problems answered themselves. A question, a comment, and the difficulties began to disappear; the dross and shoddy began to appear for what it was, and we wondered why the matter had ever seemed difficult.

I have talked, over the past 20 years, with the Justice about these men. I have heard him speak of some achievement of one of us with all the pride, and of some sorrow or disappointment of another, with all the tenderness of a father speaking of his sons. He entered so deeply into our lives because he took us so deeply into his.

The other strand in these memories is all the more vivid because of the times in which we have lived. We are the generation which has lived during and between two wars. We have lived in the desert years of the human spirit. We have lived in the barren years of disillusionment—years when the cry was "What is truth?"—years when men with a little new-found knowledge believed that they had pried into the mainsprings of the human mind and spirit, and could make mankind work for any end by playing upon its fears and appetites.

These were years during which we were with the Justice and saw in action his burning faith that the verities to which men had clung through the ages were verities; that evil never could be good; that falsehood was not truth; not even if all the ingenuity of science reiterated it in waves that encircled the earth.

We have heard him say almost in the words of St. Paul, "Whatsoever things are true, whatsoever things are honest, whatsoever things are just, whatsoever things are pure, whatsoever things are of good report—think on these things."

But to him truth was less than truth unless it were expounded so that people could understand and believe. During these years of retreat from reason, his faith in the human mind and in the will and capacity of people to grasp the truth never wavered or tired. In a time of moral and intellectual anarchy and frustration, he handed on the great tradition of faith in the mind and spirit of man which is the faith of the prophets and poets, of Socrates, of Lincoln.

And so today, whatever dark days may lie ahead, the memory of the Justice will be a voice always saying to us, "Lift up your hearts!"

INDEX